J. L. Plumb

WHAT ABOUT THE NEW TESTAMENT?

WHAT ABOUT
THE NEW TESTAMENT?

Essays in Honour of
Christopher Evans

EDITED BY
MORNA HOOKER AND
COLIN HICKLING

SCM PRESS LTD
LONDON

334 01774 2
First published 1975
by SCM Press Ltd
56 Bloomsbury Street, London
© SCM Press Ltd 1975
Printed in Great Britain by
Western Printing Services Ltd
Bristol

Contents

In place of a Preface   vii

Abbreviations   ix

1 Great Expectations? The New Testament Critic and his Audience   1
JOHN BOWDEN, *Managing Director and Editor, SCM Press*

2 Form Criticism Revisited   13
GRAHAM STANTON, *Lecturer in New Testament Studies, King's College, London*

3 In his own Image?   28
MORNA HOOKER, *Lecturer in Theology, University of Oxford, and Fellow of Linacre College*

4 Jesus, the Wandering Preacher?   45
FREDERICK H. BORSCH, *Dean of the Church Divinity School of the Pacific, Berkeley, California*

5 Miracles in the Fourth Gospel   64
EDUARD LOHSE, *Bishop of Hanover*

6 On Putting Paul in his Place   76
COLIN HICKLING, *Lecturer in New Testament Studies, King's College, London*

7 Can Apocalyptic be Relevant?   89
SOPHIE LAWS, *Lecturer in New Testament Studies, King's College, London*

8 The Place of Jesus   103
LESLIE HOULDEN, *Principal of Cuddesdon College, Oxford*

9 The Multidimensional Picture of Jesus   116
ULRICH SIMON, *Professor of Christian Literature, King's College, London*

Contents

10   Meanings   127
     GERALD DOWNING, *Vicar of Unsworth*

11   A Partner for Cinderella?   143
     DENNIS NINEHAM, *Warden of Keble College, Oxford*

12   The Uses of 'Holy Scripture'   155
     MAURICE WILES, *Regius Professor of Divinity, University of
     Oxford*

13   The Myth of the Church   165
     JOHN AUSTIN BAKER, *Canon of Westminster*

14   The Preacher and the Biblical Critic   178
     JOHN FENTON, *Principal of St Chad's College, Durham*

15   New Testament Scholarship and Liturgical Revision   187
     TOM BAKER, *Dean of Worcester*

16   Walking in Newness of Life   198
     SYDNEY EVANS, *Dean of King's College, London*

17   A Change of Diet?   207
     JANET DYSON, *Senior Lecturer in Religious Studies, Southlands
     College of Education*

18   'Who's In, Who's Out'   223
     CLARE DRURY

19   Dear Christopher, . . .   234
     ELLEN FLESSEMAN-VAN LEER

In place of a Preface

Dear Christopher,

You were once heard to say that you disapprove of *Festschriften*, as being all too often occasions for scholars to air pieces of research which would have been better left in the obscurity of the bottom drawer, and we therefore feel a little awkward about producing one ourselves as your birthday present. For someone like yourself, whose interests are so much wider than the purely academic, a collection of essays seems a particularly inadequate gift. Nevertheless we are determined not to let you reach the age of sixty-five without some expression of our affection and admiration; and since we cannot think of any more appropriate form for it to take, we offer you what we hope is a *Festschrift* with a difference. We have concentrated on raising questions rather than on dogmatizing about the answers, and we have done so deliberately as a token of our appreciation for the open-minded and open-ended character of your own writing and teaching. We have tried to take note of your warning that 'eloquent perorations are reserved either for those who believe optimistically that they have the answers, or for those who believe cynically that there are no answers to have; perorations are debarred to those for whom God's act is the last word.'[1]

As you will see, the essays have been written by a variety of friends who have known you at different times and in different roles. We have tried to make our contributions representative of your own varied interests: not only the more academic issues of New Testament exegesis and method—a field in which your critical honesty has led you continually to question the dubious and to take nothing for granted—but also your pastoral concern for others, whether as teacher, counsellor or confessor. In the academic sphere, you have set high standards for yourself and others—sometimes too high for the ordinary undergraduate, more than a little daunted by your lectures!—and none of us has ever submitted ideas to you without some trepidation. If anything we have said or written has passed your scrutiny, we feel it deserves to be taken seriously and worked out more fully. You are

vii

always ready to accept new ideas, with your ears pricked up, as it were, to hear new things: yet we know well that you are impatient with any kind of humbug. Colleagues at King's in a variety of disciplines have found you eager to 'run alongside' them, as you once expressed it, and to enter into dialogue with them. In tutorials and seminars, your infectious enthusiasm for your subject has communicated itself to men and women of all levels of ability. In the pastoral sphere, we are especially appreciative of your ability to demonstrate—to many who had been wondering!—that scholarship and faith are not incompatible. There are many, too, who in times of perplexity and distress have found in you a sensitive listener and skilful guide, willing and able to share their situation with them and struggle with them in discovering how best to cope with it.

To us, however, and to everyone else who knows you well, you are first and foremost a personal friend, and your genius for friendship is one of the most remarkable things about you. The name Christopher Evans conjures up for us a picture of a vital, affectionate, delightfully human person, prodding away at his pipe or armed with his fishing tackle, pursuing an astonishing variety of interests—cricket, football, theatre, good food and good talk—enjoying life to the full, finding himself in one unexpected situation after another, and delighting us all with the tale of his latest escapade. To you, as to no one else whom we know, belongs the gift of serendipity![2] Your exuberance and enthusiasm for life and your delight in your friends inevitably communicates itself to them, and they find themselves sharing your own joy.

To anyone as skilled in source criticism as you are, this letter should offer a fairly easy task in sorting out the various authors who have contributed to it. Although this diverse material has passed through the hands of a redactor, the result nevertheless expresses the sentiments of all the contributors to this book and of many others, among whom we would especially like to mention Ruth Nineham (collaborator in our scheme), Michael Ramsey, Eric Abbott and Alec Vidler, your friends over many years. They join with us in greeting you with gratitude and affection on your birthday.

6 November 1974

1. In *JTS*, NS 5, 1954, pp. 17f.
2. Serendipity: an assumed gift for 'finding valuable or agreeable things not sought for' (Webster).

Abbreviations

ATR	*Anglican Theological Review*, Evanston
CBQ	*The Catholic Biblical Quarterly*, Washington
Ev Th	*Evangelische Theologie*, Munich
ExpT	*The Expository Times*, Edinburgh
FRLANT	Forschungen zur Religion und Literatur des Alten und Neuen Testaments, Göttingen
JBL	*Journal of Biblical Literature*, Philadelphia
JTC	*Journal for Theology and the Church*, New York
JTS	*Journal of Theological Studies*, Oxford
NTS	*New Testament Studies*, Cambridge
SBT	Studies in Biblical Theology, SCM Press
Strack-Billerbeck	H. L. Strack and P. Billerbeck, *Kommentar zum Neuen Testament aus Talmud und Midrasch*, 5 vols., Munich 1922–56
TU	Texte und Untersuchungen zur Geschichte der altchristlichen Literatur, Berlin
ZNW	*Zeitschrift für die neutestamentliche Wissenschaft*, Berlin
ZTK	*Zeitschrift für Theologie und Kirche*, Tübingen

1

Great Expectations?
The New Testament Critic and his Audience

JOHN BOWDEN

GREAT things have been, and still are, expected of the New Testament critic, even if he does not always seem aware of the fact. Now, perhaps more exclusively than at any other time, the book which is his field of study is looked to by many as the one hopeful source of inspiration for a perplexed and post-Constantinian Christendom in crisis. And at a time when there is a widespread reaction against the institutional church, and its centuries of thought and experience are being discounted and ignored at the expense of a more direct and simplistic appeal to Jesus himself, the New Testament critic, as the interpreter and historical assessor of the gospels, is intimately involved in the never-ending task of seeking to rediscover 'the founder of Christianity'.

That might seem to be an over-dramatized claim with which to begin. But if the New Testament critic were to ask what is required of him by his widest audience—and it is wider than he might suppose—he would find it not too far off the mark. In the eyes of clergy, students and laymen he has been entrusted with an overawing series of tasks. He has to find out what happened and explain what was said in the past, in the first century AD, but he has also to present it in a way which is 'meaningful' now; he has to present what he sees to be the truth, but is expected to present it in such a way that it is edifying and constructive rather than negative and destructive; he has to unravel unusually complex problems, but is looked to for a simple and comprehensible answer. And along with all this he must remain faithful on the one hand to the canons of the academic discipline within which he works and on the other to a calling in the context of the church which goes beyond the demands of the scholarly world.

It would be easier if New Testament critics were given opportunities to explain their own views of their task and to explore the preconceptions which underlie these tangled hopes. But a forum for such discussions barely exists and can only be created with difficulty. Worse still, the New Testament critic often has to present his findings in a quite unsympathetic atmosphere. Leaving aside those hostile to Christianity in every generation who believe that he is fudging the evidence anyway,[1] he may well find those interested in and excited by his work outnumbered by others who approach it with indifference, impatience or scarcely veiled hostility. After all, every Christian is to some degree familiar with the New Testament, and many passages may have deep associations for him; he may well have found help and support in them and consequently have begun to form his own opinions on what they mean. He is therefore all too ready to brush aside the beginnings of complex explanations of what he may believe to be a simple matter, or unwilling to consider alternative explanations to his own. This poses great problems for the New Testament scholar, engaged in a discipline which has spent a long and difficult time even formulating the questions that need to be asked, let alone answering them; comparatively few others have the time or the technical training to approach the New Testament from his perspective (or with the degree of detachment that needs to be cultivated). Furthermore, scholars working in other areas, lawyers, historians, literary critics and systematic theologians, may tend to underestimate New Testament scholarship. They may not only share their experience with the New Testament critic when he asks for it, but also go on to tell him how to do his own work as well.[2]

All this, of course, would be mere inconvenience if the New Testament critic could confidently point to a steady stream of successes over the years. In fact, his achievements over the past two centuries have been remarkable, and a group of New Testament scholars, celebrating say the bicentenary of their discipline in its modern form, would have an imposing record to look back on. They might point to the way in which a sound New Testament text was established; to the forging of the tools of source criticism, form criticism and redaction criticism, to a surprising degree tailor-made for their purpose;[3] to research into the environment of early Christianity and the nature of the early church; to the exhaustive study of the life and teaching of Jesus and the way in which it was first understood; or to the reconstruction of the different individual theological views represented within the New Testament. In all these areas, and elsewhere, they could record solid progress in understanding over the years. Above all, they could point to the constant courage and integrity within New Testament scholarship, where scholars did not hesitate to press on with their researches in the face of acute personal distress and the hostility of others to the apparent outcome of particular lines of research. True, they would also be aware of the problems which had not been solved. But they would remind one another of the intractable difficulty which must hamper so many New Testament enterprises and which sharply divides the New Testament critic even from his Old Testament colleagues, namely that more often than not he just does not have enough material to work on, nor is it easy to see how this situation can be changed either by archaeological discoveries or by continued study of the range of sources already available. This is the ultimate limitation on New Testament scholarship: that the book is so small and the gaps in our knowledge of the world from which it came are still so great. Other historians or literary critics may worry at one question for a while and then move on to other issues; the New Testament critic, because he is concerned with *the* book and its subject-matter, must steel himself to go over the same well-trodden ground yet one more time.

In the company of his colleagues, the New Testament critic may find a good deal to celebrate. As so often, however, the view from outside is rather different—and in this case more pessimistic. If he is not seen as an antiquarian mechanic, tinkering around with sources, engaged in endless arguments and never really being able to give a straight answer, the New Testament critic can appear to be thoroughly destructive. The reputation earned by the four most stimulating figures of the last two centuries, F. C. Baur and D. F. Strauss in the nineteenth, and Albert Schweitzer and Rudolf Bultmann in the twentieth, is testimony enough to this. More recently, the furore following the publication of the commentary on Mark's gospel by D. E. Nineham makes illuminating reading.[4] The New Testament critic is seen to be bent on leaving a train of destruction in his wake.

A review of current results is hardly reassuring. If the 'radicals' within the discipline have been countered by 'conservatives' intent on redressing the balance, there are few places where a consensus has been achieved. Precisely because of the dearth of material indicated above, there is just sufficient evidence on which to base a very wide variety of theories, but insufficient to rule more than a very few of them out once they have been put forward. There is not even an agreed relative dating for the books of the New Testament. The majority of scholars have been content to group them within a period from AD 50 to about the beginning of the second century, but recently it has been vigorously argued that the whole of the New Testament was written before AD 70.[5] Dispute over dating here is of course more than an incidental matter; it affects any understanding of the development of the early church as well as assessments of the content of the New Testament books and their relationship to one another. As so often, the arguments here are circular: dating depends on interpretation and interpretation on dating because of the lack of decisive external evidence. In this case the shift is caused by reinterpretations of the nature of the fourth gospel and Luke/Acts on which scholars have widely differing views. John can be seen as predominantly historical, Hebrew and very early or predominantly theological, Greek and quite late;[6] 'Luke' can be seen as Paul's companion writing with considerable historical accuracy in the middle of the first century or as a representative of a later generation constructing an ideal picture with what material he can muster towards its end.[7] The chronology of Paul's career and the authenticity of the letters supposed to have been written by him are matters of the liveliest dispute;[8] and the problems in assessing the historical career and teaching of Jesus are too well known to need further mention here.[9]

More than that, the very methods which have been developed by the New Testament critic have increasingly come under fire—further fusillades appear in later essays in this volume! Source criticism, the basis of the explanation of the interrelationship of the traditions contained in the synoptic gospels, may yet prove to have hit upon an essentially correct result, but seems to have come to its conclusions by inadequate argumentation. Form criticism, concerned with individual units of material in the gospels and the church context in which they were handed down, was hotly challenged from the start and, while again apparently indispensable, is overdue for a complete re-examin-

4

ation.[10] Redaction criticism, the most recent approach, which attempts to distinguish the theological profiles of those who gave the gospels their final shape, is plagued by a multiplicity of conflicting portraits; at present whether to hope for an agreed picture of, say, Mark, or to accede to the verdict of Jeremias that 'the search for a systematic structure of the gospel is a lost labour of love'[11] would appear to be anyone's choice.

This may seem to amount to a consideration of the historical and critical problems surrounding the New Testament which ignores the question of a theological interpretation of it in wider terms. But in the latter area the disarray is no less. The story of the collapse of the attempt to establish a self-determinative biblical theology independent of history and philosophy is now becoming familiar;[12] a recent comment on the use of the New Testament in much systematic theology, that 'too often, theologians' interpretations of texts are simply fanciful meditations on modern problems with an occasional paraphrase of and reference to biblical material',[13] can, depressingly, be verified with ease. The narrower area of 'New Testament theology' has yet to acquire permanent contours. No 'Theology of the New Testament' seems to have been written in English between 1899 and 1958, and on the Continent, the field has been dominated by individual scholars in whose writings the number of presuppositions and prejudices which must colour any interpretation affects their approach to such a degree that works with the same title bear little relationship to one another.[14] In perspective these works appear as a series of glorious failures, great and distinctive interpretations which are none the less each flawed in some way; for all the shafts of light which they may shed, their overall conception is sooner or later undermined by the combined efforts of those working on less comprehensive themes. A programmatic essay by William Wrede, 'The Task and Methods of "New Testament Theology"', written in 1897, virtually unavailable in Germany but to be read in English thanks to the persuasive advocacy of Robert Morgan, makes fascinating reading; the problems it raises are as fresh and unsolved now as they were when the essay was written, and the long introduction by its editor which opens the volume is unable to foresee any constructive developments.[15]

Faced with this disagreement and disorder, it must be hard for the New Testament critic not to feel depressed when the students in his latest audience seem so disillusioned at what they see that they hesitate to plunge into a mass of detailed study with no appararent way out on the other side, and when the most flourishing wing of present-day Christianity, in the evangelical churches, seems prepared to write off the results of New Testament scholarship in favour of a fundamentalist approach which, however effective and reassuring it may be in practice, cannot begin to claim to reflect the likely truth.[16] And when he goes on to consider how few of what he might regard as his most assured conclusions have actually made a noticeable impact on the regular life and thought of the church, he might be forgiven for supposing that he was the victim of a particularly subtle campaign of obstruction.

Despite the surely incontestable demonstration by Albert Schweitzer of the impossibility of writing a life of Jesus,[17] such 'lives' continue to be attempted, and indeed, in the rebellion against the institutional church and its ethos, interpretations of Christianity based on the life of Jesus have made ground against more broadly based christologies. In recent years the categories outlined in Schweitzer's book have been increased by 'Jesus the man for others' and a repristination of 'Jesus the revolutionary'. The portraits may have been updated, but the arguments against them remain the same.

Within the church, it would be optimistic to say that even the understanding that each of the gospels was written from a distinctive perspective had penetrated very far. That the gospel accounts may not be taken apart and then harmonized into a single narrative may be commonplace to the New Testament critic; it is not to the average congregation. But how can progress be made here, or in understanding the nature of the evidence for the life of Jesus, when the New Testament critic's basic handbook to study of the gospels, the synopsis, is very seldom indeed to be found outside the circle of university teachers and the students whom they teach?

Not only are the bare necessities of study absent, but any occasional attempt that may be made to teach a new perspective on the New Testament to a wider audience is immediately negated by the un-reformed liturgical use of the New Testament, and by the abuse of it in more popular Bible readings. To break with past habits requires discipline and a change of routine if it is to be achieved; to attempt to change perspective during a regular process of almost sub-conscious conditioning is virtually impossible.

The problems which thus confront the New Testament critic are complex and stem from many causes: the enigmatic nature of his material and the subtle treatment it requires; the inadequate means and opportunities for him to present his conclusions; the resistance he encounters within the church and its life to the revolution of considerable dimensions which he is introducing; the irrational factors and the natural hesitations which influence his potential audience. It is not surprising that the only successful popularizers appear to have been those who have combined an attractively readable style with a message which has minimally affected the *status quo*. No one seems to have succeeded in popularizing 'radical' results within the mainstream of New Testament writing.[18]

So what is to be done? Are there ways in which New Testament critics can begin to close the gap between the present state of their discipline and what is ideally expected of them? A hasty retort might be that the outline of New Testament scholarship given above is highly selective and over-pessimistic, and that in any case many of the comments are concerned with areas over which the New Testament critic has no control; the question is therefore an improper one from the start.

Certainly, it can happen that an individual scholar gives the impression that he has decisively settled a fundamental question and that others have been finally discredited. But when such claims are advanced in conflicting terms from different quarters, without specifically and in detail ruling out all plausible alternatives (which the evidence seldom allows, see above), it is misguided to imply that the problems touched on above are insignificant or non-existent. And if the New Testament critic still has unfinished business to clear up, he has no excuse for putting it off by shifting the blame to others.

Paradoxically, the first and most constructive step that could easily be taken is a more general acknowledgment of the degree to which New Testament scholarship is, and must continue to remain, in a state of ignorance, and a more determined effort to educate a wider public in the art of 'living with questions'. In an unjustly neglected study of New Testament scholars' argumentation, Gerald Downing has concluded that 'with the evidence to hand and the methods available . . . the chance of any real large-scale agreement and even of relative certainty is very small'.[19] He goes on to argue that it is possible to live

7

with this uncertainty, fully and richly. It should at least be considered whether New Testament scholarship often makes unsatisfactory reading because of a pathological fear of recognizing the situation and making the venture.

Some of the recurring faults of recent writing may be listed briefly. First, there is the excessive use of adjectives expressing value judgments which are either over-emotive or plain question-begging. To say that an account is 'radical' or 'conservative' or 'reductionist' or 'constructive' or simply that it comes from Germany may serve to classify it within the range of explanations currently on offer, but does not help at all in assessing it as an interpretation of the available evidence.[20] If integrity and a concern for truth is to remain the priority of New Testament study, it is vital to avoid labels which also trigger off deep-seated prejudices, and if arguments are complex and finely balanced it is vital to avoid the *reductio ad absurdum* or the quick debating point.

Complexity in argumentation, secondly, does not necessarily require complexity of terminology. Anyone tracing the progress of New Testament writing during this century cannot fail to notice the decline in readability which has taken place (with some honourable exceptions). One factor is the widespread use of theological jargon, particularly among those writers concerned to go beyond the 'merely historical' significance of New Testament writing. Most of this jargon hinders rather than illuminates the understanding of a text.

> Terms like '*kerygma*', 'eschatology', the Word, God's act in Christ have lost nearly all precise exegetical meaning. However, not only has precise exegetical meaning been lost but meaning as such. The crisis of biblical theology is exactly the crisis of the condensed category which has lost its symbolic value and thus becomes a verbal abstraction.[21]

Is it too fanciful to suppose that New Testament scholarship might take a step forward by agreeing to abstain for a decade from the use of the word *kerygma*?[22]

An equally bad influence on the quality of writing has been the pressure of academic requirements on writers, who are encouraged to display a virtuoso technique in the assembling and presentation of material, often in enormous detail. This is not to suggest that study of the New Testament can be carried on without detailed scholarship. But with so many questions open to a variety of answers, the risk of constructing an elaborate edifice on a very shaky foundation is considerable, and perhaps more care should be taken to avoid it. It is puzzling that in recent years there has been such a flood of highly specialized monographs, written with extreme sophistication, while there is a real dearth of good textbooks on particular areas setting out the data to be taken into consideration and the possible ways of approaching them. For an introduction to source and form criticism, books available as long ago as 1930 still have to be superseded (but surely should be by now). While there is a vast literature on the 'quest of the historical Jesus' there is no single book which even begins to formulate the problem in a comprehensive way. Similarly, a good history of first-century Christianity has yet to be written; too much of what is presented as history in this period is an unhappy mixture of history and theological ideology which has the worst of both worlds.[23]

There is a good deal for the New Testament critic still to do in the historical sphere. And amid all the cries for relevance, New Testament scholarship should not be apologetic about being chiefly concerned to understand the New Testament in its own terms against its original background. Bad history writing helps no one, least of all an age like ours with its widespread tendency to understand human experience in its own narrow terms. More widely available accounts of the New Testament and its environment presented in more neutral terms might have a surprising impact, simply by communicating factual information, uncertainties and all, to an age which is not entirely uninterested either in mysteries or in the past history of religious experience.

In such an enterprise New Testament scholarship might find it easier to make alliances with other disciplines, inside and outside theology, particularly the developing science of the historical criticism of Christian doctrine.[24] And because the New Testament is not just a history book, but contains a great deal of material which requires more than strictly historical understanding, it is important that the New Testament critic should be open to the later use of the New Testament in the church, particularly when what he is accustomed to treat as historical sources became part of a canon of holy scripture.[25] Writing of the anxiety of many modern scholars to prove the Bible historically accurate (which is a very different matter from seeking to obtain a historically accurate picture of the way in which the Bible came into being, the concern outlined above), D. E. Nineham once asked whether there was 'any objection to holding that a part—perhaps even a large part—of God's revelation was through stories which God through his Spirit caused to be told about himself?'[26] He was referring to the problem of the historicity of the Old Testament. But his question might be extended to a wider field. Modern New Testament scholarship is scarcely two hundred years old, yet the New Testament was read in the church for more than fifteen hundred years before that, and this 'pre-critical' use of the New Testament has left countless marks which still remain even on today's Christianity. Is there not also a great deal to be learnt about Christian experience from the whole history of interpretation? If Christians have not always been receiving a historically accurate picture of their past from the New Testament, what have they been receiving from it?

One final word. There is still a good deal for the New Testament critic to do. But although it is not considered quite proper to mention the fact in the more clinical atmosphere of academic study, he does not have unlimited manpower or unlimited financial resources with which to carry on his work. What the long-term effect of changing requirements in university courses will be for New Testament studies remains to be seen. The effect of the new economic climate on the communication of the results of these studies is easier to forecast. Over the next decades the ways in which Christians communicate with each other will be increasingly restricted. As an academic, the New Testament critic will probably still be able to seek refuge in the haven of learned journals, and doubtless more economical ways will be developed for storing knowledge and circulating it within the academic community. But unless he is also active in making known the result of his work to a wider audience, the New Testament critic will find a far greater polarization between his world and that of the layman than already exists to the disadvantage of both sides. Can he happily contemplate a programme of 'adding to knowledge' simply for the sake of adding to knowledge? Is it too much to ask that a scale of priorities might somehow be considered?

NOTES

1. See most recently G. A. Wells, *The Jesus of the Early Christians*, Pemberton Books 1971. That this book was warmly welcomed and indeed reviewed by Hugh Trevor-Roper (who at the same time condemned C. H. Dodd's infinitely more probable *The Founder of Christianity*, Collins 1971) also substantiates other general remarks in this paragraph.

2. J. N. D. Anderson, *A Lawyer among the Theologians*, Hodder and Stoughton 1973, is a singularly bad book which illustrates this practice at its worst. A very different study (which does not really deserve mention in the same footnote), A. N. Sherwin-White, *Roman Society and Roman Law in the New Testament*, Clarendon Press 1963, much beloved by scholars assessing the historical accuracy of Acts, is most illuminating on Roman society and Roman law, but its arguments about the New Testament do not have the same authority and are by no means as conclusive as they have sometimes been taken to be.

3. For an illuminating brief study which puts these developments in their contemporary context, see C. F. Evans, *Queen or Cinderella*, University of Durham 1960; for more detailed accounts see W. G. Kümmel, *The New Testament: The History of the Investigation of its Problems*, SCM Press 1973, and, subject to the reservations on p. 8 above, Stephen Neill, *The Interpretation of the New Testament 1861–1961*, Oxford University Press 1966.

4. Before reading any of the polemic on these figures, it is quite essential also to read their work in context at first hand. For the controversy over D. E. Nineham, *Saint Mark*, Penguin Books 1963, see A. T. Hanson, 'The Quandary of Historical Scepticism', in id., *Vindications*, SCM Press 1966, pp. 74–102, and D. E. Nineham, ' . . . *et hoc genus omne*', in W. R. Farmer, C. F. D. Moule and R. R. Niebuhr (eds.), *Christian History and Interpretation: Studies presented to John Knox*, Cambridge University Press 1967, pp. 199–222.

5. So J. A. T. Robinson in an as yet unpublished paper, in contrast to the views collected in W. G. Kümmel, *Introduction to the New Testament*, SCM Press 1966. The fact that the fall of Jerusalem in AD 70 is nowhere mentioned in the New Testament has regularly attracted attention; cf. the different explanation advanced by S. G. F. Brandon, *The Fall of Jerusalem and the Christian Church*, SPCK 1951.

6. Compare, for example, A. M. Hunter, *According to John*, SCM Press 1968, with E. Käsemann, *The Testament of Jesus*, SCM Press 1968.

7. Compare, for example, the commentaries of C. S. C. Williams, A. & C. Black 1957, and R. P. C. Hanson, Oxford University Press 1967, with that of Ernst Haenchen, Blackwell 1971 (German first published 1956).

8. See especially J. C. Hurd, Jr, 'Pauline Chronology and Pauline Theology', in *Christian History and Interpretation* (note 4 above), pp. 225–48.

9. Perhaps the best recent introduction is E. Trocmé, *Jesus and his Contemporaries*, SCM Press 1973.

10. See the excellent article by M. D. Hooker, 'On Using the Wrong Tool', *Theology* 75, 1972, pp. 570–81.

11. Joachim Jeremias, *New Testament Theology*, Vol. I, SCM Press 1971, p. 38.

12. See Brevard S. Childs, *Biblical Theology in Crisis*, Westminster Press, Philadelphia, 1970, pp. 14–87.

13. J. C. Beker, 'The Function of the Bible Today', in C. D. Batson, J. C. Beker, W. M. Clark, *Commitment without Ideology*, SCM Press 1973, p. 24.

14. For English New Testament theologies see C. F. Evans, *Queen or Cinderella* (note 3 above), p. 14. Note the differences between Rudolf Bultmann, *Theology of the New Testament*, Vols I & II, SCM Press 1952, 1955; O. Cullmann, *Salvation in History*, SCM Press 1967; H. Conzelmann, *An Outline of the Theology of the New Testament according to its Major Witnesses*, SCM Press 1974.

15. Robert Morgan (ed.), *The Nature of New Testament Theology* (SBT 2.25), 1973, see especially the concluding paragraph on p. 67!

16. The evangelical understanding of the New Testament is, however, a more complicated question than might at first sight appear, see Walter J. Hollenweger, *The Pentecostals*, SCM Press 1972, pp. 292–310.

17. Albert Schweitzer, *The Quest of the Historical Jesus*, A. & C. Black 1910 (it is a pity that efforts to make the much expanded German edition of 1926 available in English have so far failed).

18. Which may in part explain why books like Hugh J. Schonfield, *The Passover Plot*, Hutchinson 1965, and John M. Allegro, *The Sacred Mushroom and the Cross*, Hodder and Stoughton 1970, made such an impact when they were written, by outsiders to Christianity.

19. F. G. Downing, *The Church and Jesus* (SBT 2.10), 1968, p. 190.

20. It is an interesting exercise to compare the argumentation in the contrasting books mentioned in notes 6 and 7 above and also the data of which each makes use.

21. J. C. Beker, *Commitment without Ideology* (note 13 above), p. 24.

22. Far more attention should have been paid to C. F. Evans, 'The Kerygma', *JTS*, NS 7, pp. 25–41.

23. See F. G. Downing, *The Past is All We Have*, SCM Press 1974, pp. 25f., 'I find very little material to help me share—or even understand for myself—"everyday life in New Testament times"—I am given either an abstract of ideas or an archivist's inventory.' At the time of writing, the Open University set text in this area is F. V. Filson, *A New Testament History*, which unfortunately illustrates the point all too well.

24. Cf. Maurice Wiles, *The Making of Christian Doctrine*, Cambridge University Press 1967; *The Remaking of Christian Doctrine*, SCM Press 1974.

25. See C. F. Evans, *Is Holy Scripture Christian?*, SCM Press 1971.

26. D. E. Nineham, 'The Lessons of the Past for the Present', in *The Church's Use of the Bible Past and Present*, SPCK 1963, p. 159.

2

Form Criticism Revisited

GRAHAM STANTON

FORM CRITICISM of the gospels is a stagnant discipline. This is a disturbing situation. For it quickly leads to a quite unwarranted confidence that this method of gospel criticism is not only asking the right questions of the text but is producing valid answers. The implications of form criticism have been discussed often enough in recent decades. Although numerous scholars, especially in the English-speaking world, have rejected the more radical conclusions of some form critics, most have accepted without critical discussion the main principles of form criticism. But a counsel of moderation is not enough: nearly all aspects of form criticism are overdue for serious reconsideration.[1]

Biblical scholars are well aware that interpretation has been and is deeply influenced by doctrinal and philosophical presuppositions. But it is all too easy to behold the speck in the eye of Augustine, Luther, Calvin or Barth, and to neglect the log in one's own eye; presuppositions cannot be dispensed with, but they must be constantly overhauled. The scholar's *methods* are also his presuppositions; they too need to be kept under constant surveillance in order to ensure that they do not lock the text rigidly into one position.

The immense difficulties which beset the path of the student of the gospels should also encourage extreme vigilance over the methods used. Christopher Evans wisely warns his undergraduate students that scholarly study of the gospels is more demanding as an intellectual discipline than any other undertaken in a modern university.

In view of the importance of form criticism for all serious study of the gospels, there has been surprisingly little debate about its fundamental assumptions and axioms.[2] The pioneer form-critical works of Rudolf Bultmann and Martin Dibelius have become standard textbooks for both German and English speaking students.[3] Few books have had such a profound and lasting effect on biblical studies. Dibelius' classic has been particularly influential in the English-speaking world and is likely to remain so now that the English translation has been reprinted. Most scholars would readily agree that neither book is immune from serious criticism, yet comparable studies of the origin and transmission of the gospel traditions have not been written since.

Form criticism has led to several new phases of scholarly study of the gospels. The so-called 'new quest' for the historical Jesus arose out of Ernst Käsemann's dissatisfaction with some of the theological conclusions drawn by Bultmann from his form-critical studies. The 'new quest' led on to a vigorous and profitable debate about the criteria which may be used to isolate traditions which are indubitably authentic,[4] but it did not, as might have been expected, encourage a reassessment of the basic principles of form criticism. Similarly, although redaction criticism is a logical development from form criticism and is closely related to it, it has not provoked a fresh appraisal of form criticism.[5] Sustained attempts to refine or replace the discipline have been few and far between.[6]

In spite of some vigorous attacks in the last two decades, the two-source 'citadel' of source criticism has not fallen, but its foundations have been re-examined and partially relaid; many scholars are now less confident than they were that the synoptic problem has been solved once and for all. A similar phase of debate about form criticism is long overdue, even though a general retreat is unlikely.[7]

In this essay we shall outline briefly some of the problems which surround several widely accepted form-critical axioms. We shall raise a number of questions and hint at few answers. But in the nature of the case that is not only inevitable but desirable.

The first premise of all form-critical study of the gospels is that behind the gospels as we now have them lie originally independent pericopae. Any reader of Mark's gospel can quickly learn to separate the individual gospel traditions from the framework in which they are set. The gospel traditions, we are frequently reminded, are like pearls on a string. This may be taken as an assured result of form-critical studies. But some of

the widely accepted corollaries are not as firmly established as is often
supposed.

Once one is able to remove the individual pearls from the string,
one's attention is focussed on the pearls, not the string. The framework
of Mark's gospel is usually held to be secondary: it may shed light on
Mark's own theological intentions, but it is of little value for the
historian.

C. H. Dodd firmly rejected this form-critical assumption and claimed
that Mark had at his disposal a skeleton historical outline of the career
of Jesus into which he fitted the individual pericopae or groups of
pericopae; the evangelist's procedure was a compromise between a
chronological and a topical order.[8] Dodd's article has frequently been
quoted by opponents of the more radical conclusions of form criticism,
but his hypothesis did not win the day. Indeed, in the wake of redaction
criticism, the view which Dodd rejected is held more tenaciously.
Although it would be difficult to defend Dodd's argument, his interest
in the origin of the Marcan framework was not misplaced.

In his detailed critical discussion of Dodd's hypothesis, D. E. Nineham
asked what *Sitz im Leben* could plausibly be posited to account for the
existence of a chronological outline of the life of Jesus in the early
church.[9] As Nineham pointed out, there is no independent evidence for
the existence of a chronological outline of the life of Jesus.[10] Nor, we
may add, is there any precedent within late Judaism for Mark's apparently 'biographical' approach, with its loose chronological and
topographical structure. When we look at roughly comparable
rabbinic traditions such as *Pirqe Aboth* or at the *Gospel of Thomas*, we are
immediately struck by the amount of *narrative* material about Jesus
which is found in the traditions on which Mark drew and which the
Marcan framework extends rather than contracts, as seems to have
happened in some circles in the early church. Indeed, on the grounds of
the criterion of dissimilarity which is so beloved of many form critics,
the framework of Mark emerges with strong claims to historicity!

Mark's method of presenting material about Jesus was by no means
as obvious an approach as it seems to modern readers of his gospel.
Very few of the numerous attempts to find a compelling historical or
theological reason for the emergence of Mark take sufficiently seriously
one of the most distinctive features of his gospel: originally independent
traditions have been set within a loosely 'biographical' framework.

There seem to be only two possible avenues open. Either we must accept that Mark acted without a precedent of any kind—and continue to search for an explanation of his method—or we may consider the possibility that Mark's achievement was rather less spectacular and original. Mark was simply extending a well-established practice: early Christian communities had long been in the habit of linking together in a loose chronological and topical structure traditions about Jesus. The latter alternative is much less fashionable than the former, but for that very reason it should be pursued all the more vigorously.

But this suggestion brings us face to face with a further corollary of the form-critical axiom that behind the gospels lie originally independent pericopae. Most form critics have accepted the dictum of M. Kähler: just as the light from the sun is reflected in every drop of the bedewed meadow, so the full person of our Lord meets us in each little story of the gospel traditions.[11] Many pericopae do make a point which is quite independent of their present context in the gospels. But they make a much greater impact and present a fuller portrait of Jesus when set alongside other pericopae.

If each gospel pericope was considered by the early church to be completely self-contained, why were so many of them retained with details which seem irrelevant to its main point? Frequently details which appear either to be irrelevant or secondary when a pericope is considered in isolation link up with others to provide a portrait of Jesus which is striking and which is often unconventional judged by the standards of the day. Particular traits, such as Jesus' attitude to women and children, his acceptance of tax collectors and other outcasts of society, his penetrating insight or his compassion and humility, emerge clearly only when several pericopae are placed together.

How would an individual pericope have been used in the early church? Whether we think of missionary preaching, catechetical instruction, debates with opponents, or worship, it is easier to imagine that traditions about Jesus were used in groups than that they were used in splendid isolation. Such groups of pericopae would be expanded or contracted according to the circumstances; if so, summaries of parts of the traditions would arise naturally.

The suggestion that groups of pericopae lie behind Mark is not new, though there has been little agreement on the nature and extent of such earlier collections.[12] But if pericopae were linked together loosely in groups which were enlarged or abbreviated in order to meet particular needs or circumstances, we should not now expect to be able to find clear traces of such groupings behind Mark's gospel. If we did not possess Mark, should we have guessed that behind Matthew's gospel lies a lengthy connected source?

The passion narratives and the Q material offer partial parallels. Many parts of the passion narratives do make sense in isolation from the rest of the passion story, but they make a much greater impact when set within a larger context. Is it not possible that the passion narratives were used in longer or shorter versions according to circumstances? Perhaps the quest for an original 'core' passion narrative which was gradually expanded by the addition of other traditions is misplaced. Q may also be seen as a partial anticipation of Mark: the Q traditions have a loose structure; some parts were very probably grouped together before the final redaction of Q.

Folklore traditions also provide some support. In its early development as a discipline, form criticism of the gospels was deeply influenced by studies of the transmission of oral folklore traditions. The 'story' element in such traditions is always strong and ought to have made form critics wary of placing too much emphasis on the individual pericope.

Mark's achievement was considerable: the 'gospel' pattern which he developed was to influence Matthew and Luke, and possibly John. But we must also recognize that Mark did not work in a vacuum. He was partially anticipated by some early Christian preachers and teachers, for they also used groups of traditions about Jesus. Even if parts of the framework were composed by Mark himself, were they not, on the whole, modelled closely on the traditions themselves?

Form criticism and redaction criticism have been held apart too rigidly as separate disciplines. The former has concentrated attention on the individual unit of tradition, while the latter has attempted to uncover the distinctive theological perspective of each evangelist. As a result we have come to accept without demur the notion that the writing of Mark is a dramatic development within the early church: no longer are we concerned with an anonymous group and individual pericopae, but with a theologically sophisticated evangelist who has created something quite without parallel. But Mark was not the first person in the early church to group together traditions about Jesus.

And why should we suppose that the traditions which he used suddenly ceased to be used by the communities which had treasured and used them for a long period?

Form critics have always insisted that the traditions on which Mark drew were oral and not written. Reference is usually made to Paul's use of technical terms for the transmission of oral tradition (I Cor. 15. 3ff. and 11.23); to the importance of oral tradition within Judaism generally; to the comments of Papias (c. AD 130): 'I supposed that things out of books did not profit me so much as the utterances of a voice that lives and abides' (Eus. *HE* III. 39.4). The earliest Christians are often alleged to have been illiterate or at best only semi-literate; in any case they are said to have inherited traditional Jewish suspicion and avoidance of any written documents apart from Torah.

The latter two points are open to question: literacy was very wide-spread in Palestine (and in the Hellenistic world generally); the Qumran and associated documents, as well as the Nag Hammadi material suggest that we have over-estimated Jewish and early Christian suspicion of writing.[13] The simple question, 'Why did Mark *write* his gospel?' has not been answered. The more strongly the role of oral tradition in the early church is stressed, the more difficult it becomes to account for the transition from oral tradition to Mark's comparatively lengthy and not unsophisticated document.

We do not wish to argue that written traditions existed before Mark,[14] but form critics have neglected to examine sufficiently carefully the relationship between oral and written tradition, and the development and use of writing in the early church. Most studies of the transmission of oral folklore traditions have been based on societies which did not have access to writing.[15] Should we not concentrate our search for possible parallels to the transmission of the gospel traditions on societies which had access to writing, but in which oral tradition was still very much alive?

To what extent did Mark's decision to *write* a gospel lead automatically to a change of perspective? This is a most important question which form critics have not usually stopped to ask. The transition from oral to written tradition is normally assumed to have been a natural and smooth one: the fact of writing *per se* is of comparatively little significance. Mark wrote a *gospel* from traditions about Jesus which had

long been used in close support of the preaching of the church: so
argued M. Dibelius and many other form critics. The standard form-
critical view can even appeal to Irenaeus, for he claimed that the
evangelists set down in writing the apostolic preaching (*Haer*. III. 1.1).

E. Güttgemanns has recently launched a spirited attack on this view
of the origin of the written gospels.[16] He asserts that form critics have
mistakenly believed that there is continuity between oral and written
tradition; the way back from the 'literary' form of the gospel to the
individual oral traditions is much more precarious than form critics
have supposed.[17] Güttgemanns claims that studies of folklore traditions
carried out in Yugoslavia by M. Parry and A. B. Lord prove that there
is a decisive difference between oral and written tradition: they belong
to quite different *genres* which are not to be confused.[18] Mark's gospel is
both more than and quite other than the sum of its parts. In short, we
should concentrate our attention on the 'gospel' form, on the structure
and intention of Mark, rather than continue the futile attempt to study
the individual oral pericopae with our present inadequate methods;
the future lies with redaction criticism, not form criticism.[19]

Güttgemanns' work is to be welcomed warmly; it is one of the few
recent attempts to reopen discussion of basic form-critical principles.[20]
But his attempt to drive a firm wedge between oral and written
tradition is unconvincing: the work of M. Parry and A. B. Lord does
not support the far-reaching conclusions he has drawn from it.

Parry and Lord sought to shed new light on the origin of the Homeric
traditions: Homer is the most talented representative of a tradition of
oral epic singing.[21] They began collecting material in the 1930s, when
the Yugoslav oral epic was accessible, alive and distinguished; it has
now almost completely disappeared, killed by the spread of literacy
and the influence of written 'authoritative' texts. Lord's brilliant book
includes a chapter on the relationship between writing and oral
tradition. He repeatedly emphasizes that the use of writing in setting
down oral texts does not in itself have an effect on oral tradition.[22] The
transition from oral to written techniques is 'a process, or better the
acceleration or aggravation or extension of a process that continually
goes on in oral composition'.[23] An oral tradition dies, not when
writing is introduced, but when 'published' song texts are spread
among singers and begin to be thought of, not as the recording of a
moment of the tradition, but as *the* song.

The standard form-critical view associated particularly with M. Dibelius is not refuted, but finds some support from the work of Parry and Lord. There is no reason to suppose that Mark's gospel is quite other than the sum of its parts. Indeed their work provides some further points of interest for students of Mark's gospel. The introduction of writing leads to longer songs, greater thematic freedom and a frequent tendency towards episodic structure. 'When a tradition or an individual goes from oral to written, he, or it, goes from an adult, mature style of one kind to a faltering and embryonic style of another sort.'[24] It is perfectly possible for writing to exist side by side with oral tradition, just as it is possible for an oral poet steeped in oral tradition to write his own text. There is no reason to doubt that it was not the writing of Mark's gospel, but the later slow acceptance of Mark as a fixed and authoritative text which led to the death of oral traditions about Jesus. Matthew and Luke, after all, were able to combine written and oral traditions without difficulty.

Güttgemanns' position is also undermined by such evidence as we have of the relationship of written and oral tradition in Judaism. Not surprisingly, he has paid scant attention to Jewish traditions, though they are surely at least as relevant as studies of Yugoslav oral epic poets! The Mishnah very probably reproduced collections of notes which had already been written before; 'Tannaim' continued to repeat Tannaitic texts orally long after these had been reduced to writing.[25] The Jewish evidence poses its own particularly difficult problems, but it ought not to be ignored.

We have been assuming, without discussion, that studies of folklore and Jewish traditions are of relevance to the student of the gospels; we must now take up briefly this most important form-critical principle. Form critics have analysed the gospel traditions according to their 'form' and have then used this analysis to trace the history of the traditions.[26] The formal analysis of the traditions was deeply influenced by alleged parallels in Jewish, Hellenistic or folklore traditions. The similarities are often striking, but form critics have often paid insufficient attention to the dissimilarities. The form and content of the oral traditions have often been considered separately. But form and content are interdependent; their relationship needs to be examined much more carefully.

The distinctive and unique situation in which traditions about Jesus were transmitted inevitably means that parallels from other oral traditions must always be partial and must always be treated with care. Studies of traditional Jewish techniques of teaching and transmission of tradition are relevant, but the early Christians were not attempting to transmit the teaching of rabbi Jesus and to develop a 'school of inter-pretation'.[27] Hellenistic pedagogical method is relevant, but even though the intelligence and the education of the earliest Christians is regularly underestimated, they are unlikely to have been acquainted with sophisticated Hellenistic literary techniques. Study of folklore traditions is relevant, but K. L. Schmidt's famous description of the gospels as *Kleinliteratur* rather than *Hochliteratur* can be pressed too far. The gospel traditions were neither a saga nor a song-cycle honouring the memory of a long-dead hero; they were not preserved, as were most folklore traditions, by inward-looking 'conservative' communities; they are not *traditional* in the sense that the Yugoslav oral poems are.[28] We have no exact parallels to the gospel traditions; for even if we were to confine our attention to the transmission of other Christian oral traditions, the evidence is so much later than the gospels and so sketchy that it is of little use.

This is a counsel of warning, not of despair. The traditions about the actions and teaching of Jesus were transmitted in quite unique cir-cumstances and this factor must be considered in analysis of their form and history. But the earliest Christian communities were always open to a variety of influences, for they were certainly not enclosed in glass cases. To what extent did the unique circumstances of the early church and the unique content of its traditions about Jesus influence the form in which those traditions were transmitted? The form critic can never hope to be in a position to answer that question with absolute con-fidence, but it is a question which he avoids at his peril.

Closely related to the problems which are involved in the formal analysis of the traditions is yet another form-critical assumption which needs careful scrutiny. The 'form' of the gospel traditions is usually linked closely to their use in early Christian communities. Traditions about Jesus were retained and used only in so far as they met the needs and interests of the early church.

In a sense the latter observation is a truism: it was a very long time before the development of the canon encouraged the Christian church to retain documents which were of little interest and which sometimes seemed to be of little direct relevance! But what were the needs and interests of the early church? Form-critical study of the gospels always involves a circular argument. The form critic must either study the traditions with a particular understanding of the early communities in mind, or he must attempt to use his analysis of the traditions to shed light on the needs and interests of the early church. M. Dibelius adopted the former alternative and R. Bultmann the latter.

The dangers are obvious, but not always heeded: it is all too easy to allow a particular view of the needs of the early church to influence judgment of the *Sitz im Leben* of various parts of the tradition, or *vice versa*. The dangers of a circular argument cannot be avoided entirely, but they can be minimized by paying close attention to evidence from outside the gospels. The epistles, Acts and Revelation give us some insights, admittedly often only partial, into the self-understanding of Christian communities. The gospel traditions belonged to the same Hellenistic communities as Paul and John.[29] Unless we accept that there were two 'branches' in the early church, one of which transmitted traditions about the life of Jesus, while the other, the Pauline branch, took no interest in such traditions,[30] such evidence as is found outside the gospels must be taken very seriously indeed.

One example must suffice. For some time now many scholars have followed R. Bultmann's lead and claimed that a number of sayings attributed to the historical Jesus in the gospels originated as sayings of the risen Christ speaking to the church through early Christian prophets. This may well have happened. But such evidence of prophetic activity as we have from outside the gospels does not suggest that the influence of Christian prophets was as pervasive as is often supposed. The epistles and Acts indicate that the apostles, not early Christian prophets, were the leaders of the communities; 'another group, however important, can hardly have possessed the authority to speak in the name of the risen Lord and have such declarations accepted.'[31]

We do have some evidence from outside the gospels which can partially avoid circular arguments, but the form critic must frequently acknowledge that our knowledge of the early church is limited.[32] Gaps in our knowledge must not be filled by our own understanding of the nature and role of the church.[33]

The relationship between the 'form' of a given tradition and its *Sitz im Leben* in the early church cannot be determined as easily and as confidently as some form critics have supposed. Judgments about the *Sitz im Leben* of a pericope have often differed considerably. But there are more important reasons for caution. Recent research into oral tradition points to a much more flexible situation. Almost every 'form' of oral tradition may be used in a wide variety of ways. Similarly, any given situation can utilize very different forms.[34]

There is evidence from within the New Testament itself which confirms this principle. The christological hymns which are quoted in the Pauline or post-Pauline epistles have survived only because they were found to be useful in a secondary paraenetic setting: the same 'form' of tradition has more than one *Sitz im Leben*.[35] The Pauline epistle is a distinctive literary *genre*; it was found to be useful in very different circumstances in the post-Pauline period; in the Pastoral Epistles the *Sitz im Leben* has changed while the *genre* has remained constant.[36]

Hence the form critic cannot be confident that his observation of a change in the form of a pericope suggests a new *Sitz im Leben*. Nor can he assume that similar forms of traditions were used in the same way in the early church. It is very probable that gospel traditions were used in a wide variety of settings and circumstances with little or no change in their form being necessary.

The long-standing debate about historicity continues. In the last few years the tide of opinion has swung firmly behind a more moderate approach than that usually associated with the earlier form critics. Three factors have been particularly influential. The work of H. Riesenfeld and B. Gerhardsson was attacked vigorously: there are serious weaknesses in their similar positions. But their work has served to remind us that even though the early church did not proclaim Jesus the rabbi, traditions about Jesus were transmitted for some time in a Jewish milieu which took tradition seriously. The debate about the appropriate criteria which may be used to isolate authentic traditions has shown how absurd it is to maintain that the only indubitably authentic traditions are those which can be paralleled neither in contemporary Judaism nor in the early church. But perhaps the most important factor has been the work of H. Schürmann, a scholar whose writings are not yet widely known in the English-speaking world. He has argued that the origin of some of the gospel traditions is to be located not merely within the life of the primitive church, but in the community life and missionary preaching of the disciples *before* Easter.[37] Schürmann has opened a new phase in the debate about the ultimate origin of the gospel traditions; he has done so not by rejecting form criticism, but by using several form-critical principles in a fresh and illuminating way.

Our comments on the historicity of the traditions have deliberately been very brief. But we do not mean to suggest that this is an unimportant issue or that it is so intractable that little or nothing can usefully be said. All too often debates about historicity have distracted attention away from discussion of the central axioms of the form-critical method. Some agreement about the limitations and possibilities of the discipline itself must precede any fruitful debate about the historicity of the traditions.

A number of form-critical axioms have been touched on.[38] Few can be shown to be false, but the optimism and confidence of some scholars is ill-founded. As we have hinted more than once, the evidence often does not allow us to be certain; new evidence is unlikely to be forthcoming. On the other hand, such evidence as there is has not always been scrutinized sufficiently rigorously. Form criticism is a most useful tool; it is unlikely that a replacement for it will ever be found. But it is a blunt tool which urgently needs resharpening.

NOTES

1. For a useful but uncritical exposition of form criticism, see E. V. McKnight, *What is Form Criticism?*, Fortress Press 1969.

2. There are notable exceptions which prove the rule: H. Riesenfeld, 'The Gospel Tradition and its Beginnings', *Studia Evangelica* I (TU 73), 1959, pp. 43–65; B. Gerhardsson, *Memory and Manuscript*, Lund 1961; T. Boman, *Die Jesus-Überlieferung im Lichte der neueren Volkskunde*, Göttingen 1967; E. Güttgemanns, *Offene Fragen zur Formgeschichte des Evangeliums*, Munich, 2nd ed. 1971.

3. R. Bultmann, *Die Geschichte der synoptischen Tradition*, first published 1921; 8th ed., Göttingen 1970. (The *Ergänzungsheft*, 4th ed. 1971, includes a discussion of recent literature by G. Theissen.) ET, *History of the Synoptic Tradition*, 2nd ed., Blackwell 1968. M. Dibelius, *Die Formgeschichte des Evangeliums*, first published 1919; 6th ed.,

Tübingen 1971; ET, *From Tradition to Gospel*, 1934; reprinted by James Clarke, 1971.

4. See, for example, H. K. McArthur, 'A Survey of Recent Gospel Research', *Interpretation* 18, 1967, pp. 39–55; N. Perrin, *Rediscovering the Teaching of Jesus*, SCM Press 1967; M. D. Hooker, 'On Using the Wrong Tool', *Theology* 75, 1972, pp. 570–81; R. S. Barbour, *Traditio-Historical Criticism of the Gospels*, SPCK 1972, pp. 14ff.; W. O. Walker, 'The Quest for the Historical Jesus: a Discussion of Methodology', *ATR* 51, 1969, pp. 38–56.

5. See J. Rohde, *Rediscovering the Teaching of the Evangelists*, SCM Press 1969, and R. H. Stein, 'What is Redaktionsgeschichte?', *JBL* 88, 1969, pp. 45–56. Redaction criticism also needs careful reappraisal. See C. J. A. Hickling's interesting discussion of Marcan redaction criticism in *Religious Studies* 10, September 1974, pp. 339–46. On Luke, see G. N. Stanton, *Jesus of Nazareth in New Testament Preaching*, Cambridge University Press 1974, pp. 31ff.

6. W. G. Doty has assembled a thorough bibliography and has discussed the history of form criticism: 'The Literature and Discipline of New Testament Form Criticism', *ATR* 51, 1969, pp. 257–321. The cynic might suggest that preoccupation with the history of a scholarly discipline is a sign of its stagnation.

7. As examples, see W. R. Farmer, *The Synoptic Problem*, Macmillan 1964; D. L. Dungan, 'Mark—the Abridgement of Matthew and Luke', *Jesus and Man's Hope* I, ed. D. G. Buttrick, Pittsburgh Theological Seminary 1970, pp. 51–97; A. Gaboury, *La Structure des Évangiles Synoptiques*, Leiden 1970; D. Wenham, 'The Interpretation of the Parable of the Sower', *NTS* 20, 1974, pp. 299–319.

8. C. H. Dodd, 'The Framework of the Gospel Narratives', *ExpT* 43, 1931–2, pp. 396–400; reprinted in a collection of Dodd's essays, *New Testament Studies*, Manchester University Press 1953.

9. D. E. Nineham, 'The Order of Events in St Mark's Gospel—an examination of Dr Dodd's Hypothesis', *Studies in the Gospels: Essays in memory of R. H. Lightfoot*, ed. D. E. Nineham, Blackwell 1955, pp. 223–39. Cf. C. F. D. Moule's comments in *JTS*, NS 7, 1956, pp. 280ff.

10. Nineham dismisses too readily Dodd's appeal to the speeches in Acts, though he correctly concludes that Acts 10.37–41 and 13.23–31 afford only the most limited support to the historicity of Mark's order: ibid., pp. 228ff.

11. *The So-Called Historical Jesus and the Historic Biblical Christ* (originally 1896), ET Fortress Press 1964, p. 81. Cf. G. Bornkamm, *Jesus of Nazareth*, ET Hodder 1960, p. 25.

12. For a thorough recent discussion (though with largely negative results) see H. W. Kuhn, *Ältere Sammlungen im Markusevangelium*, Göttingen, 1971.

13. We urgently need a full-scale study of the extent of literacy and of the uses to which writing was put in Judaism and Hellenism in the first century AD. Although B. Gerhardsson's *Memory and Manuscript* is sub-titled *Oral and Written Transmission in Rabbinic Judaism and Early Christianity*, his comments on *written* tradition are brief. But see G. Widengren, 'Tradition and Literature in Early Judaism', *Numen* 10, 1963, pp. 42–83; C. H. Roberts, 'Books in the Graeco-Roman world and in the New Testament', *The Cambridge History of the Bible*, Vol. I, ed. P. R. Ackroyd and C. F. Evans, Cambridge University Press 1970, pp. 48–66.

14. But see R. H. Gundry's defence of this possibility, *The Use of the Old Testament in St Matthew's Gospel*, Leiden 1967, pp. 182ff.

15. See, for example, the influential study of Jan Vansina, *De la Tradition Orale: Essai de Méthode Historique*, Musée Royal de l'Afrique Centrale, Tervuren, Belgium

1961. Most of the evidence on which he draws comes from societies without writing.

16. E. Güttgemanns, *Offene Fragen zur Formgeschichte des Evangeliums*, Munich, 2nd ed. 1971. Somewhat surprisingly, Güttgemanns does not refer to the Irenaeus passage, even though he strongly criticizes Dibelius' 'preaching' theory.

17. Ibid., pp. 78ff.

18. See especially A. B. Lord, *The Singer of Tales*, Harvard University Press 1960.

19. Güttgemanns uses the structural linguistics of Ferdinand de Saussure in an attempt to break new ground in gospel criticism.

20. As yet it has not received the attention it deserves; this is partly because the use of modern linguistics takes most New Testament scholars into new and difficult terrain. But see the critical review-article by H. Thyen, 'Positivismus in der Theologie und ein Weg zu seiner Überwindung?', *EvTh* 31, 1971, pp. 472–95.

21. With Güttgemanns' use of the work of scholars primarily interested in Homer, we have once again a cross-fertilization of New Testament and classical studies.

22. *The Singer of Tales*, pp. 124ff.

23. Ibid., p. 130.

24. Ibid., pp. 132ff.

25. J. Kaplan, *The Redaction of the Babylonian Talmud*, Bloch Publishing Company 1933, pp. 272ff. Cf. also the article 'Mishnah' in *Encyclopaedia Judaica*, Jerusalem 1971.

26. T. W. Manson's often-quoted attack on form criticism does not do justice to the form critic's attempt to use his analysis of the traditions to reconstruct their history. Manson claimed that 'a paragraph of Mark is not a penny the better or the worse for being labelled "Apophthegm" or "Pronouncement Story" or "Paradigm" ' ('The Quest of the Historical Jesus—Continued', *Studies in the Gospels and the Epistles*, ed. M. Black, Manchester University Press 1962, p. 5).

27. Cf. W. Wiefel, 'Vätersprüche und Herrenworte', *Novum Testamentum* 11, 1969, pp. 105–120.

28. Cf. the concluding words of A. B. Lord's book: 'Yet after all that has been said about *oral* composition as a technique of line and song construction, it seems that the term of greater significance is *traditional*. Oral tells us "how", but traditional tells us "what", and even more, "of what kind" and "of what force".' *The Singer of Tales*, p. 220.

29. Cf. E. Käsemann, *New Testament Questions of Today*, SCM Press 1969, pp. 40f. and 49.

30. This view has been suggested by several scholars. See, for example, U. Wilckens, 'Hellenistisch-christliche Missionsüberlieferung und Jesustradition', *Theologische Literaturzeitung* 89, 1964, cols. 518ff.

31. D. Hill, 'On the Evidence for the Creative Role of Christian Prophets', *NTS* 20, 1974, p. 274. The same point is made by F. Neugebauer, 'Geistsprüche und Jesuslogien', *ZNW* 53, 1962, pp. 218–28.

32. Cf. F. G. Downing, *The Church and Jesus* (SBT 2.10), 1968.

33. In particular our notion of what 'preaching' should be today can easily be read back into the New Testament. It would be very instructive to investigate the debates about the nature and role of the church which took place in the first two decades of this century; the first form critics' understanding of the primitive church may well have been influenced by contemporary discussions. I owe this point to Dr. H. Willmer.

34. H. Kuhn, 'Zur Typologie mündlicher Sprachdenkmäler', *Bayerische Akademie der Wissenschaften, Phil.-Hist. Klasse, Sitzungsberichte 1956*, Heft 5, Munich 1960, p. 21.

35. R. Deichgräber, *Gotteshymnus und Christushymnus in der frühen Christenheit*, Göttingen 1967, pp. 190ff.

36. W. G. Doty, 'The Literature and Discipline of New Testament Form Criticism', *ATR* 51, 1969, p. 307.

37. 'Die vorösterlichen Anfänge der Logientradition', *Der historische Jesus und der kerygmatische Christus*, eds. H. Ristow and K. Matthiae, Berlin 1962, pp. 342–70. Schürmann's main arguments have been accepted by a number of scholars. See especially E. Trocmé, *Jesus and his Contemporaries*, SCM Press 1973; the main thesis of Trocmé's book may be seen as a considerable extension of Schürmann's view.

38. Two further widely accepted form-critical axioms need reconsideration: the early church was not interested in the 'past' of Jesus and the gospels are not biographies; both are discussed in some detail in my book, *Jesus of Nazareth in New Testament Preaching*, Cambridge University Press 1974.

3

In his own Image?

MORNA HOOKER

SPIES at King's College London report that the Professor of New Testament Studies, exasperated by excessive undergraduate reference to the 'wrong tool', exploded with a denunciation of the wretched woman with her wrong tools,[1] declaring that the real problem was that the right tools were used in the wrong way. He is, of course, correct—the real problem is the misuse of tools; though if someone applies a sledgehammer to a nut with disastrous consequences, it may fairly be said that the wrong tool has been used for the particular job in hand. Whichever way one describes it, New Testament scholars do often show a remarkable—dare one say 'naive'?—confidence in the particular scholarly method which happens to be in vogue at any time, and tend to use it to the near exclusion of other methods. As a result, successive generations of scholars are classified according to the method which they pioneered or used, so that source critics were followed by form critics, who in turn gave way to redaction critics; the categorization implies that no one may examine the material in more than one way!

This picture is of course an over-simplification. It is obvious that every scholar builds on the foundation of those who have gone before, and accepts the results of previous work as the basis of his own. Both the historian of the tradition and the redaction critic rely on the conclusions of the source critic regarding the relationship of the documents, and their investigations follow on naturally from the insights of the form critic. To this extent, each scholar may claim to be 'using' various disciplines. Nevertheless, there is always a danger in assuming that the results in a certain area are 'assured'; conclusions which are not constantly re-examined become the presuppositions upon which new hypotheses are based. It is not enough to accept the conclusions reached yesterday and move on to new methods; for yesterday's problems may look rather different if viewed from today's position, and may yield different answers. The questions must therefore be continually reformulated and grappled with, however tiresome this may be: the New Testament scholar must not simply set certain questions aside as 'solved', but like a juggler, endeavour to keep all his balls in the air—sometimes, indeed, adding new ones to the number in play, but never allowing any of them to drop.

A study of the history of biblical interpretation demonstrates the way in which the answers which are given to questions in any particular period are largely determined by the outlook of those who ask the questions. If it is true to say that those who have hunted for the historical Jesus have often looked down a well and seen a reflection of their own faces, it is also true that students of the gospels have tended to picture those who wrote them in their own image. When source criticism was in its heyday, and B. H. Streeter and his friends presented their solution of the synoptic problem in terms of a four-document hypothesis, the evangelists appeared, through their eyes, in the guise of Oxford scholars, poring over their sources, meticulously piecing together the evidence of various documents, and taking care to record all available material and to lose no scrap of evidence. The scope of the hypothetical Q could therefore be determined with some confidence, and even the other sources used by Matthew and Luke—envisaged now as documents—could be reconstructed. Not only were the evangelists seen in the likeness of Oxford scholars in their method of working, but the underlying motives of scholars and evangelists were also understood to be remarkably similar: the evangelists, it was assumed, carefully preserved historical material about the Lord, since their concern was primarily to record what happened; they therefore provided valuable evidence which would lead the scholar back from the evangelist to the historical Jesus and his authentic words.

Form criticism, by contrast, threw the emphasis neither on the evangelists nor on the figure of Jesus, but on the interim period and the units of tradition. Its exponents saw the evangelists as collectors of pericopae, each of which confronts those who hear it with the word of the gospel. Once again, the philosophy of the scholar is reflected in the picture which is drawn—not, this time, in any portrait of the evangelists, now mere faceless stringers of pearls—but in the presentation of the 'community', that strange collective entity with the face and philosophy of a Lutheran preacher.

The implications of the form-critical approach for the search for the historical Jesus have been under continual discussion for the past fifty years; the hopes of the English source critics for recovering the real Jesus and his authentic words crumbled before the advance of the new method. Strangely, its relevance for source criticism itself is less often realized; the important role of the individual units of tradition—and possibly of small collections of units in the community—suggests that the idea of a monolithic Q is an unnecessary and indeed unlikely explanation of the phenomena it was devised to explain.[2] But if the existence and shape of a document Q is uncertain, it is, to say the least, remarkable to find a redaction critic writing a recent book on 'The Theology of Q' without really considering the question whether Q ever existed![3] The old questions must be constantly asked, and the old answers be continually questioned.

Redaction critics, too, may fairly be said to have recreated the evangelists in their own image. For many of them, it is axiomatic that the evangelists had no interest in history, but were creative theologians; their supposed creativity has surely met its match in the imaginative ability of many redaction critics! Redaction criticism, in its turn, ought to open up again some of the questions 'solved' when certain presuppositions held good. If the evangelists were as free with their material as is now being suggested, do the reasons once given for the priority of Mark, for example, still hold good?

As an illustration of the extent to which one's presuppositions and basic method influence one's conclusions, we may take the different interpretations given by different scholars to Mark 2.1–3.6. H. B. Swete, in his commentary on Mark published in 1898, believed that 'the writer intended to follow the relative order of time' and that there is 'a progress in the history of the Galilean Ministry, as it is depicted by St Mark, which bears the stamp of truth'.[4] He was therefore able to treat the links between the sections in 2.1–3.6 as historical. Most commentators in the past fifty years have accepted the conclusion of the form critics that the section is a pre-Marcan collection of conflict stories, grouped together because of their common theme. Recent emphasis on the evangelists as men with theological purposes, and not mere gatherers of tradition, however, would seem to suggest that this grouping may be due to Mark himself, and should be seen in the context of the structure of the whole gospel; it may be in the plan of Mark's book that we shall discover the motive for bringing these particular narratives together. Hardly surprisingly, we find Eduard Schweizer, who writes his commentary from the viewpoint of a redaction critic, attributing most of the collection to Mark himself.[5] These three very different explanations of the Marcan arrangement demonstrate the way in which assumptions about the material determine the interpretation which is given: responsibility for the ordering of events has shifted from the historical Jesus to the early community and finally to the evangelist. The final stage in this progression may indeed be to place the emphasis on the interpretation of the commentator (where, one suspects, it is in reality already hovering!) and to say with some literary critics that the original author's own purposes are immaterial, and that the meaning of what is written is found in the interpretation given to it by the reader.

It is in fact reasonable to suggest that Jesus, the community, the evangelist and the modern interpreter all play their part in the understanding of any gospel passage, and that the relative importance of each factor varies from one passage to another. We shall hear the voice now of one, now of another. But how does one distinguish between these voices, and decide who is playing the major role? The difficulty of knowing whether the material mediated to us by 'the community' reflects only the beliefs of the community, or whether it speaks to us also about the historical Jesus, is matched by a similar difficulty when we turn to redaction criticism. Can we distinguish between the beliefs of the redactor and those who went before him? A recent guide to redaction criticism says:

> In order for redaction criticism proper to develop we had to learn to trace the various stages through which tradition has passed. Only then was it possible to recognize the nature and extent of the redac-action. In other words redaction criticism proper is dependent upon the ability to write a history of the tradition.[6]

The author of this guide is confident that we have this ability: the tools to do this, he says, 'were developed through the . . . discipline known as form criticism'.[7] Yet it is precisely in this attempt to trace the history of the tradition that we have seen the difficulties and dangers of coming to any certain conclusions; if the tools we use in tracing the tradition turn out to be inadequate, and if the method involves circular arguments and presuppositions, then we must recognize that we are in danger of building our redaction-critical house on foundations of shifting sand.

The redaction critic does, of course, have one great advantage over those whose primary concern was to trace the history of the tradition in the oral period. When he comes to Matthew and Luke, at least, he is able to point to actual verbal changes which an evangelist has made in his sources. Or is he? He may feel that present scholarly opinion makes it reasonable for him to assume the priority of Mark, and therefore to argue that any changes made by Matthew and Luke to the Marcan wording are significant. Already, however, difficulties arise: is it the text of Mark as we know it (in so far as we do know it!— perhaps here, too, we are over-confident) that was used by the later evangelists? Where they diverge from Mark, is it because their theological motives compel them to make changes? Are the alterations due to other reasons—perhaps stylistic or accidental? Most important of all, are such divergences perhaps not primarily alterations of Mark, but due to the fact that an evangelist has chosen to follow a tradition other than Mark's, even where the two gospels are to some extent parallel? This particular difficulty occurs most frequently in Luke: suggestions that Luke prefers a non-Marcan source to Mark tend to be treated with suspicion, since they are usually understood to be part of the unpopular proto-Luke hypothesis. Nevertheless, it is undeniable that Lucan parallels to Mark are frequently remarkably dissimilar. If we assume that Luke is deliberately altering his source, then we are likely to see these changes as evidence for his theology, and perhaps build important conclusions on them; if, however, Luke has not changed Mark, but in fact preferred to use another source, then—although his choice of source may be significant—we shall need to enquire carefully about the reasons for his choice.

An obvious example of this particular problem is Luke's 'omission' of Mark 10.45. On the basis of his failure to reproduce this saying, Luke has been accused of having no *theologia crucis*, and of deliberately altering Mark's interpretation of Christ's death.[8] Yet an examination of the Marcan section and its parallels in Matthew and Luke suggests that, while Matthew is clearly following Mark at this point, Luke is using a different version of the saying, for there is little verbal similarity.[9] Moreover, he has placed the pericope in a different setting, where it is in some ways more appropriate. These two factors seem to indicate that Luke was not consciously using Mark at all at this point—and therefore not altering or 'toning down' his interpretation of the significance of the cross. Now of course it may still be argued that the fact that Luke has preferred his non-Marcan source at this point can tell us something about his theology. But we must be very cautious how we use this kind of argument: for Luke may have had many reasons for doing what he did—among which must be included the fact that he often uses non-Marcan material in preference to Mark. The use of an alternative tradition, together with his placing of this particular pericope in a different setting (where possibly it was already embedded), suggest that it may simply not have occurred to Luke that he was 'altering' Mark or that he was rejecting a Marcan emphasis, and he might well have been astonished by the verdicts of his commentators and the motives attributed to him.[10] Too often, the discussion about this passage isolates the Lucan verse from its context, and overlooks the fact that while Mark 10.45 is the climax of a pericope about glory, which points out the paradoxical path which the Christian disciple must follow, the Lucan version is set in the account of the Last Supper, and the theme of the significance of the death of Jesus for his followers is present in the context, immediately before and after the pericope: the death of Jesus is linked with the coming of the kingdom, in which Jesus has the right to apportion places,[11] and he gives these places to those who have continued with him in his 'trials'—though in the supreme trial immediately following, Jesus stands alone, his disciples having failed him. As in Mark, the themes of honour, lowliness, service, sharing the suffering of Jesus and the central role of his lonely death—in Mark a 'ransom' for many, in Luke a 'covenanting' to the disciples—are all present.[12]

The question of the changes made to the Marcan material by the later evangelists is difficult enough. The problem becomes even more complex, however, when Mark is left behind, and the only source the redaction critic has for comparison is the unknown and unknowable Q. If Q ever existed in the solid form once envisaged, then the discussions as to whether Matthew or Luke has preserved its wording more exactly in various places might offer us some interesting evidence for the theological motivations of those two evangelists. But the more significant are the differences between the Matthean and Lucan forms of a saying, the more doubtful is it whether either evangelist is making deliberate changes, and the more possible is it that the tradition has come to them in different forms. Once again, the choice of material which an evangelist makes may be important (especially if he is consciously rejecting an alternative version of the tradition) but it is less significant than changes which he may deliberately have made in the tradition he received, in order to fit his theological purpose. Those who argue that Luke used Matthew and not Q are in a much better position for showing the significant changes which have been made to the material by Luke; but if their basic assumption about Luke's sources is wrong—and the arguments for it are far from convincing—their interpretation collapses.[13]

The redaction critic therefore faces a formidable task: in order to understand his author, he needs to be able to trace the history of the tradition which has been used; yet at every step, both at the oral and at the written stage, the uncertainties are such that he must beware of any easy solutions. It is dangerously over-confident to assert:

> Our knowledge of the redactional activity of Matthew and Luke is ... both firm and extensive; we not only have one of their major sources, Mark, but we can also reconstruct another, the sayings source, Q.[14]

How then is the redaction critic to proceed? In many cases what he in fact does—or tries to do!—is to allow the evangelist to speak for himself; to study the structure and language of a gospel, and to deduce from this evidence the purpose and position of the author. This approach has produced some illuminating insights in the hands of cautious scholars such as R. H. Lightfoot.[15] Yet this method, too, has its dangers. For it is all too easy to see patterns where none exist, and to impose our own interpretation on the material; when Mark is interpreted with the help of algebraic formulae,[16] or John with the aid of liturgical calendars which still fit even when shifted through six months,[17] then one is bound to ask whether the interpreter has not taken over from the evangelist. Sometimes the redaction critic ignores awkward pieces of evidence which do not fit his theory: Conzelmann, for example,[18] has often been justly criticized for making a generalization in speaking of the absence of Satan from the ministry; perhaps even more important is his failure to consider the significance of Luke 1–2, since, whatever their origin, these chapters now stand at the beginning of Luke's work, and may well provide vital information about his purpose.[19]

At other times, the redaction critic's analysis will lead him to speak of an evangelist's 'characteristics'. Undoubtedly each writer has his characteristics, but it is often extremely difficult to be certain what belongs to the evangelist and what to his source. Over-confidence in one's ability to distinguish the two can lead to false conclusions when the discovery of 'characteristics' is then used as a tool to separate sayings which have come to the evangelist as part of the tradition from sayings which he has created.[20] Even if we did conclude that a saying in Mark, for example, contains Marcan characteristics, this does not mean that it was a Marcan 'creation'; Mark may well have left his own finger-prints on the tradition which he has handled. Form critics have often fallen into the trap of supposing that when they have unearthed the earliest recoverable form of a saying and reconstructed its setting in the community, they have also discovered its origin. Redaction critics can easily fall into a similar trap, in supposing that a Marcan form means a Marcan origin. In the analysis of a book's structure, too, we find that very different interpretations are given according to the prior assumptions—or 'critical method'!—adopted by the investigator. Whereas source critics, for example, have tended to regard inconsistencies in a document as indications of a piecing-together of traditions by editors who were unconcerned by apparent contradictions, redaction critics assume that the redactors were rational men, and the same inconsistencies can therefore be explained as important indications of theological intent![21] But Mark and his successors were handling traditional material, and though each of them used it in his own way, it is unwise to assume that they carefully organized every detail of its arrangement. It is possible to concentrate on the evangelists to such an extent that one ignores the prior history of the tradition—and that means, inevitably, a distorted understanding of the evangelist and his aims.

Perhaps the greatest danger before the redaction critic, however, is that of imposing his own philosophy upon the material, and seeing the gospel in the light of his own situation. The modern New Testament critic has weathered the storm which assailed his faith when he first discovered that the gospels are not biographies, and do not present him with 'history as it happened'; for many Christians, the discovery that the gospels are primarily theological documents, telling us as much about the faith of the community as about the things which Jesus did and said, has proved a liberating experience. Yet liberation from the shackles of historicity and its problems has led some to a position where they happily cut the ties with the historical Jesus and refuse all historical props to faith. This kind of criticism has often been brought against Bultmann, whose interest has been with the tradition—and with its history! The same tendency is now seen in redaction criticism: the evangelists, too, are understood as interested only in 'what it means' and not in 'what happened'.

The swing of the pendulum is seen in a comment by Perrin on Mark: 'After several generations of being read mistakenly, as a historian, he has earned the right to be read as a theologian.'[22] With this statement we must surely agree. But the pendulum is given a remarkable push in a revealing comment which Perrin makes on a study in Marcan theology written by Ernest Best, which he describes as 'a strange book in that the author combines redaction criticism with the assumption "that Mark believes that the incidents he uses actually happened"!'[23] Now this is really an extraordinary statement. Why should the fact that Mark is a 'theologian' preclude him from writing about events which he thought had happened? Can a 'theologian' write only about imaginary events? This is obviously sheer nonsense. Against Perrin, we must quote Perrin himself: 'Mark has the right to be read on his own terms.'[24] And what is the most obvious thing about Mark's method of writing? It is that he presented his theology in a form which 'misled' generations of scholars into believing that he was writing an historical account! This, says Perrin, 'is mute testimony to the skill of Mark as an author'.[25] Mark may well be more skilful than has sometimes been allowed—but not if he succeeded only in concealing his purpose until the twentieth-century critic uncovered it! Was he perhaps using his skill to do precisely what he seems to be doing? He certainly gives the impression that he is writing *Heilsgeschichte*, and that theology and history are for him inextricably bound together. Is it not likely that he has chosen 'to introduce his particular theology of the cross' in narrative form because it is an exposition of what he understands to have actually happened? Perrin continues: 'That he chose to do this in the form of narrative rather than theological treatise is his business.'[26] It is perhaps sufficient comment on this to quote again his own remark made a few lines later: 'Mark has the right to be read on his own terms'!

When we turn to Luke, it is impossible to deny that his theology is presented as being grounded in history: he, certainly, believed in *Heilsgeschichte*. Is it, perhaps, the modern theologian's unease with the idea of God at work in history which has led to the accusation that Luke has 'historicized' the material? Yet even in Lucan studies, we find the assumption that theology and history do not mix appearing in a new guise in Perrin's summary of Conzelmann's views: 'Luke is in no way motivated by a desire to exercise historical accuracy, but entirely by his theological concept of the role of Jerusalem in the history of salvation.'[27] But does not Luke also have 'the right to be read on his own terms'? His own statement of intent in 1.1–4 scarcely seems to support this antithesis between historical accuracy and theology!

It may not be an accident that this kind of one-sided emphasis on theology over against history has grown up in connection with a stress on the Hellenistic influence on the Christian community; yet we would surely expect those soaked in the tradition of the Jewish scriptures to place more emphasis on history than is now often allowed. The dismissal of the past and its importance for the evangelists is in part also the result of stressing the *Sitz im Leben* of the evangelist himself; this concentration on the period of the redaction and denial of historical interest on his part continues a tendency already seen in form criticism. Undoubtedly the early Christian writer selected and used material which spoke to his condition—and, he presumably hoped, to that of his readers—but did his interest stop there? Luke's answer, in 1.1–4, is clearly 'no'. And since Mark chose to write his 'gospel' in the form of an account of 'what happened then', he also does not appear to have thought 'now' and 'then' unrelated. The twentieth-century critic must not build the first-century evangelist in his own image, and assume that because he himself has despaired of discovering certainty regarding the historicity of his material, and has come to terms with this by placing more and more emphasis on its theological meaning, the evangelists did the same.

Such extreme expressions of the antithesis between 'theology' and 'history' are not necessarily part of the redaction-critical approach: indeed, they must be regarded as over-enthusiastic statements which distort the picture by exaggerating certain aspects neglected in previous study.[28] Our discussion has concentrated in particular on Perrin's *What is Redaction Criticism?* because this is offered as an introduction to the discipline for the 'ordinary student'. It is unfortunate that the account is so likely to mislead its readers.

The evangelist, we have already suggested, must be allowed to speak for himself; we must not impose our ideas upon him. But it is extraordinarily difficult to hear what he is trying to say. We have lost his *Sitz im Leben*; just as there is disagreement about the setting of the pericopae, so there is no certainty about the situation of the books, and the variety of interpretations presented by commentators demonstrates the difficulty. We try to put ourselves into the evangelist's shoes, and only succeed in forcing him into ours! Some have seen liturgical interests as paramount; the gospels are linked with lectionaries, and the epistles with baptismal rites. But where is the evidence for this kind of liturgical organization at this early period? And where is the evidence in the material itself? It surely appears only when one wears liturgical spectacles. The most popular model in current exegesis, however, is a doctrinal one: the New Testament writers' main concern was to combat 'false christologies'. The fourth gospel and the Colossian 'hymn' have long been interpreted in this way,[29] and Paul is certainly frequently found in debate with opponents of one kind or another—now understood to be 'gnostics' as often as they are Judaizers, teaching a false christology. Recently Mark has been understood as a defence against 'heresy'. This theory has been most fully expounded by T. J. Weeden, who argues that Mark presents us with two contrasting christologies—first, in chapters 1–8, a *theios-aner* christology, and secondly, in the rest of the gospel, his own suffering-Son-of-man christology; the Caesarea Philippi incident describes a conflict between these opposing christologies, and 'since there is no historical basis for a christological dispute of this nature having taken place between Jesus and the disciples, the only way to account for Mark's consuming interest in it is that it has some existential importance for the situation in his own

/ community'.[30] If we ask Weeden what evidence there is for such a dispute in Mark's own situation, he will no doubt simply refer us to Mark himself: it has become axiomatic that the gospel material is direct evidence for the evangelist. Yet even if we grant this initial assumption, there are grave difficulties with Weeden's thesis: that the disciples' understanding of Jesus is represented as *inadequate* is clear, but that it is *wrong* is by no means evident. If Mark is trying to attack a false christology which he has put into the mouth of Peter, then he was remarkably unsuccessful, since innumerable readers of his gospel, from Matthew onwards, have interpreted him completely otherwise! Certainly the disciples fall under Mark's disapproval; but this is not because they uphold a *theios-aner* christology (whether the *theios-aner* theme is as significant for the New Testament as the current fashion for the title suggests is also questionable), but because they are blind to the significance of Jesus' words and actions. There is nothing in Mark's gospel which supports the idea that he is presenting us with a wrong interpretation in chapters 1–8 which must be rejected: the story of the two-stage opening of the blind man's eyes in 8.22–26 suggests, on the contrary, that a proper understanding of Jesus as presented in these chapters is a necessary first stage before the mystery of the suffering Son of man can be understood.

The danger of reading later christological beliefs back into the gospels has long been recognized by New Testament scholars; the documents must not be read through Chalcedonian spectacles. But we may wonder whether this current 'heresy hunt' is not also something of an anachronism. Were there already 'false christologies' to combat? No doubt whose who wrote the documents now incorporated in the canon sought to emphasize certain aspects of the gospel as they understood it. Mark perhaps felt it necessary to remind his readers that as disciples of Jesus they must expect to suffer—but did he feel this because they were *forgetting* this aspect (like the Corinthians), or because he wished to assure them that their present sufferings, of which they were possibly very much aware, were a necessary part of their discipleship, and that if they were faithful they would receive their reward? The emphasis of a particular theme does not mean that we have to look for a 'heresy' which is being opposed. Weeden's analysis brings out the two themes in Mark's presentation of Jesus—his mighty acts, and the paradoxical path of suffering, which his disciples must also follow. Mark's writing is of course christological, since the whole New Testament is christological, attempting to express this new faith centred on Jesus: Mark does not need 'heresy' to make him write in this way.

False teaching certainly creeps into the Christian communities—though it is in the later New Testament epistles that we find the defences against it being set up. But does not this notion belong to a situation where Christian truth has established some kind of norm, and 'heresy' is a deviation? And can this be already the situation when Mark was written? In looking for the setting of the New Testament books it is apparently all too easy to overlook the obvious—that is, the fact that most of them were written before the final break with Judaism came: that the most pressing and urgent controversy which faced these men was the controversy with the orthodoxy of Jewish faith and practice. There was as yet no 'Christianity'; the movement was still a Jewish sect—claiming to be in the succession of Judaism, its members indeed the only true adherents to the Jewish religion. These early writers are concerned to establish that Jesus is the Messiah of God—and that if 'the Jews' do not accept him, then it must be because they are blind and deaf, and have cut themselves off from the promises of God; it is for these authors vitally important to demonstrate that their belief is entirely in accordance with the scriptures—which remain for them authoritative, since it is God's word through Moses and the prophets—and indeed that it is only they who really understand the scriptures, since 'Israel' has failed to grasp their meaning. This may well be the kind of controversy which lies behind Mark, where it is the Jewish people who demonstrate the false understanding of Jesus, the disciples who—in the end—have their eyes opened: if the disciples seem slow in understanding, then we may at this point agree with Weeden in supposing that this reflects in part the situation of Mark's own time; the process of showing how Jewish heritage and Christian experience could be reconciled was not completed in a day, and it was a process which was continued in many different ways, as the New Testament itself demonstrates.

The same kind of controversy is reflected elsewhere in the New Testament. That Paul had much to say on this particular topic is obvious. The other great theologian of the New Testament, John, is also concerned to show how Jesus fulfils all that Judaism promises, and completes the role of the Torah, which pointed forward to him.

Matthew, too, with his enigmatic comments on the law, is interpreted
by commentators in many ways, but his words cease to seem contradictory when we stop trying to make him answer our questions, and
allow him to put his own: What is the relation of the Christian community to the law? And of Christ to Moses? Are Christians law-
breakers? Or are they in fact the true doers of the law in contrast to
Israel? The letter to the Hebrews also, which is often said to be addressed to those in danger of lapsing into Judaism, was perhaps more
probably written by someone who was grappling with the problem
'Why then the Old Testament?' and who solved it by seeing the cultic
system as a foreshadowing of the work of Christ. We forget too
easily the difficulty—and the excitement!—of discovering and demonstrating how Christ fulfilled the scriptures, which could be interpreted
in a variety of ways—taken atomistically as simple proof-texts, used
allegorically or typologically, or commented on by *midrash*. The
Jewish scriptures are for these writers part of God's revelation, of which
Christ is the fulfilment; since God is not fickle, the two cannot be
contradictory, and the scriptures must point to Christ. With this
dominating concern it is understandable why, for example, Luke
might wish, as Christopher Evans suggested,[31] to present the central
section of his gospel as a Christian Deuteronomy.

This formulation of Christian belief against the givenness of the Old
Testament is the particular setting which suggests itself to me as a
likely background for much of the New Testament. In a book devoted
to asking questions, it would be improper to indulge myself by
exploring this theme any further. I must content myself with revealing
my own particular presuppositions. Perhaps I, too, am reading my
own concerns into the minds of the New Testament writers, and
interpreting their work and their use of scripture in the light of present-
day discussion about how Christians should use the Christian Bible!
It is at least arguable, however, that in regard to this particular problem
of relating the givenness of the past with the exhilarating experience
of the present, we today have much in common with the writers of
the New Testament.

NOTES

1. M. D. Hooker, 'On Using the Wrong Tool', *Theology* 75, 1972, pp. 570–81.
2. See C. K. Barrett, 'Q: A Re-examination', *ExpT* 54, 1943, pp. 320–23.
3. R. A. Edwards, *The Sign of Jonah* (SBT 2.18), 1971.
4. H. B. Swete, *The Gospel according to St Mark*, Macmillan 1898, p. liii.
5. E. Schweizer, *Das Evangelium nach Markus* (Das Neue Testament Deutsch), Göttingen 1967, ET, *The Good News According to St Mark*, SPCK 1970, in loc.
6. N. Perrin, *What is Redaction Criticism?*, SPCK 1970, p. 13.
7. Loc. cit.
8. For a recent example of this approach, cf. R. A. Edwards, op. cit., p. 37: 'Luke has been careful to modify the very significant statement in Mark 10.45.'
9. Bultmann regards Mark 10.45 as a dogmatic reformulation of a more primitive saying preserved in Luke 22.27. See *The History of the Synoptic Tradition*, ET Blackwell 1963, p. 93. Luke's version has parallels also with the tradition recorded in Mark 9.34f. and Luke 9.46–48.
10. There is another factor which enters into our judgment on Luke's intention in this passage, and which demonstrates the importance of our own assumptions in handling the material; for the answer we give to the question of Luke's handling of the saying depends to a large extent on our interpretation of the Marcan version! Those who understand Mark 10.45 in the light of Isa. 53 naturally regard the absence of the 'ransom' saying from Luke as significant; if the Marcan saying is understood in the tradition of Old Testament ideas about God's redemption of his people at the Exodus and from the Exile, and the hope of a future redemption, then the contrast between Mark 10.45 and Luke 22.27 is not so great. See C. K. Barrett, 'The Background of Mark 10.45', *New Testament Essays: Studies in memory of T. W. Manson*, ed. A. J. B. Higgins, Manchester University Press 1959, pp. 1–18; M. D. Hooker, *Jesus and the Servant*, SPCK 1959, pp. 74–9. We may also note that Luke adds to the Marcan framework of the journey to Jerusalem the story of Zacchaeus (19.1–10) which leads up to another saying about the Son of man: 'The Son of man came to seek and to save that which was lost.' Here we have what seems to be a typical Lucan emphasis on salvation as already present in the ministry of Jesus, and had Luke inserted it before the story of Bartimaeus, it might have been argued that he was deliberately substituting this for the saying in Mark 10.45 linking the saving activity of the Son of man with his death: but Luke places the Zacchaeus incident in Jericho, and has Jesus heal Bartimaeus on the way *into* Jericho, instead of on the way out!
11. In Mark 10.40, Jesus does not have the right to apportion the two chief places next to himself, though sharing his suffering is understood as a necessary qualification for sharing in his glory.
12. A similar argument to that about Luke's treatment of Mark 10.45 is often used regarding his failure (according to the shorter text, which surely has the better claim to originality) to copy Mark's saying over the cup in 14.24. Once again, however, this ignores the setting in which Luke places the giving of the cup in vv. 17f., the cup from which Jesus will not drink, and which is firmly associated with the coming of the kingdom. The pericopae immediately following, as we have already seen, link the kingdom with the theme of the covenant. Luke's expression of the association between the cup and the covenant may not be as succinct as Mark's, but is his understanding so very different? Is the difficulty with Mark's version perhaps not the significance

which is given to the death of Jesus, but rather the apparent identification of wine which is drunk with blood?

13. The case for Luke's use of Matthew was argued by A. M. Farrer, see 'On Dispensing with Q', *Studies in the Gospels: Essays in memory of R. H. Lightfoot*, ed. D. E. Nineham, Blackwell 1955, pp. 55–88. Those who have used this thesis as the basis for redaction-critical work include M. D. Goulder, 'Characteristics of the Parables in the Several Gospels', *JTS*, NS 19, 1968, pp. 51–69, and J. Drury, *Luke* (J. B. Phillips' Commentary), Collins 1973.

14. N. Perrin, op. cit., p. 57.

15. See especially R. H. Lightfoot, *The Gospel Message of St Mark*, Oxford University Press 1950.

16. Cf. A. M. Farrer, *A Study in St Mark*, Dacre Press 1951. Farrer subsequently revised his own interpretation of Mark in *St Matthew and St Mark*, Dacre Press 1954, 2nd ed. 1966.

17. Cf. A. Guilding, *The Fourth Gospel and Jewish Worship*, Oxford University Press 1960. Some of the difficulties of this interpretation are discussed by L. Morris in *The New Testament and the Jewish Lectionaries*, The Tyndale Press 1964.

18. H. Conzelmann, *The Theology of St Luke*, ET Faber 1960.

19. Cf. P. S. Minear, 'Luke's Use of the Birth Narratives', *Studies in Luke–Acts*, ed. L. E. Keck and J. L. Martyn, SPCK 1968, p. 121, and M. D. Hooker, 'The Johannine Prologue and the Messianic Secret', *NTS* 21, 1974, pp. 51f.

20. An example of this is to be found in Perrin's discussion of Mark 9.1, op. cit., p. 48: he notes that 'Mark speaks of seeing the parousia here in 9.1, again in 13.26, and for a third time in 14.62'; moreover Mark uses the words 'power' and 'glory' in 'parousia contexts'; hence 'the reference to "seeing" the parousia and the use of the words "power" and "glory" in this kind of context' are Marcan characteristics. One confusion in this argument is immediately obvious: Mark 9.1, with its reference to 'seeing' and to 'power', is not a 'parousia' saying at all, but describes the coming of the kingdom of God: it is Matthew who transfers it to the Son of man. There are therefore *two* Marcan parousia sayings which promise that men will see the Son of man coming with clouds; these two sayings are similar, and they occur in similar contexts, promising future vindication in spite of present humiliation and suffering. There seem to be three possible explanations: (i) Mark has created both sayings, and the reference to 'seeing' is therefore a Marcan characteristic, as Perrin suggests. (ii) One saying came to Mark in the tradition, and he doubled it, in drawing the parallel between the situation of persecuted Christians and Jesus himself. (iii) Both sayings are traditional, and the reference to 'seeing' the Son of man is a natural one, for the words are in both places clearly referring to Daniel's vision; since the sayings have their setting in the context of suffering, it is not surprising that they are found, like the prediction of the passion, in Mark alone. It seems rash to conclude that the first of these suggestions is the only possible explanation, and that the saying in Mark 9.1 about the kingdom of God coming with power must be a Marcan creation!

21. See, for example, Q. Quesnell, *The Mind of Mark: Interpretation and Method through the Exegesis of Mark 6.52*, Rome 1969.

22. Perrin, op. cit., p. 53.

23. Ibid., p. 83, quoting E. Best, *The Temptation and the Passion: Marcan Soteriology*, Cambridge University Press 1965, p. xi.

24. Op. cit., p. 53.

25. Ibid., p. 52.

26. Ibid., p. 53.

27. Ibid., p. 29.

28. There are signs that Perrin himself does not always mean what he seems to say. In an article in *Exp T* 82, 1970, for example, entitled 'The Literary *Gattung* "Gospel"—Some Observations', he speaks of a gospel (of which form Mark is in his estimation the only pure example) as 'a narrative of an event from the past in which interests and concerns of the past, present and future have flowed together' (p. 7).

29. But see M. D. Hooker, 'Were there False Teachers in Colossae?', *Christ and Spirit in the New Testament: Studies in honour of C. F. D. Moule*, ed. B. Lindars and S. S. Smalley, Cambridge University Press 1973, pp. 315–31.

30. T. J. Weeden, *Mark—Traditions in Conflict*, Fortress Press 1971, p. 69.

31. C. F. Evans, 'The Central Section of St Luke's Gospel', *Studies in the Gospels* (see note 13), pp. 37–53.

4

Jesus, the Wandering Preacher?

FREDERICK H. BORSCH

I

IN his classic study of more than a half century ago Wilhelm Bousset characterized Jesus in his ministry as 'the wandering Preacher'.[1] In so doing he was making use of a distinct and well formed impression that emerges from the pages of the gospels and which has ever since influenced Christian piety, forms of missionary strategy and biblical scholarship. With regard to this scholarship, and by way of illustrating the effects of this understanding on the ideals of Christian practice, it can suffice to quote from but one of many more contemporary examples. In what has now become another classic study of Jesus, Günther Bornkamm, when speaking of the meaning of discipleship in the New Testament, finds that the disciple is called '... to follow Jesus from place to place, and to accept the fate of a wanderer with all its privations'.[2]

Although it would appear that critical scholarship has raised almost every conceivable question concerning Jesus and his ministry, it may seem remarkable that this aspect of the context of his public life has rarely been subject to serious debate. Along with many other students of the New Testament, we would subscribe to the following methodological statement:

> No understanding of the teaching of Jesus is possible without the recognition of the significance of its original historical context, and the precaution of constantly seeking to discover that context and to take it into account is one that is most necessary for us to undertake.[3]

Scrutiny of the place that itinerancy played in the context of Jesus' ministry may conceivably assist us better to interpret certain sayings and themes attributed to him and to identify themes and emphases which we might critically prefer to regard as those of the early communities or the evangelists rather than of Jesus himself. The process may also be of help in determining and properly understanding the legitimacy of the bases of this characterization of Jesus' style of ministry for the pietistic and evangelical considerations mentioned above.

While not proposing to suggest that Jesus was in some way rigidly localized in his activities, we shall ask whether the picture describing itinerancy as the dominant mode of his ministry has been rightly drawn. Might the characterization of him as a 'wandering preacher' be in some sense a caricature and an exaggeration? In the following pages we shall present many of the factors which can be adduced in favour of a largely itinerant style of ministry and then bring forward alternative considerations. While our data and evidence are not of the kind that will allow us to draw any definitive conclusions, we shall finally wish to make some brief observations arising from this research.

II

Although it is true that, outside a few suggestions in Acts, the New Testament writings other than the gospels do not describe Jesus as an itinerant, this silence can be largely discounted as evidence for or against itinerancy.[4] These letters and other materials are little concerned with the details of Jesus' historical ministry, and one can spin all too many theories to fill in the gaps. The conception of Jesus as an itinerant is, however, pervasive in the gospels. In negative terms, none of the evangelists would seem to intend to indicate that Jesus during his public ministry lived for any period of time in any one place. In positive terms, through the criterion of multiple attestation, we find references to Jesus being in various locales associated with different forms of narrative and discourse materials. Though such references are often generalized and could, in some instances, be rather easily detached from the main pericopae, the impression they give is clearly one that was important to the early churches. To some extent the evidence may be discounted through the realization that oral tradition does not regularly localize a saying or story.[5] Such a concern is more often that of a writer, one who is interested in some form of a consecutive narrative and who owns to at least a measure of a historicizing attitude. Nevertheless this approach to the materials supports the picture of itinerancy at least in general terms.

Similar results are obtained when the criterion of multiple attestation is applied to the sources. While the scope of this article does not permit us to study the many passages in great detail, a review of them indicates that the conception of Jesus as an itinerant has a place in the traditions of all four gospels and in the so-called Q material.

In the material that is for the most part common to the synoptic gospels we may begin with the baptism and temptation narratives. Although the stories are now highly idealized and the second of them may be more mythical than legendary, they do suggest that at some stage, perhaps at the beginning of his public ministry, Jesus travelled to an area outside his home region.[6] Such a journey and/or a period in which he was associated with John the Baptist (and perhaps a baptist group) would not, however, necessarily be indicative of the general style of Jesus' own preaching and healing activities.

The synoptic gospels then inform us that Jesus went to Galilee, Matthew tells us that at this point he left Nazareth and went and dwelt in Capernaum. Luke here introduces a form of the pericope, found later in Matthew and Mark, containing the saying to the effect that 'a prophet is not without honour, except in his own country'. Luke specifically locates the incident in Nazareth; Matthew and Mark speak more vaguely of 'his own country', perhaps with the meaning 'his native town', but conceivably with reference to Galilee in general or possibly to Capernaum rather than Nazareth.[7] If historical, the story could well suggest that Jesus had spent some time preaching and healing outside 'his own country' (whatever that means). The saying, however, is well known in the ancient world and may have originally been used by the churches as a way of comprehending Jesus' rejection either by Jews in general or more specifically by individuals who had known him.[8]

The next information of concern to us is the call of the two sets of brothers, Simon and Andrew and James and John. The statement that they 'followed him' (and similar statements elsewhere in the gospels) may not be of as much significance as it would at first seem, 'since [the expression] was in common use by the Jews as a term for discipleship'.[9]

Perhaps of more importance is the indication that they relinquished their profession, possessions and even family to be associated with Jesus. With this may be compared Mark 10.28–30 and parallels in which Peter reminds Jesus of all that the disciples have left, including homes and relatives, to be with him, and Jesus promises a reward for such sacrifice. Two observations can be made here. Privations of this kind would also be consistent with some form of sectarian or group existence, and the critical historian will recognize a general tendency on the part of hagiographers (here the evangelists and/or their traditions) to exaggerate the sacrifices made by their heroes.[10] This is not to say that Jesus' disciples were not ultimately called upon to make genuine acts of renunciation, but it is to ask whether such acts were clearly understood to be essential to their initial commitment. (To both of these matters we shall later return.)

In Mark 1.35=Luke 4.42 we are told that Jesus went to a lonely place to pray. Though the evangelists may well have understood this and similar reports elsewhere in the gospels (especially in Luke) in terms of a semi-nomadic existence, such a withdrawal is not necessarily inconsistent with a localized ministry. Following upon this we are, however, informed (Mark 1.38=Luke 4.43) that Jesus expressed the desire to go on to other towns 'for this is why I came out' (Mark) or 'for I was sent for this purpose' (Luke). All three of the gospels then give a summary description of travels through Galilee[11] and preaching in synagogues.[12] It is our opinion that this sense of missionary zeal must be viewed as constituting the strongest evidence indicative of an itinerant ministry. We say this apart from the question of the authenticity of particular passages, because such an understanding of Jesus' activity could well be regarded as coherent with possibly authentic themes stressing the urgency of the proclamation of the coming kingdom. Although it is probably rightly regarded as part of the Marcan redactional process, with such statements should also be taken the summary remark in Mark 1.45 indicating that the spread of the news about Jesus later made it impossible for him to enter a town openly.

There is then the picture of Jesus sending out his disciples, with very little to encumber them, to preach and to heal (see Mark 3.14f.; 6.7–11; Matt. 10.1, 5–23; Luke 9.1–5; 10.1–20). With this presentation of the mission of the pre-resurrection community should probably be associated the Matthean theme that Jesus' followers were at this time to go only 'to the lost sheep of the house of Israel' (Matt. 10.5f.; see 10.23). But it is also just at this point that our chief and most controversial question must be raised: to what extent might the conception of Jesus' eagerness to communicate his message *through the medium of journeys and travels* and the commissioning and sending out of disciples (either a small group of twelve or a larger group as in Luke's commissioning of the seventy) be regarded as either exaggeration or a reading back into the traditions of ideas drawn from post-resurrection experiences and missionary zeal?

While most scholars are able to see a number of anomalies (such as the continued passivity of the disciples) and evident signs of the influence of later Christian experience in the passages describing the commissioning of Jesus' followers, they remain convinced that an essential activity of pre-resurrection disciples is at the heart of the descriptions.[13] They are impressed by the fact that there are clear indications of separate bits of tradition in this regard in all three synoptic gospels as well as the Q material, and they note the seemingly impractical strictness of the restrictions on the equipment the disciples are to take with them, most stringently presented in Q. This latter feature is seen as fitting with the eschatological urgency of Jesus' own sense of mission.

Unfortunately we do not here have the scope to enter into the intricacies involved in debating the many issues raised by these passages. We do not doubt that the several lines of tradition are informed by the idea of missionary travels on the part of Jesus and his disciples, but the reason for this is precisely the issue we wish to focus upon in the next section. One could also argue that the very strictness of the regulations implies the idealization rather than the authentic character of such missionary commandments. Palestinian in origin they may be,[14] but Bultmann maintains that the section dealing with the missionary charge 'must in the end be included in the regulations of the Church'. Contending that Mark gives but an excerpt of what is more fully preserved in Q, he argues that Mark has read the materials back into the ministry of Jesus for the very reason that they were no longer applicable to the mission in the Hellenistic world, 'and Matthew and Luke followed him in that'.[15]

In terms of other material generally held in common by the synoptic gospels, we need not especially concern ourselves with the record of the journey to Jerusalem. Obviously such a journey took place, and it would have led through countryside and towns like Jericho, where various incidents and occasions for teaching or preaching could well have occurred. Indeed, the point can be made that the impression of this journey could have been rather formative with respect to the early traditions, perhaps colouring other memories and lending a tone of peregrination to them.

Although the material widely regarded as a common source for Matthew and Luke is often classified as a collection of sayings, it apparently could have contained some narrative material. Yet, as far as one can tell, this was not of a kind that provided any continuity. The story of the healing of the centurion's servant begins with the words 'he entered Capernaum', but there are few if any other references of this type. We have already noted the fragments of a missionary charge in the common Matthean and Lucan traditions. There are also several passages dealing with the privations proper to a disciple: Matt. 6.25–33=Luke 12.22–31 on worldly anxieties; Matt. 6.19–21= Luke 12.33f. concerning true treasures (where Luke alone explicitly advises the selling of possessions); and Matt. 10.37=Luke 14.26 on the requirement of placing discipleship ahead of family relationships. While we cannot here critically sift through this material with the question of authenticity in mind, it would probably be generally agreed that there are to be found here some sayings that could reach into the pre-resurrection circumstances. We would only note that, while such advice could correspond with an itinerant style of life, it is not by any means necessarily applicable only to such a mode of living. Similar instruction in other religions and philosophies has been given to individuals and groups who led a very stabilized and localized existence. A classic example would be the advice of Henry David Thoreau, whose very point it was that such a style of life is easier to maintain and true meaning is more readily to be discovered by staying in one's own backyard.

Probably the most significant Q passage for our purposes is Matt. 8.19–22=Luke 9.57b–60. It is first instructive to note that both Matthew and Luke independently set the pericope within their own generalized context of travelling. In Matthew Jesus has just given 'orders to go over to the other side'. Luke prefixes 'as they were going along the road' (to Jerusalem).

Matt.8.19-22	Luke 9.57b-60
19. And a scribe came up and said to him, 'Teacher, I will follow you wherever you go.' ²⁰And Jesus said to him, 'Foxes have holes, and birds of the air have nests, but the Son of man has nowhere to lay his head.' 21. Another of the disciples said to him, 'Lord, let me first go and bury my father.' ²²But Jesus said to him, 'Follow me, and leave the dead to bury their own dead.'	. . . a man said to him, 'I will follow you wherever you go.' ⁵⁸And Jesus said to him, 'Foxes have holes, and birds of the air have nests; but the Son of man has nowhere to lay his head.' ⁵⁹To another he said, 'Follow me.' But he said, 'Lord, let me first go and bury my father.' ⁶⁰But he said to him, 'Leave the dead to bury their own dead; but as for you, go and proclaim the kingdom of God.'

Although the two evangelists and the Q tradition understand 'follow me' to be involved with itinerancy and make this explicit, we have previously seen that the expression can well be interpreted outside of such a context. The authenticity of both of these sayings of Jesus has, of course, been disputed. The remark concerning the foxes and birds is sometimes regarded as a converted 'I' statement or as an original use of 'son of man' as periphrasis which escapes the problem of the Son of man designation and, for some, makes it fit more easily into their view of Jesus' own words and ministry. Often it is noted, however, that the saying has the proverbial quality of folklore and that similar descriptions are made of heroic figures before they achieve their eminence.[16] Even if the statement is to be regarded as in some way authentic or as a primitive reminiscence about Jesus, it may well need to be applied as a generalized reference to his relative poverty and not as a literal description of his circumstances.[17] In addition, some scholars suggest that the logion may originally have had a symbolic frame of reference which would render it insignificant for the purposes of our discussion.[18]

The rather mysterious logion concerning the leaving of the dead to bury their own dead is more difficult to deal with, since its meaning remains somewhat unclear. Does it reflect a misunderstanding of an original maxim which meant 'leave the dead to the burier of the dead' or was it metaphorical in intent, 'the dead' referring to those who were not disciples?[19] If it is to be interpreted more literally, it probably presupposes that the father is in fact not yet dead, but rather is near to the point of death. In these terms the request of the would-be follower of Jesus is but a matter of common decency and proper filial loyalty, a virtue highly valued in Judaism. Seen in this light, one could well believe that the remark attributed to Jesus is to be read hyperbolically (in a fashion similar to other gospel statements regarding family relationships), and is intended to assert the priority of the call of the kingdom of God, rather than as an explicit, literal commandment. As such an admonition it need not have been a call to adopt an itinerant style of life.

Finally in connection with Q material, we should mention the passage (Matt. 11.21–23a=Luke 10.13–15) in which woes are pronounced on the three neighbouring towns of Chorazin, Bethsaida and Capernaum. To this pericope we shall return when discussing a possible locale for the major portion of Jesus' ministry.

We have of necessity already taken brief notice of indications that the individual synoptic evangelists augmented the general picture of Jesus' itinerant ministry. Mark records a visit to the region of Tyre and Sidon (found also in Matthew) and another vague reference to a journey through the Decapolis. Matthew, along with references such as in 11.1 to teaching and preaching in their cities, presents a theological-evangelistic plan limiting missionary activity to the Jews until after Jesus' death, when the command is given (28.19f.) to make disciples of all nations.[20] Luke, in addition to editorial changes expanding the scope of Jesus' ministry[21] and the inclusion of several traditions peculiar to him which mention different locales, adopts the literary device of a much fuller description of the final journey to Jerusalem.[22] Into this journey he inserts material placed in other contexts by Mark and Matthew. While debate can, of course, be presented on specific points, we regard at least the great majority of these narrative references as the redactional work of the evangelists or formulations by the communities which passed the traditions along to them. We also would suggest that the inclusion of some of the place names in the stories is probably to be regarded as a manifestation of the 'George Washington slept here' syndrome; i.e., there would have been a strong tendency, as local communities of Christians were established, to come to believe that Jesus might once have visited their town.

We must not pass beyond this survey of the synoptic material without reference to the numerous generalized descriptions of movements and passages ('as he was going away', 'as he was going along a road', 'as he passed on from there') and the rural background of seashore, hills and countryside against which Jesus' ministry is often placed. Nor can we neglect the introductory phrases which mention travel across the Sea of Galilee or in and out of Bethsaida and, especially, Capernaum. Our argument will be that many of these references only substantiate the fact that the traditions and the redactors owned to the general impression that Jesus was an itinerant (and also provided an aid to the narrative task) or that they are not inconsistent with, and to a degree may even support, the possibility of a more localized ministry.

The overall effect of the fourth gospel tends to support the portrait of Jesus as a wanderer. Upon closer examination, however, that support persists almost entirely in the form of a generalized delineation; the details are, for the most part, contradictory to those of the synoptics. The fourth evangelist does place some of Jesus' public ministry in Galilee. We are also informed that Jesus 'went about in Galilee'. Capernaum is several times mentioned, as is passage on the Sea of Galilee. But this gospel otherwise cites localities not found in the synoptics, makes definitive a ministry in Samaritan regions only touched upon by Luke, and, of course, most at variance, tells of four or five visits to Jerusalem and infers that Jesus had genuine acquaintance with the geography and certain of the residents of Jerusalem and its environs. There has been considerable critical debate regarding the possibility that the fourth gospel gives better information than the synoptics on this latter point. Previous visits to Jerusalem might help to explain certain incidents which the synoptics place during Jesus' one and only journey to Jerusalem. Certainly it would be understandable if someone with his belief in the inbreaking of the new age made more than one visit to the holy city. On the other hand, one has to take into account the fourth evangelist's theological concerns, which were far more important to him than historical details. Having inherited and developed traditions which centred upon controversy between Christians and Jews, he would naturally wish to focus that controversy by placing much of it at the heart of historical Judaism and so amid its leaders. There is evidence, too, that this evangelist had taken over traditions which had grown in a Jerusalem-centred Christianity and which would therefore emphasize and perhaps exaggerate the extent of Jesus' ministry there. Moreover, it is clear from the manner in which John presents his narrative that he had little precise chronological or geographical information concerning Jesus' movements.

Even should we accept the theory that Jesus made two, three or more journeys from Galilee to Jerusalem in his ministry, we could not necessarily infer from this that his regular mode was one of itinerancy. In this regard it is of considerable interest that there are imbedded in the fourth gospel clear clues that even in Jerusalem Jesus remained known as a Galilean.[23] No prophet was to come from that region. But Jesus did, and concerning his ministry there this gospel adds little to the general picture gained from the synoptics concerning his style of ministry in Galilee.

III

To this point we have reviewed evidence which tends to support the long-standing Christian tradition that presents Jesus as a homeless preacher and teacher. While we have sought to neutralize and question this testimony, we do not thereby suggest that it is totally without foundation. We do wish now, however, to offer reasons for believing that the presentation may be an exaggeration—that for theological reasons and the purposes of narration, and because of the intervening experiences of the Christian churches, it was easier and more desirable for the framers of the traditions about Jesus to remember and exaggerate whatever journeys he may have taken than it was to present him as one who spent the great majority of his public life in one fairly restricted locale.

Among the designations applied to Jesus in the gospels are those of teacher and rabbi. We shall not here debate the question whether Jesus was actually given the honorific and unofficial address of rabbi during his lifetime, but probably all scholars would agree that Jesus could aptly be described as a teacher, even if this general designation does not fit him into any precise category. Certainly he cannot simply be equated with the scribal class of his time, for there are ways in which he seems to have been regarded more as a prophet[24] and a wisdom figure[25] than as a preserver and interpreter of scriptural traditions. Since the character of our evidence and quite possibly Jesus' own style of ministry do not permit us sharply to delineate him in terms of office or some one function, we cannot make any definitive arguments on this basis. It is, however, worth noting that, while other Jewish teachers of his period did from time to time make travels, they were, so

54

far as we know, more often identified with a locality and a relatively stabilized style of life. Students or followers came to them. In this connection we may observe that the gospels actually provide considerable testimony that individuals and crowds *came to* Jesus or *were brought* to him and that the report concerning him *went out* from where he was teaching.[26] While this would not necessarily be inconsistent with an itinerant mode (crowds coming to him as he arrived at new preaching and healing stations), it could imply that people came and were brought to him more often than he journeyed to meet them.

Supposing for the moment that such was the case, we next need to ask the important question why the alternative impression grew so strongly in all the traditions. Here we wish, recognizing its limitations, to apply the same criterion of *diversity*, which has been used with regard to the sayings attributed to Jesus, to the issue of the nature of his ministry. Our argument will be that itinerancy was a style either adopted by or perhaps in some cases forced upon a number of the early heroes of Christian evangelism. As such this mode may well have become a kind of ideal for the Christian leader. In these circumstances, it would have been most natural to assume for and to apply to Jesus himself such a form of ministry, and the requirements of historical scholarship would obligate us to raise inquiry about the accuracy of the description of Jesus' activities in this regard.

Once again our evidence is not nearly as complete as we would desire, but what testimony we have is reasonably consistent. Not only from the Acts but from Paul's own letters we know that he made a number of journeys during the best known and remembered portion of his life. While he did stay in particular cities for as much as two or three years and probably used Antioch as a base, what was most remembered and that which Luke glamourized were his travels. Paul himself stresses the privations he suffered as a result. Memory of these is also enshrined in the Pastoral Epistles.

Although Acts informs us only about Peter's travels within Palestine, strong early tradition and a reference of Paul's (I Cor. 9.5) make it clear that Peter also engaged in longer missionary journeys. That the extent of these may have been exaggerated would be a part of our argument. Journeying was the ideal for early Christian evangelists.

It may be suggested that for a time some of the leadership of the church was centralized and stabilized in Jerusalem. If, however, Acts is to be believed, this pattern began to be disrupted after a relatively short period, perhaps less than a decade. At least some of these disciples, we are told, 'were scattered because of the persecution that arose over Stephen [and] travelled as far as Phoenicia and Cyprus and Antioch' (Acts 11.19). Tradition indicates that James, the Lord's brother, and others remained in Jerusalem until the sixties, but that, after his martyrdom and the ensuing troubles, the community was further scattered.[27] It is also important to observe that even during the period when a community of Christians may have enjoyed some stability in Jerusalem, Luke tells us that leaders of the church went out on missionary forays. Peter and John were sent to Samaria and returned 'preaching the gospel to many villages of the Samaritans' (Acts 8.14, 25).

Of course, it was part of Luke's purpose in Acts to present a programmatic picture of the Christian mission, beginning 'in Jerusalem and in all Judea and Samaria' and extending 'to the ends of the earth' (Acts 1.8). In doing this he concentrates on the activities of Peter and Paul, but we also hear of the travels of their companions and of Barnabas and Mark apart from Paul. There are hints that Apollos might have been itinerant, and the so-called 'we passages' may in part be intended to associate the reader with Paul's missionary work. A significant report is also given regarding Philip's activity. He was among those scattered after Stephen's martyrdom and 'went about preaching the word' (Acts 8.4). His travels took him to Samaria, along the desert road leading from Jerusalem to Gaza, and later to Azotus, from where 'passing on he preached the gospel to all the towns till he came to Caesarea' (Acts 8.40). Finally in the Acts we should take cognizance of Luke's inclusion, with a report of the early proclamation of the church, of the model for Christian missionaries, Jesus of Nazareth who 'went about doing good and healing all that were oppressed by the devil' (Acts 10.38).[28]

The general picture which Luke presents, both in Acts and in his gospel, undoubtedly held a strong attraction for his first readers. The zeal and willingness to sacrifice which these missionary travels represented were inspiring examples to later disciples, even if they were not able fully to emulate their heroes.[29] But we may surmise that it was not Luke alone who had this interest. It is a well-grounded hypothesis of New Testament scholarship that all the gospels were written more out of a concern with the contemporary mission of the church than with history as such or reminiscence. That these evangelists should have wished to present and to emphasize Jesus himself as the chief exemplar of the heroic, missionary style of life would be most understandable in the context of the tasks they had set themselves.

It may also be true that all these gospel writers (whose primary audience in each case was probably set in the Hellenistic world), as well perhaps as the actual Christian missionaries, were in some measure influenced by the itinerant practice of contemporary exponents of other religions and philosophies. Apollonius of Tyana, a preacher and worker of miracles who is said to have travelled extensively, would probably provide the best known illustration.

Turning back to the pre-resurrection circumstances, we may ask questions having to do with the practicality of some of the scenes presented to us. Jesus is most often described in the company of close followers. Without debating the issue of whether he in fact chose twelve primary disciples, we can well believe that he was remembered as often having followers from the fishing villages of northern Galilee with him. The impression is, of course, given that these disciples gave up everything (homes, families and employment) to be with Jesus. The logistics of the situation might suggest, however, that we may be dealing with didactic exaggeration. Some form of support would be needed for the members of such a group. We shall in a moment argue that there are signs indicative of a relatively restricted sphere of activity for Jesus and his disciples. That lack of family attachments was not always a requirement for the first disciples seems clear when Paul compares his own circumstances to those of 'the other apostles and the brothers of the Lord and Cephas' who had accompanying wives (I Cor. 9.5). The tradition also remembers that Simon and Andrew had a house, and Simon a mother-in-law in Capernaum. Mark (1.29–31) tells us that they went there after they had come to 'follow' Jesus, although the tradition probably did not record when the healing of Simon's mother-in-law took place.

Counter-proposals can be made. A number of Jesus' companions seem to have been fishermen, and fishing is not a year-round activity.[30] Several of them at least were young men, perhaps without family responsibilities. Such considerations obviously make it possible that journeys of some duration could have been made. We only raise the question whether an itinerant style of life, even if the eschaton was felt fast to be approaching, would represent the best historical interpretation of the circumstances of these men.[31]

In concluding this section we may pose a question which might be asked by proponents of the thesis of a more fully itinerant ministry: if Jesus had a far more localized sphere of ministry, why do the gospels not indicate this and instead prefer to give this impression of Jesus as a wanderer? We believe we have already given good reasons why the evangelists and their traditions would have preferred the latter. One could also maintain that the relative localization of Jesus' public activities might have been unconsciously avoided in order to convey the idea that Jesus had proclaimed his message to a great many of the Jews, and perhaps to avoid any embarrassment over the fact that the new Christian faith did not grow strongly in Jesus' home area.[32] Beyond this, however, we would contend that the gospels may well preserve evidence of that relative localization. At least three indications are given that Capernaum could have been a kind of home for Jesus. Though the meaning of ἐν οἴκῳ in Mark 2.1 is disputed, it could reflect the belief that Jesus for a time led a stabilized existence in Capernaum.[33] John 2.12 tells us that Jesus came to Capernaum at one point in his ministry with his mother and his brothers and his disciples, perhaps suggesting a family association with that town. Matthew 4.13 relates that Jesus left what is regarded as his original home, Nazareth, and came and lived (κατῴκησεν) in Capernaum.

Perhaps of more significance are the several, if somewhat random, references in all the gospels and in Q to Capernaum and the impression, even though it may not always be intentional, that a number of the incidents in Jesus' life took place there.[34] As indicated above, it would certainly appear from the synoptics that the home of Peter and Andrew was there. One may also gain the feeling that the story line keeps returning to this town as for example in Mark 9.33: 'They came to Capernaum, and when he was in the house. . . .'

The fourth gospel maintains that Peter and Andrew as well as Philip were from Bethsaida, but this may not even be a contradiction, for Bethsaida was but a short walk from Capernaum. It is quite conceivable that fishermen, especially those who hired out, would move their temporary residence during the fishing seasons.

Indeed, it is important to have the geography of the north coast of the Sea of Galilee in mind. Though exact sites of the ancient cities are sometimes still disputed, it is clear that Capernaum, Bethsaida and Chorazin were all within a very few miles, less than a walk of an hour or two from one another. Thus, when these three towns are denounced in the Q passage (Matt. 11.20–24 with Luke 10.13–15), one can understand this as a denunciation of one vicinity and not three disparate locales. The passage does more than imply that Jesus conducted a number of his activities there. Should the passage be viewed as inauthentic, it might be regarded as even more significant, perhaps giving evidence that later Christians were attempting to compensate for the failure of Christianity to grow in Jesus' own home locale.[35]

That Jesus should sometimes be in Bethsaida (Mark 6.45; 8.22; Luke 9.10; John 1.44) along with Capernaum, and go to the Plain of Gennesaret but a very few miles south or even to Magdala (Matt. 15.39; probably Mark's Dalmanutha in 8.10 and presumably the home of Mary Magdalene) would hardly be inconsistent with a localized ministry. The gospels may give the impression (it may well have been that of the evangelists) that Jesus was travelling fair distances by being active in such locales. In fact, he may have been doing little more than staying at home.

Similar remarks could be made about the pastoral background of hills, countryside and seashore against which Jesus' activities are often set. Such would fit well with the region neighbouring Capernaum. And to pass by boat from Capernaum to Bethsaida would be a natural means of travel and a relatively swift journey, though the evangelists may quite possibly have believed that much greater distances on and about the Sea of Galilee were involved.

IV

The scope of this article has left us with insufficient room for detailed exegesis, nor have we been able to follow all the avenues of investigation. The gaps in our study and in the information available to us obviously leave a number of issues unresolved and offer possibilities open to further informed guesswork. There continues to be some evidence in favour of the itinerant character of Jesus' ministry. We do hope, however, that an intriguing and significant alternative has been raised and that others will be interested further to examine with us the possibility that the picture of a fully itinerant ministry is at least an exaggeration and somewhat of a stylization. Should this be considered a legitimate hypothesis, we can here briefly note some of the corollaries which would flow from it.

Since the context in which a ministry is conducted and sayings and stories are told is so important for their understanding, we may have provided ways in which different questions can be asked about some of the statements attributed to Jesus on discipleship and other matters. In the course of this study we have tried to give a few examples of how logia seen from the angle of this hypothesis might appear in a different light, and how new lines of inquiry with regard to the issue of authenticity might be opened. In a similar manner we may thus gain insight into certain of the concerns of the early Christian communities and the evangelists and some of the influences which were operative on them.

Though it is possible that our observations may seem to make the mysterious figure of Jesus yet more mysterious, it is also conceivable that the discovery of an intelligible, alternative mode of ministry for him may be salutary. The lives of Paul and others are more than sufficient examples for Christians who feel called away from home to follow their Lord. The demands the gospel makes, and the realization that the kingdom of God must come before all else, if all else is to have true value, are no less strong (in some ways they may become more acute) to a Christian whose ministry is set in one locale. If we read our gospels with this alternative possibility in mind, Jesus may emerge as a historical figure less remote and more fully incarnated into the life of his contemporaries. While the evangelists, for their purposes, may have wished to emphasize Jesus' distinctiveness from his fellow men, historical criticism, without lessening the significance of his impact, may offer ways of understanding that significance which present more parallels with the life that most people experience.

As (through the Qumran finds and, derivatively, the Nag Hammadi materials) further insights become available to us concerning certain sectarian groups active in Palestine in Jesus' time, scholars may wish to continue to explore the possibility that Jesus himself was a member and leader of such a group. Our evidence for the most part indicates that these groups, often adopting patterns of communal living, led relatively localized lives during their respective existences. That Jesus with his immediate followers might have shared in such an experience on the north shore of the Sea of Galilee is a possibility which we believe to be worthy of further research.[36]

While many of the issues here raised remain problematic and perhaps always beyond the range of historical knowledge, it is a pleasure to offer this short study in tribute to the scholar who introduced me to the critical study of the gospels. He first taught me the value in gospel research, not only of asking questions, but of asking questions about the questions.

NOTES

1. Wilhelm Bousset, *Kyrios Christos* (1st German ed. 1913), ET Abingdon Press 1970, p. 117.

2. Günther Bornkamm, *Jesus of Nazareth*, ET Hodder and Stoughton 1960, p. 146.

3. Norman Perrin, *Rediscovering the Teaching of Jesus*, SCM Press 1967, p. 52.

4. References to Jesus' lowliness or poverty in Phil. 2.5ff. and II Cor. 8.9 are almost surely to be read in a theological rather than any historical sense.

5. This is not always the case, however. Sometimes a place name becomes fixed in the oral tradition. It may even be used as a way of remembering or referring to a particular story or saying. Thus in b Bab. Batr. 174ᵃ a rabbi refers to a particular case by means of the catch-word Sidon. The case-story is found in M Git. VII.5 beginning with the words, 'A man in Sidon once said to his wife . . . ' (cf. B. Gerhardsson, *Memory and Manuscript, Oral Tradition and Written Transmission in Rabbinic Judaism and Early Christianity* [Acta Seminarii Neotestamentici Upsaliensis XVII] Lund and Copenhagen 1961, pp. 136ff.). An example from the gospels might be the healing of the centurion's son or servant at Capernaum in both Q and John.

6. The synoptics are vague with regard to the place where John did his baptizing. All are clear that it was not in Galilee. Matthew and Mark seem to suggest a location on the Jordan relatively near to Jerusalem. The fourth gospel, though still indicating a place with fairly ready access to Jerusalem, may, with its reference to Aenon near Salim (3.23), point to a more northerly locale.

7. The comparable passage in John 4.43–4 is particularly confusing. The plainest meaning of the words would suggest that Samaria rather than Galilee was Jesus' own country, but this may not be what John intended.

8. See below p. 59 and n. 35. For a more theological presentation of the theme, cf. John 1.11.

9. Rudolf Bultmann, *History of the Synoptic Tradition*, ET, rev. ed., Blackwell 1968, p. 29, with reference to Strack-Billerbeck I, pp. 187f.; 528f.

10. Note Luke's emphasis in 5.11: 'they left everything and followed him.'

11. The stronger textual tradition in Luke reads 'the synagogues of Judah' which for several reasons should probably be regarded as original. Probably Luke intends it as a more general geographical reference, and it can be seen as part of his tendency regularly to associate Jesus with Jerusalem and its environs.

12. Cf. also Matt. 9.35 and Mark 6.6.

13. See D. E. Nineham, *The Gospel of St Mark* (The Pelican Gospel commentaries), Penguin Books 1963, pp. 167–71.

14. So Nineham, op. cit., p. 168.

15. Bultmann, *History*, p. 145.

16. Cf. Bultmann, *History*, p. 98. We may note that the saying is also to be found in the Gospel of Thomas as logion 86.

17. Cf. the discussion of H. E. Tödt, *The Son of Man in the Synoptic Tradition*, ET SCM Press 1965, pp. 120–3 and *passim*, where the saying, which he insists referred from the beginning to Jesus as the Son of man, is seen as a creation within the Q community. We have elsewhere argued that the saying might only be regarded as coming from the context of Jesus' ministry if one derives it from the background of lore concerning a mythical Son of man figure. Cf. F. H. Borsch, *The Son of Man in Myth and History*, SCM Press 1967, p. 325.

18. In this light *foxes* would refer to Herodians and *birds* to Gentiles. 'The saying may originally have meant, "Everyone else has his place in Israel, except the true king of Israel, the Son of man." ' So J. C. Fenton, *The Gospel of St Matthew* (The Pelican Gospel Commentaries), Penguin Books 1963, p. 128.

19. See again Fenton, ibid., p. 129.

20. The plan could be regarded as, at least in part, emerging within the tradition Matthew inherited. Cf. E. Käsemann ('The Beginnings of Christian Theology' in *New Testament Questions of Today*, SCM Press 1969, p. 87) on Matt. 10.5f.: 'What we are really hearing in this saying, too, is the voice of the strictest form of Jewish Christianity.'

21. See Luke 4.15 (synagogues) and the references to being in or passing through cities and towns in 5.12; 8.1; 13.22.

22. On this view that Luke presents this section as a kind of Christian Deuteronomy cf. C. F. Evans, 'The Central Section of Luke's Gospel' in *Studies in the Gospels: Essays in memory of R. H. Lightfoot*, ed. D. E. Nineham, Blackwell 1955, pp. 37ff.

23. See John 7.41, 52, to which may be added the references to Jesus as from Nazareth: 1.45f.; 18.5, 7; 19.19.

24. There are too many different prophetic styles in the Bible to make valid generalizations, but it certainly would not necessarily be expected that a prophet, even one with an eschatological message, would be a wanderer. One could wish more were known about John the Baptist in this regard.

25. On the possibility that the wisdom form of sayings in the gospels may have been given impetus by Jesus himself, cf. R. G. Hamerton-Kelly, *Pre-existence, Wisdom, and the Son of Man* (Society for New Testament Studies Monograph Series 21), Cambridge University Press 1973, p. 241.

26. E.g., Mark 1.28, 32, 40, 45; 3.8; 6.33; 8.1; 9.17; 10.13; Matt. 8.34; 9.26, 28, 31f.; Luke 4.14.

27. Eusebius (*HE* III. 1–5) suggests that because of persecution Christian missionaries 'were scattered throughout the whole world'. He relates the tradition that a band of Jerusalem disciples afterwards came to dwell in Pella of Perea.

28. The list could go on. Acts 20.4 tells of seven more companions of Paul on one of his travels, and Paul's letters imply a number of journeys by other companions and helpers of his. Then there are the many unknown disciples who must first have taken the gospel to Damascus, Antioch, Caesarea, Rome, etc.

29. Among other evidences that the itinerant style of Christian ministry did, however, persist one may cite *Didache* xi–xiii. It would seem from this that there were some who abused the hospitality owed to an itinerant prophet, but the true prophet is 'worthy of his food', a theme found also in I Tim. 5.18; I Cor. 9.14 and Matt. 10.10 = Luke 10.7; and perhaps alluding to itinerant ministries.

30. On the conditions and circumstances of the classes of Galilean fisherman, cf.

W. Wuellner, *The Meaning of 'Fishers of Men'*, Westminster Press 1967, pp. 26–63. That Jesus himself is said to have had an occupation is somewhat beside the point, since it is easier to understand how one dedicated person could give up his livelihood and be supported by others.

31. One might also bring into consideration the indication from the synoptic gospels that Jesus' public ministry may have been quite short in duration. (The fourth gospel would, however, seem to suggest two to three years.) This might make the logistics of an itinerant ministry more feasible. We doubt, however, whether any of the evangelists had much real information on this point.

32. See below on the denunciations of Chorazin, Bethsaida and Capernaum.

33. The phrase can be translated either 'at home' or 'in a house'. In the parallel passage, without mentioning Capernaum by name, Matthew (9.1) speaks of Jesus coming to 'his own city'.

34. For a careful listing of these and related discussion, see E. F. F. Bishop, 'Jesus and Capernaum', *CBQ* 15, 1953, pp. 427–37.

35. It is possible that Mark 6.3–6 and par. should be interpreted in the same manner.

36. On some of the evidence concerning the sectarian movements and several of the possible implications of this for gospel studies, cf. F. H. Borsch, *The Son of Man in Myth and History* (note 17 above) and *The Christian and Gnostic Son of Man* (SBT 2.14) 1970.

5

Miracles in the Fourth Gospel

EDUARD LOHSE

THE author of the fourth gospel, like the other evangelists, gives an account of miracles which Jesus performed during his earthly life. After the narrative of the turning of water into wine at the wedding in Cana and the cleansing of the temple, we are told: 'Many believed on his name, for they saw the signs which he did' (2.23). Yet it is precisely this faith based on miracles which is criticized in the following sentence: 'But Jesus did not entrust himself to them, for he knew them all . . . since he knew what is in man' (2.24f.). Faith that is based on miracle is thus only a weak and unreliable faith, a sort of 'flash in the pan', blazing up quickly but soon going out. Thus Nicodemus, who admiringly lays weight on Jesus' miracles (3.2), remains unbelieving and uncomprehending before Jesus' demand for the new birth (3.1-10). Jesus reproves the crowd of people eager for miracles, who, by contrast with the nobleman from Capernaum, are willing to believe only on the basis of signs and wonders (4.48). When the crowd, attracted by Jesus' unprecedented acts, approach him out of curiosity (6.2; cf. 12.18) and wish to make him king solely because of the impression made on them by the sign which he had accomplished (6.14f.), all that Jesus can do is to withdraw himself from them and escape into solitude (6.15). While many imagine that they can deduce from his miracles that he is the Christ (7.31), it is precisely because of this that the Jewish authorities decide that he must die (11.49-53). At this the crowd's faith, kindled by Jesus' miracles, immediately dwindles and disappears, so that the evangelist, in his retrospect over Jesus' activity, has to state: 'Such mighty signs had he done before their eyes, and yet they did not believe in him' (12.37)—an enigmatic state of affairs which can only be explained by the prophetic words about God's hardening of the nation's heart (12.38–40). By this means the evangelist points to a critical assessment of a faith born out of miracles; indeed, he denies such faith both permanence and lasting value.

Hence one might be inclined to ask whether for the evangelist miracle can have any significance for Christian faith at all. Yet to this question he gives an unambiguous answer when he writes at the conclusion of his work: 'Many other signs Jesus did in the presence of his disciples, which are not written in this book. But this'—obviously including the reports of Jesus' miracles!—'has been written so that you may believe that Jesus is the Christ, the Son of God, and that believing you may have life in his name' (20.30f.). On the one hand, then, faith based on miracles is regarded as weak and impermanent, yet on the other hand it is precisely the news of Jesus' signs that should awaken faith. What significance, therefore, have the miracles of Jesus in the framework of the fourth gospel?[1]

I

In order to answer this question we shall first consider the narratives to which there are synoptic parallels.[2] For through comparison of the synoptic and Johannine pericopae it is possible to indicate the distinctive nature of the Johannine version. The narrative of the healing of the nobleman's son at Capernaum (4.46–54) is unmistakably related to the story of the centurion at Capernaum (Matt. 8.5–13 par. Luke 7.1–10).[3] We cannot indeed assume any literary dependence of the Johannine pericope on the synoptic one or on a version of it in the sayings-source Q. It is more likely that a narrative passed on in oral tradition has been recorded both in Q and in the fourth gospel, in each case provided with particular emphasis.[4] According to the synoptics, a Gentile centurion addresses himself to Jesus and intercedes on behalf of his servant, who lies ill at home. Jesus does not in fact visit the Gentile's house, but expresses amazement at his faith and utters a word of power through which the servant is immediately healed. According to John it is different. Here there comes to Jesus, while he is in Cana, an official in the royal service whose son is fatally ill in Capernaum. The encounter thus takes place at a considerable distance from the place where the sick child is lying, so that the subsequent miracle is enhanced in its significance as an astonishing event.[5] It is not a Gentile but a Jew who approaches Jesus. Hence the refusal of his request, which is the immediate response, has to be explained in another way. Jesus declines on the grounds that 'Unless you see signs and wonders,[6] you will not believe', v. 48. Mere miracle-based faith, seeking only visible supernatural happenings, is thus not recognized as genuine faith. Yet the father does not allow Jesus to send him away, but on the contrary renews his intercession for the fatally ill child with all the greater urgency. Jesus now replies with the majestic command, 'Go your way, your son is alive'. 'So the man believed the word that Jesus spoke and went away', v. 50. Thereby a significant progress is indicated from miracle-based faith to faith as trust.

On the way home the father is met by his servants, who convey to him the report that his son has suddenly recovered. They act as undoubted witnesses for the miracle that has taken place, since it must have remained unknown to them that Jesus' word was the cause of the healing. Here also, therefore, emphasis is placed on the greatness of the miracle, far surpassing the event described by the synoptics. But the father, who sees the words of Jesus fulfilled, becomes a believer with his whole household, v. 53. This can only mean that he recognizes Jesus as sent by God and so has arrived at real faith, which has been born from encounter with Jesus' word. Thus the evangelist has undertaken, first of all, to enhance the miraculous event. At the same time, however, he has also joined to the story the reference to the faith which responds to and trusts the word of Jesus. The miracle story has thus become a testimony which points to Jesus as the Saviour of the world (4.42), and invites us to a faith which does not ask for supernatural events, but grounds itself upon the word of Jesus.

In ch. 6 the evangelist again takes up an inherited tradition, in which the miraculous feeding and Jesus' walking on the water were already joined.[7] But the synoptic and Johannine versions of the tradition have been formed independently, so that it is impossible to assume any literary relationship. In both cases it is more likely that an oral tradition about Jesus, handed on in a fixed form, has been worked over.[8]

The crowd which had seen the signs performed by Jesus on the sick— of which the healing of the nobleman's son is an example—follows Jesus and his disciples in tense expectation. When Jesus sees so many people, he asks Philip, 'Where can we buy bread so that these men may eat?' (6.5). Here the difference from the synoptic story stands out strikingly. According to the latter, the disciples suggested to Jesus that he should dismiss the people so that they might buy bread in the surrounding villages. According to John's gospel, however, Jesus takes the initiative, addressing Philip with the question which—as the evangelist adds—was intended to put Philip to the test; for Jesus knew from the start what he wished to do (6.6). Philip's reply is that not even 200 *denarii*—a sum of money which according to Mark 6.37 was regarded by the disciples as sufficient—would be enough for every individual to have even a little. Thus the evangelist, by mentioning this sum of money, refers to tradition; yet he enhances this feature in order to make the magnitude of the subsequent miracle stand out the more strongly. It is only in the Johannine narrative that we find Andrew's remark that a boy is at hand who has five loaves of barley bread and two fishes. 'But what is this among so many?' (6.9).[9] This doubting comment causes the feeding of the five thousand to appear all the more miraculous. Jesus gives orders for the crowd to recline, and after saying the thanksgiving over the food, distributes it. The disciples pass the food on, and all have enough. The miracle itself is not described at all; only in closing is it reported that twelve baskets were filled with the remaining fragments. The nature of the miraculous feeding as a sign is more exactly defined by the evangelist through his having joined the story of the feeding with the discourse about the bread of life: the living bread which allays all hunger is Jesus (6.35, 48, 51). He who to his disciples revealed himself as master of the wind and the waves (6.16–21)[10] does not produce for the crowd a sign of compelling probative force to legitimate himself, so that all must bow before him. On the contrary, the sign effected by Jesus is heightened by the evangelist as far as its miraculous character is concerned, in order to direct all attention to the word of Jesus as the bread of life, which only he who believes can receive.

The Johannine pericopae which permit comparison with synoptic parallels thus indicate that the fourth evangelist gives Jesus' miracles an even greater prominence than do the other evangelists. But the significance of the signs that are carried out is grasped adequately only when they are taken as directing attention towards the witness borne by the words of Jesus, who is the Saviour of the world and the bread of life.

II

Comparison and contrast with the synoptic narratives has enabled us to see some specifically Johannine traits in the understanding of Jesus' miracles. We must now investigate the remaining miracle stories of the fourth gospel in relation to their presentation of the signs of Jesus.

The first action through which Jesus 'manifested his glory' is, in the order of events in John's gospel, the miracle of the wine at Cana (2.1–12). The mother of Jesus, Jesus himself, and his disciples are guests at a wedding in Cana of Galilee. When the wine gives out, Jesus' mother draws his attention to the fact, and makes the unspoken request that he should perform a miracle. Jesus, however, refuses to comply. His hour has not yet come. But his mother gives the servants a hint to do everything that Jesus asks from them. He gets the servants to fill six large stone vessels, each holding 80–120 litres (about 18–25 gallons) with water, and then says that they are to take some of it to the ruler of the feast. The miracle itself is not described, but the fact that one has occurred is noted by the astonished ruler of the feast: a huge abundance of the best wine is suddenly available.

The narrative exhibits features which are typical of a miracle story. The miracle is carried out in spite of an initial refusal. The large capacity of the vessels is explicitly mentioned, and at the conclusion the miracle is attested by an unsuspecting witness. But some features of the story remain curiously unrealistic. Jesus roughly contradicts his mother. Both are in a position to give orders to the servants in somebody else's house, even though they are only guests, and the servants obey. Apparently they understand at once what is going to happen, and therefore are perfectly willing to pour a huge quantity of water into the vessels. Jesus' miracle does not, like those in the synoptic gospels, bring help in a situation of concrete necessity, but can on the contrary only be described as a 'luxury miracle'.[11] The Johannine account of this event has obviously been shaped with the aid of motifs from the cult of Dionysus. These ideas could be the more easily taken over, in view of the fact that wine had for a long time been seen in Israel as an attribute of the time of salvation.[12] The evangelist lays special emphasis on the character of the story as a sign, and therefore states at the conclusion that Jesus manifested his glory in this, the first of his signs, and that his disciples believed in him.[13] The only adequate response to this announcement consists, therefore, in faith in Jesus, who thus revealed his glory.

The two healing stories in chs. 5 and 9, constructed largely on parallel lines, are also shaped by the theme of the revelation of Jesus' glory. Among the many sick men lying by the pool of Bethesda[14] Jesus sees one who has already suffered helplessly for thirty-eight years. This mention of the duration of the illness is one of the typical features of a miracle story, and merely serves to stress the magnitude of the healing which at once occurs.[15] The sick man does not address Jesus with a request; on the contrary, Jesus knows, without a word being spoken, the severity and long duration of the illness, and utters the challenging question: 'Do you want to become well?' (v.6). At this, the lame[16] man begins to bemoan his suffering, and Jesus simply issues the brief command, 'Take up your bed and walk' (v.8).[17] His order produces an immediate effect: the man stands up, takes up his bed, and leaves, thus demonstrating to everyone that a miracle has happened. But in John's gospel his walking does not serve, as in the synoptic story of the healing of the paralytic, as proof that the healing is complete. Instead it is given a further significance, which becomes obvious in the evangelist's next remark, 'but it was the sabbath on that day' (v.9b). When, after being healed, the man picks up his bed and walks away, he is, in the eyes of the Jews, doing work, and thus committing an impious breach of the sabbath. It is of course Jesus who is ultimately responsible for this; but he rebuts the criticisms levelled against him.[18] Just as the Father's activity knows no respite, so Jesus' work of revelation cannot have a limit set to it even on the sabbath. Jesus' time on earth is limited (cf. 9.4), so that he must now act and work unhindered. Thus this story, too, becomes a revelation of Jesus' majesty. The long discourse which follows the miracle story and the conflict story asserts the authority with which he has been invested. Jesus' word interprets his action, and establishes the latter's meaning as a demonstration of his work of revelation.

This feature is even more strongly brought out in the narrative of the healing of the blind man in ch. 9.[19] While the synoptics, too, several times report healings of the blind, the fourth evangelist—going beyond anything the synoptics say—states that Jesus encounters a man who has been blind from birth (9.1). If the power of sight can be granted even to him, the miracle must seem all the more impressive.

Such an occurrence is altogether unheard of (9.32). The disciples' question whether the blind man's suffering is to be attributed to his own sin or to his parents' is shown by Jesus to be inappropriate. This man's blindness, he says, occurred in order that the work of God might be seen in him (9.3). The sole purpose of the suffering and the healing is that Jesus' glory should shine out through them. By this means the reader is confronted at the very beginning of the story with its significance as a sign. This is underlined when it is then said that Jesus is the light of the world (9.5). Jesus' command to the blind man to wash in the pool of Siloam is given an allegorical interpretation by the evangelist: Siloam means 'sent' (9.7). This can only mean that Jesus alone is the man sent from God who has come as the light of the world.[20]

In the argument about the miracle which then develops between Jesus, the Jews, the man who has been healed, and his parents, everything centres on the question whether or not Jesus can legitimately claim to be God's messenger. After the subsequent accusation (as in ch. 5) of a breach of the sabbath, the Jews first of all try to dismiss Jesus' sign by disputing whether it happened at all. They allege that the man who has been healed is not identical with the parents' blind son, but fail in this perverse attempt (9.18-23). The evangelist has thus made it evident that Jesus' miracle has really happened and that its reality cannot be doubted. Consequently the question posed by Jesus' sign is whether or not the claim of revelation is understood. The Jews and the Pharisees are blind in their unbelief; this is why their sin remains (9.39-41). The man who has been healed, on the other hand, comprehends what has happened to him, and is finally led to perceive that Jesus is the Son of man (9.35-38) with whose arrival the eschatological crisis has irrupted.[21]

The climax and conclusion of the public activity of Jesus comes with the raising of Lazarus.[22] The two sisters, Mary and Martha, send a message to Jesus to say that their brother lies sick, thus conveying their hope that Jesus will come to their aid with a miracle (11.3). But Jesus does not come. On the contrary, he says that this sickness is not fatal—that is, death is not the end and the meaning of this sickness—but rather it is for God's glory, in order that by it the Son of God may be glorified (11.4). Whoever believes in him will behold the glory of God (11.40). After Jesus has waited some days, he says to his disciples, 'Our friend has fallen asleep' (11.11). In antiquity this expression was often used as a euphemism for death, but here it is used to create the possibility of a misunderstanding, which immediately takes place on the part of the disciples. They think that Jesus is talking about ordinary sleep (11.12f.). Jesus removes this misunderstanding by stating unambiguously 'Lazarus is dead' (11.14). Death seems to have had the last word—all the more so when, on his arrival in Bethany, Jesus receives the news that Lazarus has already been lying in the grave for four days (11.17, 39). According to the popular view, the soul of a dead man stayed near the grave for three days, but from the fourth day decomposition set in and death became the undisputed victor. Jesus approaches the grave, orders the stone closing it to be rolled back, and cries out with a majestic voice, 'Lazarus, come out!' (11.43). Then the dead man comes out. Bound hand and foot, he staggers out—a smaller miracle within the greater. Jesus orders him to be unbound and allowed to go, so that the amazing event becomes apparent to everyone (11.44).

In the case of this story, which he took over from tradition and whose features he further accentuated,[23] the evangelist does not, as in the other chapters, append a discourse to Jesus' action. On the contrary, he introduces into the narrative at this point a conversation between Jesus and Martha, in which the meaning of the sign is explained. 'I am the Resurrection and the Life,' says Jesus; 'he who believes in me will live even though he dies. And everyone who lives and believes in me will not die for ever' (11.25f.). To the question whether she believes this, Martha replies with the confession of faith: 'I believe that you are the Christ, the Son of God, who has come into the world' (11.27). This, then, is what the sign indicates: Jesus alone—no one and nothing else— is the Resurrection and the Life. This gift is received in faith, and cannot be striven after by any other means. In connection with this, various writers have raised the critical objection: if this is so, then the resurrection of Lazarus is completely superfluous.[24] But against this it must be pointed out that the factuality of the miracles in John's gospel is as strongly emphasized as it is because the evangelist is anxious to show that Christ really is what the deeds of Jesus, as signs, affirm him to be.[25] The signs and the words of Jesus are thus inseparably linked. The miracles, whose performance as something astonishing is so impressively stressed, point towards the words, and underline the claim which the latter make. Hearer and reader alike are thus inescapably confronted with the decisive question 'Do you believe this?'

To that question the Jews give a negative answer. Alarmed by the impact of Jesus' signs (11.47), they decide that he must die. The resurrection of Lazarus sets in motion the passion of Jesus and brings him to the cross. If the signs of Jesus reveal both God's glory and his own, the glorifying of Jesus must ensue in his lifting up on the cross (12.16, 23, 28; 13.31f.; 17.1, 4f.). His earthly activity, in which his glory shone through his signs, is gathered into a unity with his crucifixion and exaltation. Hence it is that the believing church confesses 'We beheld his glory' (1.14).

III

The miracles of Jesus are thus firmly embedded in the context of the fourth gospel. The evangelist emphasizes the greatness of the miracles by indicating the distance between Jesus and the sick child, the long duration and the severity of the illness, the huge vessels of water, the hungry crowd numbering thousands, and finally the fact that Lazarus is already dead. It is not needy men[26] who occasion Jesus' actions; rather, Jesus takes the initiative which leads to the miracle, since it is his intention to reveal his glory. The greatness of the miracle which takes place before the eyes of many witnesses points to the unprecedented event of the Word's becoming flesh, of Jesus' coming into the world. The actions of Jesus therefore do not have a merely symbolic or allegorical meaning.[27] Rather, the reality of the signs is as trenchantly emphasized as it is because they are to draw attention to the event of the revelation of God in Christ.[28]

Adopting an Old Testament concept, the evangelist calls Jesus' miracles 'signs', and it is his intention in doing so to say that each sign is not to be considered simply by itself, but 'has significance only as a pointer to something quite different'.[29] The miracles of Jesus indicate that he is the bread of life, the light of the world, the resurrection and the life. By so doing they address the reader directly in a way which demands response in the confession of faith. The words and deeds of Jesus in this way interpret one another, and together form the witness to the revelation of Jesus' glory.[30]

The Jews, however, demand of Jesus a sign offering overwhelming proof of his claims (2.23; 6.30, etc.).[31] Jesus declines to perform this

72

sign (4.48 etc.); for his signs are intended to evoke the free decision of faith. Hence Jesus' miracles exert no incontrovertible power before which all must bow, but rather, like his preaching, consistently provoke a double reaction (7.40f.; 9.16; 10.19; 11.45f.). On the one hand stands faith, which understands the signs of Jesus as a revelation (2.11; 4.46–54). But on the other hand, the signs of Jesus release the embittered hatred of the Jews, which brings him to the cross.[32]

In his conduct, Jesus reveals the works of God (9.3). The disciples who see them (7.3) are to do the work of God, which is to believe in him whom God has sent (6.29). As they grasp the unity of the deeds and words of Jesus and believe in him because of them (14.11), so they are given the promise that he who believes in Jesus will be able to do the works that he does and even greater ones (14.12). This means that, after Jesus' departure to the Father, they will bear testimony before the world, by their confession of faith and by their preaching, to the completed revelation of God. But the representatives of the present world-order, who also have seen Jesus' signs, close their minds to the challenge which is contained in them. They harden themselves in blindness and disobedience (9.29–41; 12.37 etc.), and try to do away with Jesus (10.31). The works that the Father has given him to do bear witness to him (5.36; also 4.34; 9.4; 17.4). As this takes place, however, the eschatological crisis is fulfilled in which belief and unbelief, light and darkness, life and death are separated out from one another. Against the background of this ultimate decision, with which the reader finds himself confronted, the evangelist unfolds the witness of the signs of Jesus 'in order that you may believe that Jesus is the Christ, the Son of God, and in order that, believing, you may have life in his name' (20.30f.).[33]

NOTES

1. There is a wealth of material on the *religionsgeschichtlich* background and theology of miracle in C. F. D. Moule (ed.), *Miracles*, Mowbray 1965.

2. Cf. E. Haenchen, 'Johanneische Probleme', *ZTK* 56, 1959, pp. 19–54 (= *Gott und Mensch, Gesammelte Aufsätze*, Tübingen 1965, pp. 78–113).

3. Cf. E. Schweizer, 'Die Heilung des Königlichen', *EvTh* 11, 1951/2, pp. 64–71 (= *Neotestamentica*, Zürich 1963, pp. 407–15).

4. It is unnecessary to discuss here the problem of the 'signs source', which, it has

been suggested, constituted a written collection of miracles of Jesus which the evangelist had before him, since the present investigation is concerned with the significance of the miracles of Jesus in the context of the whole gospel. The hypothesis that such a source existed remains uncertain, though it has again been vigorously put forward by J. Becker ('Wunder und Christologie', *NTS* 16, 1969–70, pp. 130–48). It is in any case obvious that the miracle stories are distinct from the Johannine discourses both stylistically and in terms of content. It must at least be allowed for that the evangelist has made use of, and joined together, different traditions or groups of traditions.

5. If 2.1–12 and 4.46–54 were originally contiguous in the signs source, it would be necessary to assume from 2.12 that in the source the healing, too, took place in Capernaum. In that case the evangelist would have introduced Jesus' journey to Cana in order to bring about an enhancement of the miracle.

6. The linking of signs and miracles (according to an Old Testament model, cf. Ex. 7.3; Deut. 4.34, etc.) is found only here in John's gospel.

7. Cf. J. Jeremias, 'Johanneische Literarkritik', *Theologische Blätter* 20, 1941, p. 42, where attention is drawn to the following parallel sequences:

John 6.1–15	Feeding	Mark 6.30–44
6.16–25	Walking on the water	6.45–52
6.26–31	Request for a sign	8.11–13
6.32–65	Discourse on the bread of life	8.14–21
6.66–9	Confession of Peter	8.27–30
6.70	Saying to Peter	8.33

8. Contrast S. Mendner, 'Zum Problem Johannes und die Synoptiker', *NTS* 4, 1957–8, pp. 282–307, where the somewhat unconvincing thesis is maintained that the Johannine feeding narrative was only secondarily introduced into the fourth gospel in dependence on the synoptic account.

9. In Mark 6.38 it is said only that there are five loaves of bread and two fishes to hand.

10. The miraculous character of what has taken place is also particularly strongly accentuated in the story of the walking on the water and the miraculous coming to land: the moment that the disciples find themselves in the boat in the middle of the lake, Jesus comes across the water to them. No sooner has he reached them than the boat is already at the shore.

11. W. Bauer, *Das Johannesevangelium*, 3rd ed., Tübingen 1933, p. 46.

12. Cf. J. Jeremias, *Jesus als Weltvollender*, Berlin 1930, pp. 28f.

13. Nevertheless, there is no sacramental reference to the eucharist; contrast O. Cullmann, *Early Christian Worship* (SBT 10), 1953, pp. 66–71.

14. On the topographical question see J. Jeremias, *Die Wiederentdeckung von Bethesda*, Göttingen 1949.

15. Thus an allegorical interpretation of the number would be irrelevant.

16. The nature of the illness is indeed not stated, but according to v. 8 we should take it to be lameness.

17. Cf. Mark 2.9, 11 and J. Buse, 'John 5.8 and Johannine-Markan relationships', *NTS* 1, 1954–5, pp. 134–6. The far-reaching agreement between Jesus' command in John's gospel and in the synoptics does not, however, prove literary dependence. It is more likely that the miracle-working word of the Lord has been handed on consistently in the orally transmitted tradition.

18. The conflict story about the breach of the sabbath concludes in 7.15–24.

19. The miracle story in ch. 9 is to a great extent modelled on the one in ch. 5.

In both of these incidents an incurably ill person is healed on the sabbath. Both of the healings take place at a pool. In both cases the initiative lies with Jesus, who manifests his glory through the greatness of the miracle. In both cases there ensues a long dispute between Jesus and the Jews, in the course of which Jesus and the man who has been healed meet one another a second time. In ch. 9 the man becomes a believer in and a disciple of Jesus.

20. Here the allegorical interpretation is asserted by the evangelist himself. But the view of E. Hoskyns and F. N. Davey, *The Fourth Gospel*, 2nd ed., Faber 1947, p. 335, Cullmann, op. cit., pp. 102–5, and others, in agreement with the interpretation maintained from Tertullian onwards, that a reference to baptism is to be found here, reads into the text what is not there. K. Kundsin's suggestion (*Topologische Über-lieferungsstoffe im Johannesevangelium*, Göttingen 1925, pp. 37f.) that Siloam was in the evangelist's day a baptistery for the Jerusalem church, is quite arbitrary.

21. 10.19–21 probably reached its present position as a result of a misplacement of pages, and should follow 9.41.

22. Cf. R. Schnackenburg, *Das Johannesevangelicum* II, Freiburg 1971 (ET in preparation), pp. 428–33, on the traditio-historical and historical problem of the story of Lazarus.

23. Cf. Hoskyns, op. cit., p. 111: it was unnecessary for the evangelist to find out whether the tradition counted as historically reliable or not. The question facing him was not so much that as whether to include the traditional story of the raising of Lazarus in his book or to omit it.

24. J. Wellhausen, *Das Evangelium Johannis*, 2nd ed., Berlin 1908, p. 51; similarly, recently, J. Becker, art. cit. (see note 4), p. 146.

25. Cf. W. Wrede, *Charakter und Tendenz des Johannesevangeliums*, 2nd ed., Tübingen 1933, p. 8; E. Schweizer, *Ego Eimi*, 2nd ed., Göttingen 1965, p. 140.

26. 4.46–54 is an exception. That the father comes to Jesus with his request is a feature embedded in the story as handed on in the tradition.

27. So Bultmann, *Theology of the New Testament* II, SCM Press 1955, pp. 44f.; id., *The Gospel of John*, Blackwell 1971, pp. 331, 401 n. 3.

28. By saying this, however, the evangelist does not by any means show that he is enslaved to a 'naive docetism', as though a god were walking on earth; contrast E. Käsemann, *The Testament of Jesus*, SCM Press 1968, pp. 26, 66, 70, etc.

29. Cf. E. Schweizer, op. cit., p. 138.

30. Cf. C. H. Dodd, *The Interpretation of the Fourth Gospel*, Cambridge University Press 1953, p. 372.

31. A prophet had to authenticate himself by a sign, cf. Strack-Billerbeck II, p. 480.

32. E. Käsemann, op. cit., p. 22, rightly stresses that it is not permissible to transfer responsibility for the miracle-stories narrated in the fourth gospel to the tradition (as Becker does, art. cit., *passim*); for the evangelist ultimately took over this tradition in order to show that it is impossible to have the glory of Christ without his miracles.

33. The translator (the Reverend C. J. A. Hickling) gratefully acknowledges the help of Dr Kurt Gartner in preparing this version, and of Bishop Lohse himself in reading and checking it.

6

On Putting Paul in his Place

COLIN HICKLING

'THE trouble with Paul has always been to put him in his place.'[1] Some members of the Corinthian and Galatian churches would have agreed with some feeling (whether we should include anyone in Jerusalem is a more delicate matter). For the modern student of Christian origins the problem is indeed safer than it was for them. We do not risk the scathing invective experienced by Peter in person and by the Galatian congregations through the written word. We may even fail to note to what extent there is a problem at all. It is still difficult for us to appreciate that Acts, however much or little history it contains, is a work of interpretation as well as of reportage. This fact necessarily obliges us to penetrate behind its account of Paul if we can. Once that is attempted, the problems become inescapable.

Yet 'placing' Paul, however difficult, is an undertaking we cannot shirk. The fundamental question we have to ask is: 'How often was Paul right?' He was the most original of men, and at the same time one of the most rootless. He was a Jew to the core brought, at least at one moment (1 Thess. 2.16), to the point of predicting the perdition of his race; he was a citizen of the Hellenistic world community who found himself bound to accept the damning charge of preaching folly (I Cor. 1.18) and of doing so with powers of rhetoric that were 'contemptible' (II Cor. 10.10); he was a Christian bitterly attacked by fellow-Christians as being altogether too original, and as having sold the pass where morals were concerned (Rom. 3.8). It was this man who gave the Christian faith of the first generation—or one version of it— the systematic shape which determined to a great extent the direction

76

of the whole subsequent development of Christian doctrine. To such an extent, indeed, is this the case that the question whether he was right is one more predictably to be found on the lips of critics of institutional Christianity than on those of scholars. Yet it is inevitable that the question should be put at some point. For, unless we espouse a simplistic doctrine of biblical inspiration, we cannot deny the possibility that some of those whose views Paul so hotly opposed may have held them not only in good faith but for good reasons. Placing Paul against his background—cultural, religious, and historical—is thus a necessary enterprise if his originality is to be seen in the proper perspective, and if his claim to represent authentic tradition (I Cor. 11.16; 15.3; Gal. 2.2b) is to be evaluated even tentatively.

It will be useful, then, at least to identify the problems as exactly as possible, and to suggest within what limits solutions may be looked for.

In one respect, a problem has long been identified. Successive stages in Pauline interpretation have seen Tarsus and Jerusalem as symbolizing the most formative influences on his mind. Paul has been presented to us as a Christian Stoic (and it is certainly a coincidence that Stoic thought found a home in Tarsus over so long a period), or at least as essentially Hellenistic in his world-view and assumptions. He has also been presented to us as a Christian rabbi, and this has for some time been perhaps the most influential approach to the interpretation of his thought.

To say this, however, is to approach the issue too starkly: the options as they have been sometimes stated need more exact definition. Culturally and linguistically, the frontier between Palestine and the rest of the world was in many ways not significant as far as Judaism is concerned[2] (and the same may be true of Christianity: between the world of the synoptic tradition and that of Paul it may well be that the effective difference is sociological, the gap between the countryside and the city, and to some extent between the predominantly proletarian and the better-to-do). Moreover, it is at last being recognized[3] that our knowledge of first-century Pharisaic doctrine and practice is far from secure: what we know about Paul we know with greater certainty than is the case with our knowledge about the Pharisees, and some imprecision attends every attempt to interpret his aims and methods by theirs.

Some matters, however, seem clear. Paul was by religious background a Diaspora Jew of his day, and the Diaspora had important links with the centre at Jerusalem. The situation of Paul before his conversion—and perhaps in certain ways after it—had much in common with that of Philo.[4] Like Philo, Paul may have been fully aware of contemporary Pharisaic exegetical method[5] while at the same time making use of the concepts of some forms of Hellenistic spirituality in the course of expounding his theology.[6]

Culturally, too, it is hard to 'place' Paul. Much suggests that he moved in somewhat well-to-do and leisured circles as one who was at home in them.[7] Yet it is difficult to determine his social status: the Roman citizenship ascribed to him by Acts does not take us very far. The related question of the degree and nature of his participation in the intellectual life of his time is also obscure. Did non-theological considerations amounting to intellectual snobbery play a greater part than we realize in the contempt he evoked in Corinth? The scorn, already noted, with which his spoken word was received by some (and also, perhaps, the grudging and not unambiguous[8] admission of his literary powers, II Cor. 10.10) may have been judgments pronounced in terms of strictly literary canons such as were increasingly coming into vogue at about this time. Paul may have appeared unfashionable—we should hardly be surprised to learn that!—and something of a boor. Resources now seem to be available for attaining a sharper focus in these aspects of the portrait of Paul: and while by no means of central importance, they are more than peripheral. The whole man in Paul—above all!—was involved in what he was as a messenger of the gospel, and if we could place him culturally with greater accuracy than has hitherto been attempted, we might well gain light on more specifically religious and theological aspects of what he was at the same time.

More crucial than either of the questions so far discussed, however, is that of the 'placing' of Paul in the two contexts which most concern the student of Christian origins, namely the history of the Christian movement, and that of the development of its ideas. In both these enquiries, vital as they are to the historian and to the apologist alike, a distorting factor has been provided by Paul himself; while in relation to the first of them the author of Luke-Acts, too, has (as we have already noted) added to the historian's problems. For these problems are not, in the first place, problems of lack of information. Paul's contribution to the source-material for the historian is unique: had his letters not survived, the available evidence would be fragmentary in the extreme. On most interpretations, Acts also preserves sources whose value may be considerable, difficult as it is to know how far the author had modified them in redaction. The basic problem is one of perspective. How can we put Paul in his place, when Paul is almost all we have?

The first aspect of this problem to be considered can be put in the following terms. To what extent is Paul's domination of the New Testament canon accidental? It is a familiar speculation[9] that Onesimus, the runaway slave of Philemon whom Paul hoped to reconcile to his master—and whose services he nevertheless hoped to regain subsequently (Philemon 13: whether Onesimus was to receive emancipation in the process is regrettably unclear)—became the editor of the collection of Pauline letters. After reconciliation had been effected, he went on to achieve an ecclesiastical career which ultimately brought him to the episcopal oversight of the church at Ephesus in the time of Ignatius. In the course of this somewhat remarkable ascent (the bishop of Ephesus during the very years when, on a widely held view, the fourth gospel was being compiled there, must have been for several reasons a person of some significance) he collected the letters which now form the 'undisputed' Pauline epistles, composing Ephesians to form the introduction. Onesimus, on this view, was a kind of Boswell on an incomparably greater scale: by publishing his dead protector's letters (as Boswell did with Johnson's table-talk), he gave permanence to a brilliance and personal influence which had been magnetic, but which might nevertheless have left no trace but for the piety of the admirer. (Indeed, given the importance of Paul's letters in determining the direction of later Christianity—and still more, if the view is taken that the collected letters formed the nucleus of the emergent New Testament canon—Onesimus might be claimed to be, after Paul himself, the most influential single figure in the whole of Christian history.)

The speculation and its corollary are fascinating, though perhaps too suggestive of the historical novel to command complete assent: moreover, we should need to envisage Onesimus as surviving to be at least a septuagenarian bishop. But even if we abandon the hope of giving a name to the editor of the collection of Pauline letters, it seems likely that we can assume he existed, and assume also that he worked of set purpose to perpetuate more than simply his master's memory. It was Paul's teaching, indeed, that was being canonized, rather than (in a different sense of the word) his memory, for hagiographical interest would have suppressed some of the less dignified outbursts.

But here is the problem. Why did the disciples of Apollos (for example) fail to do the same?[10] The presence in the canon of the Pauline letters—and therefore their dominant place in a canon which gives no other single writer the same prominence—is essentially accidental, in the sense that this man's spiritual (and literary) heirs succeeded in their task of piety, while those of his contemporaries either omitted to undertake the same task, or, if they did undertake it, failed to achieve their design. It is hard to believe that Paul's personal ascendancy over his admirers, and his influence upon them, were so much greater than was the case with any others that the survival and publication of his letters was, as it were, the inevitable ultimate achievement of the man himself. Paul's dominant place in the New Testament canon is therefore not a necessary reflection of his achievement. For this reason, we cannot rule out the possibility that his position in the canon may distort our appreciation of his true place in the history of early Christianity. Other missionaries, teaching significantly different interpretations of the Christian message, may have had a greater importance than we now realize. Indeed, we know that some of them did. We think of them as Paul's opponents, but this may not do full justice to their achievements.[11]

In the same way, Paul's domination of the second part of the narrative of Acts may be misleading. Philip, Peter, ultimately Barnabas, disappear from the unfolding story of the gospel's progress, until it is Paul alone, accompanied by his entourage, who leads that progress to Europe and finally to Rome. History, however, is seldom so exclusively in one man's hands. It is historians who prefer to have it so. What motives prompted the author to accord Paul this prominence? Was he, too, anxious to preserve the memory of the recently martyred apostle? Or was he, in his own way, all too busy with 'putting Paul in his place' as subordinate to the Jerusalem church, and going to his martyrdom as one who had striven for the priority of the Jews in the reception of the gospel, and who had been eager in his own personal observance of the feasts and ceremonies of the Law?[12] At all events, if Acts is at all concerned to 'put Paul in his place', that place is still a very prominent one, and the historian must ask to what extent Acts' hagiography at this point corresponds to the facts.

We are thus in the position of a man who wishes to look at a land-scape of which a superb mountain forms one part. He finds it extra-ordinarily difficult to get far enough back from the mountain to be able to see the whole view. It is for this very reason that he is unable to estimate the height and contours of the mountain in relation to the rest of the scenery, which indeed is so overshadowed that it is hard even to see it.

To say this is already to indicate the main puzzle which confronts us both in the Pauline letters and in Acts. Was Paul both the pioneer and, for an appreciable period, the sole agent of the Gentile mission outside Palestine? Or did he enter upon a scene where a certain amount had already been achieved?

Acts, in outline at least, gives an affirmative answer to the first question, and there is much in Paul's own writing which appears to support the same view. Thus it has been possible to argue that both Paul himself, and subsequently the three leaders of the Jerusalem church, believed that God had charged him, and him alone, to bear the gospel to non-Jewish humanity as a whole. 'Paul,' says Munck, 'as the apostle to the Gentiles, becomes the central figure in the story of salvation,'[13] and Rom. 15.16 should be translated as expressing Paul's belief in his call to be, uniquely, *the* servant of Christ Jesus for the Gentiles.

The immediate context of this last phrase, however, reveals Paul's awareness (to which Munck surely does less than justice[14]) that others had worked in parts, at least, of the Asiatic and European mission field before him. Romans 15.20f. shows that Paul knew of a successful preaching of the gospel which was independent of his own, and one, moreover, which, like his own, had been carried out among Gentile populations; for it would be straining the sense of these verses to assume that Paul believed Christ to have been called on ('named') before his own arrival, and the foundation of Christian faith laid, only in areas of solely Jewish population.[15] II Cor. 10.14f., too, implies the existence of Gentile congregations already evangelized by others, over whom Paul disclaims any attempt to establish his authority (unless indeed this passage is a wholly *ad hominem* attack on the 'poaching' that had actually been attempted in Corinth by Paul's successors there, and the action Paul renounces is purely hypothetical).[16] Further support for the view that non-Pauline communities existed already in regions he visited is perhaps supplied by I Thess. 1.7. The tenses which Paul uses in writing of his work in Thessalonica and its results would appear to make his reference apply in a fairly limited way to the events which followed immediately after the conversion of the Christians there. But this in turn became immediately—before, that is, Paul's subsequent work in Corinth had been more than begun—an example 'to all those who were believers in Macedonia and in Achaia'. Paul's churches in those regions, it might be deduced, were neither the only nor the first ones, and Stephanas' household was the 'firstfruits of Achaia' (I Cor. 16.15) only in the sense of being the first converts there won by Paul.[17] Further, there was a church at Cenchreae of which Phoebe was a 'servant' (Rom. 16.1). Cenchreae is indeed the port of Corinth, and the church there may have been an offshoot of the one in Corinth itself, and hence a Pauline foundation. But the fact that Paul commends Phoebe does not necessarily imply that this church's existence resulted solely from his work.

Most obviously of all, however, Rome itself had been evangelized by others than Paul, a fact which, interestingly enough, Acts itself reveals (28.15), even though the overall plan of the book seems to culminate in Paul's arrival and preaching in Rome as the first herald of the gospel in the capital of the civilized world. Even if we lacked any other indications of the existence of other missionary work in the Gentile world parallel to and independent of that of Paul, the early evangelization of Rome would make us pause before accepting the impression given us by Acts and by so much in the Pauline letters, that Paul's was the only—or the only significant—work that had been done. Romans makes it clear enough that the Roman church (or house-churches)[18] were well-established when Paul wrote; he does so, indeed, with perceptible respect and even embarrassment (Rom. 1. 11-13). He is uneasily aware that he writes to them as having no authority over them, and as knowing himself—as we have seen—to have been slandered to them. Rom. 1-11 is an *apologia pro doctrina sua* offered, we may well feel, in a situation making the formulation of this *apologia* a matter for considerable deliberation.

Do I Peter 1.1 and Rev. 1.11 offer further evidence of missionary achievement independent of Paul's? The answer, of course, depends on the dating of both documents; though, even if we place both works fairly late, we may reasonably assume that the churches addressed must have been established for some years beforehand.[19] What seems clear is that Paul was not the pioneer that Acts (e.g. 26.17f.) wishes to make him, and that a reading of some parts of the letters might also imply that he was. He was the most outstanding individual missionary, in the sense that he left heirs who secured the success of his somewhat controversial interpretation—as it clearly was—of the Christian gospel. That he was the only missionary outside Palestine is contradicted by the existence of a Christian population in Rome, and possibly also by the evidence that has been considered relating to regions in which Paul himself had worked; nor should we neglect the evidence of the synoptic, and particularly of the Marcan, tradition, that stories about Jesus were handed on in Gentile churches as well as in Palestinian Jewish ones, with no indication whatever (rather the contrary) that those churches owed their existence to Paul's teaching.

The significance of the collection on behalf of the church in Jerusalem should not, then, be exaggerated. Paul's ecumenical gesture[20] was designed to represent the community of faith with Jerusalem of those Gentile Christians for whose conversion Paul had been responsible. He was not in a position to go to Jerusalem as an ambassador for the entire Gentile Christian world.

Closely bound up with the question of Paul's place in the history of the expansion of Christianity is that of his place in its theological development. The issues here are indeed too complex to be reviewed even in outline in an essay such as this. Form criticism of several passages has led some writers,[21] following Bultmann, to find Paul quoting and modifying confessions which he inherited. What was their source? How significant were the modifications he made? Is the form-critical method, in any case, a sufficiently delicate instrument to serve the purpose to which it has been put in these cases? If Paul wanted to say what he did, there were perhaps no words so apt, and no form of expression so schematic, as those of a sentence which inevitably looks like a confessional formula. Until questions like these have reached widely agreed solutions, it will be difficult to form any reliable estimate of the degree of creativity in Paul's Christian teaching, and of the latter's relation to what others already believed (apart, of course, from the positions adopted by his opponents; and even these are considerably less certain than some recent writers, particularly on II Corinthians, have supposed).

Again, do the other New Testament writings, emerging as they do from the decades following those during which Paul was working and writing, show evidence of theologies lying behind them which were contemporary with Paul's but distinct from it? The deutero-Pauline works seem to do so: the links which have been demonstrated[22] between Ephesians and Qumran, for example, might indicate the presence of another theology; the synthesis between this and the Pauline heritage may not be quite true to either type of thought. Further, some of the traditions which were drawn on by the synoptic evangelists show a fairly wide divergence from Pauline teaching, most notably in relation to christology[23] and the law of Moses.[24] Here, of course, the fundamental problem is that of Paul's contact with traditions of the teaching of Jesus.[25] If he was at all aware of these, and of theologies making use of them, it is possible that we should view Paul's doctrines and those of his contemporaries as, in part, competing interpretations of the tradition about Jesus. By selection and by emphasis each presented his own impression of what is central. Thus Paul stands over against some of the material peculiar to Matthew[26] (and also, over against James) through a kind of intuition of the primacy of one doctrine, namely that of the absolute gratuitousness of grace—a doctrine which curiously and significantly echoes Jesus' teaching about the kingdom promised to those least deserving of reward on any calculable basis.[27] But to argue, as we surely could, that Paul's was the most perceptive and faithful interpretation[28] is not to relegate all others to lack of historical importance. These other Christianities did not survive, except in the sense that they have left traces in the works of later writers. But they were not for that reason alone any the less important in the times and places of their first propagation.

Paul is thus even harder to 'place' in the beginnings of doctrinal history than he is in his other contexts. Yet here, more urgently than anywhere else, the quest for greater clarity must be pursued. To the extent, after all, that Pauline formulations dictated subsequent developments, he did ultimately win his battle with his opponents. More than that, it was perhaps Paul who first introduced into Christian history the notion of doctrinal orthodoxy. When he reproved Peter and his companions at Antioch, as he tells us (Gal. 2.14) that he did, for 'not behaving correctly with regard to the truth of the gospel' (οὐκ ὀρθοποδοῦσιν πρὸς τὴν ἀλήθειαν τοῦ εὐαγγελίου), he was perhaps enunciating for the first time the concept of a norm by which one might judge not only conduct—that indeed was a familiar matter in the debates over *halakah*—but also the theology motivating it. Paul's intolerance perhaps introduced into Christianity—for good or ill—an acerbity which was of a different order from what could obtain in Judaism; for toleration was impossible (in spite of Phil. 1.18, which remains a very remarkable statement on Paul's part) over issues involving beliefs about the nature of God himself. It is all the more necessary for the doctrinal historian and the apologist to attain an objective assessment of the issues between Paul and his contemporaries as far as this can be done. We may believe that Paul *was* right, but we should not do this simply because he says so.

All of us, then, stand too close to Paul to be able easily to gain an objective impression. For some, temperamental as well as theological reasons render him the most modern of the voices they hear in the New Testament. Others, finding Paul less congenial, may nevertheless accept too uncritically the doctrinal pre-eminence accorded to him by his place in the canon. For all of us, the attempt to set him in his context must lead to a better appreciation of him as a historical figure. It might also contribute to the clarification of the urgent problem of continuity and interpretative innovation in the church's witness to Jesus himself.[29]

NOTES

1. E. A. Judge, 'St Paul and Classical Society', *Jahrbuch für Antike und Christentum* 15, 1972, p. 19.

2. As is shown by M. Hengel, *Judaism and Hellenism*, ET SCM Press 1974.

3. See J. Neusner, *The Rabbinic Traditions about the Pharisees before 70*, Leiden 1971. Part 1, pp. 1–10.

4. Cf. S. Sandmel, *The Genius of Paul*, Farrar, Straus & Cudahy 1958, and J. Klausner, *From Jesus to Paul*, Allen & Unwin 1944, pp. 450–66. Note, however, by contrast, the suggestion of U. Wilckens ('Die Bekehrung des Paulus als religionsgeschichtliches Problem', *ZTK* 56, 1959, pp. 281–7) that the Judaism of Paul had been not that of the Pharisees but of the circles which produced apocalyptic.

5. Cf. E. Bréhier, *Les Idées Philosophiques et Religieuses de Philon d'Alexandrie*, Paris 1950, pp. 54–61; H. Hegermann, 'Das hellenistische Judentum', in J. Leipoldt and W. Grundmann (eds.), *Umwelt des Urchristentums*, Berlin 1971, I, p. 333.

6. Cf. E. R. Goodenough with A. T. Kraabel, 'Paul and the Hellenization of Christianity', in J. Neusner (ed.), *Religions in Antiquity*, Leiden 1968, pp. 39–68.

7. Cf. E. A. Judge, art. cit., p. 28. The whole subject indicated in this paragraph is

discussed in Judge's article in a wide-ranging way which indicates many directions for further research.

8. Both βαρύς and ἰσχυρός receive a number of pejorative meanings in Liddell and Scott's *Lexicon* (including in both cases 'indigestible'!); it is possible that both adjectives were a little double-edged. On Paul's performance as an exponent of rhetoric, in the light of contemporary standards, see E. A. Judge, 'Paul's Boasting in relation to Contemporary Professional Practice', *Australian Biblical Review* 16, 1968, pp. 37–50, and other articles by the same author there cited.

9. J. Knox, *Philemon Among the Letters of Paul*, University of Chicago Press 1960, pp. 63–93, and C. L. Mitton, *The Formation of the Pauline Corpus of Letters*, Epworth Press 1955, pp. 50ff. See now a brief criticism of these views in K. M. Fischer, *Tendenz und Absicht des Epheserbriefs*, Göttingen 1973, p. 14 n. 1.

10. Unless, of course, he was the author of Hebrews. In that case one has to account for the survival of the letter and its ultimate inclusion in the canon, and some phenomenon comparable with what must have happened in the case of Paul might be imagined. If, however, Hebrews is to be regarded as in some sense deutero-Pauline, its relatively late arrival in the corpus suggests that the 'school of Paul' had an extended history and drew, in the course of its development, on a variety of traditions.

11. The multiplicity of the earliest forms of Christian faith and practice, to which attention was drawn by C. F. D. Moule, *The Birth of the New Testament*, A. & C. Black 1962, pp. 153–177, has been re-emphasized as a necessary presupposition for New Testament research by the republication of J. M. Robinson, 'Kerygma and History in the New Testament' and H. Koester, 'Gnomai Diaphorai: the Origin and Nature of Diversification in the History of Early Christianity', in J. M. Robinson and H. Koester (eds.), *Trajectories through Early Christianity*, Fortress Press 1971, pp. 20–70, 114–157.

12. These views of the purpose of Acts were argued respectively by e.g. S. G. F. Brandon, *The Fall of Jerusalem and the Christian Church*, SPCK 1951, and J. Knox, *Marcion and the New Testament*, University of Chicago Press 1942, pp. 117–20. Some more recent commentators see no such polemic in the author's mind. According to E. Haenchen, Acts regards Paul as a 'representative' of the apostles ('*so etwas wie ein Apostel-Stellvertreter*'): 'with him . . . there draws to its close a . . . special time, when the Church was still pure' (*The Acts of the Apostles*, ET Blackwell 1971, p. 147); while for J. C. O'Neill the Paul of Acts is Paul as the church remembered him before the publication of the letters—the apostle who became a martyr in Rome, *The Theology of Acts*, 2nd ed., SPCK 1970, pp. 183–5. Cf. also C. K. Barrett, *New Testament Essays*, SPCK 1972, pp. 92ff.; H.-J. Michel, *Die Abschiedsrede des Paulus an die Kirche Apg 20, 17–38*, Munich 1973, pp. 77–83.

13. J. Munck, *Paul and the Salvation of Mankind*, ET SCM Press 1959, p. 49.

14. Ibid., p. 52: there have been other missionaries, but Paul alone is 'the priest who is to prepare the Gentiles' offering'. This last phrase rightly places the significance of the collection at the centre of the problem of Paul's self-understanding; cf. K. F. Nickle, *The Collection* (SBT 48), 1966, pp. 100–143, where indeed the importance of Paul's initiative is if anything somewhat neglected. But it is surely not necessary to take τῶν ἐθνῶν so comprehensively; the collection could have been thought of (as presumably it was) as a gesture on the part of Paul's churches—largely, indeed, Gentile in origin—rather than as representing the entire non-Jewish world. It should be added that the anarthrous λειτουργόν in v. 16 is ambiguous, and could, but need not, imply the uniqueness of Paul's ministry (cf. Blass-Debrunner, *Greek Grammar of*

the New Testament, ET Cambridge University Press 1961, §254, p. 132). For a critique of Munck's (and Cullmann's) views see J. Knox, 'Romans 15:14–33 and Paul's Apostolic Mission', *JBL* 83, 1964, pp. 1–11.

15. As might be understood if the 'division of labour' in Gal. 2.9 gave Paul his sphere of work exclusively among non-Jews (which is not the view of Acts, admittedly) rather than exclusively outside the borders of Palestine; cf. J. Munck, op. cit., p. 119. H. Schlier rightly points out (*Der Brief an die Galater*, 4th ed., Göttingen 1965, p. 79 and n. 6) that Paul's words indicate direction of missionary activity rather than exclusive delimitation. In Rom. 15.19f. Paul could, on this showing, have had in mind any centre of population, with or without a large Jewish element, which he might have evangelized on the basis of his commission.

16. C. K. Barrett, in a lengthy discussion of this verse and its context (*The Second Epistle to the Corinthians*, A. & C. Black 1973, pp. 265ff.), offers a different reconstruction of Paul's missionary situation: by heading westwards beyond Rome to Spain, 'Paul would be able to avoid the province of others (such as Peter, his Jerusalem colleagues, and their dependants)', p. 268. Barrett has to admit, however, that 'Rome would constitute a possibly embarrassing exception'. His exegesis appears to rely to a considerable extent on taking κανών ('rule, standard; ... limit, boundary; ... "province", sphere of action', Liddell and Scott) in a strictly geographical sense: 'Corinth was part of the virgin territory that Paul claimed as his special mission field.' If, however, the reference is in some way to the agreement in Jerusalem as limiting Paul's work to those who were neither Jews nor proselytes, there would be room for reference here to congregations in Greece founded by missionaries other than Paul on the basis of secessions from the synagogues. It is of course an embarrassment for this solution that Acts represents Paul as having done precisely this at Corinth itself, Acts 18.4, 8; but—as has been again suggested in this essay—Acts may have its own reasons for showing Paul in this light. Even apart from this, however, Paul could have thought of his κανών as defined in other than simply geographical terms. It consisted, perhaps, in those hitherto unevangelized Gentile cities in which God had predestined him to preach; the existence of already established Christian congregations in neighbouring centres would not thus be ruled out. Cf. E. Käsemann, *An die Römer*, Tübingen 1973, p. 378 (on Rom. 15.20 f.).

17. The references to Aquila and Priscilla might give support to this. Acts 18.2 describes Aquila as a Jew, and the sequel presumably includes them both among those converted at v.8, since they accompany Paul to Syria, and at v.28 complete Apollos' oddly inadequate Christian instruction. But is it not more likely that they were already Christians when Paul met them, as implied by E. Käsemann, op. cit., p. 394? The New Testament evidence about Aquila and Priscilla permits, in Käsemann's view, the conclusion 'that both should be reckoned among the most important early Christian missionaries working in the Diaspora', which would considerably strengthen the view here being argued.

18. Cf. P. S. Minear, *The Obedience of Faith* (SBT 2.19), 1972, pp. 7f.

19. It is curious that two of the churches addressed in the Apocalypse were also respectively the recipient of a letter from Paul (Laodicea) and one of his most important centres of work (Ephesus), while Smyrna, Sardis, and perhaps Philadelphia were relatively near. Was it the intention of the author to address—whether as an actual communication with these Christians or symbolically—an area in which Paul's influence was known to be dominant? Or were there distinct and even rival churches in some of these cities?

20. Cf. J. Munck, op. cit., pp. 301–5.

21. E.g. recently W. Kramer, *Christ, Lord, Son of God* (SBT 50), 1966, and H. Thyen, *Studien zur Sündenvergebung* (FRLANT 96), 1970, pp. 152–217.

22. See K. G. Kuhn, 'The Epistle to the Ephesians in the Light of the Qumran Texts', in J. Murphy-O'Connor (ed.), *Paul and Qumran*, Chapman 1968, pp. 115–31; J. Coppens, ' "Mystery" in the Theology of St Paul and its parallels in Qumran', ibid., pp. 151–6; F. Mussner, 'Contributions made by Qumran to the Understanding of the Epistle to the Ephesians', ibid., pp. 159–78. Cf. E. Käsemann, article 'Epheserbrief', *RGG*[3] II, 1958, col. 518, and K. M. Fischer, op. cit. (see note 9), pp. 109–200, for these and other non-Pauline elements in Eph.

23. It is an over-simplification to find in Mark a so-called 'θεῖος ἀνήρ' christology, as do J. M. Robinson, art. cit. (see note 11), pp. 48–51 and T. J. Weeden, *Mark: Traditions in Conflict*, Fortress Press 1971. Nevertheless, the miracle stories of the synoptics imply a christology significantly at variance with Paul's.

24. Granted that Rom. 7.12, 8.4 and 13.8–10 are not isolated texts, but indicate a positive view of the law on Paul's part, there is still a wide disparity between Paul's doctrine and that of the special material in Matthew, cf. especially 12.37.

25. A new approach to the problem is offered by D. L. Duggan, *The Sayings of Jesus in the Churches of Paul*, Blackwell 1971. For a recent survey of the wider issues, see J. Blank, *Paulus und Jesus*, Munich 1968.

26. In spite of C. H. Dodd's useful indication of unsuspected parallels in theological interest, 'Matthew and Paul', *New Testament Studies*, Manchester University Press 1953, pp. 53–66.

27. Paul's doctrine of justification also explicates the meaning of Jesus' resurrection, as Christopher Evans has pointed out in an extraordinarily penetrating exercise in fundamental hermeneutics, 'The Faith of an Exegete', *Theology* 77, 1974, pp. 287–90.

28. Cf. J. Bowker's perceptive comment on Jesus' attitude to the Pharisees: 'It is not the actions of men which create the actions of God, but the actions of God which create and transform the actions of men ... In this, as in almost all else, Paul, far from distorting the teaching of Jesus, expressed and continued it with greater accuracy', *Jesus and the Pharisees*, Cambridge University Press 1973, pp. 44f.

29. For comments on an earlier draft of this essay I am grateful to the Rev. John Bowden and Dr Morna Hooker, and to a group of students at King's College, London, some of them Professor Evans' pupils: Judith Long, Malcolm Herbert, Roy Screech and Tom Hurcombe.

7

Can Apocalyptic be Relevant?

SOPHIE LAWS

'W E are caught by surprise and are unprepared when systematic theologians discover that the material we work with has relevance'; but the surprise of the biblical scholar is the greater when the systematic theologian lights upon material he has not been working with to any extent, and without waiting for him to analyse it, takes it up and incorporates it into a dogmatic scheme that is thereby declared to be a biblical theology. H. D. Betz's wry comment[1] was evoked by his survey of the use of the idea of apocalyptic in the theology of the Pannenberg group; for apocalyptic, that ball which seemed to fall squarely into neither the Old Testament nor the New Testament court, has been taken up in the last decade by the systematic theologians, Wolfhart Pannenberg himself,[2] and to a lesser extent Jürgen Moltmann[3] and Carl Braaten.[4] The biblical scholar might perhaps blame systematic theology itself for his neglect of this section of his material, for, when the prevailing climate of theology was existentialism, apocalyptic, with its mythology and its objectifying of the activity of God, hardly recommended itself as fruitful ground for exegesis or hermeneutic. However, the initiative of the systematic theologian to rediscover it would seem to receive a measure of confirmation and approval from the side of the biblical scholar in Ernst Käsemann's celebrated declaration that 'apocalyptic was the mother of all Christian theology'.[5]

The use that each of these scholars makes of their common material is somewhat different. For Pannenberg, apocalyptic is the biblical exemplar of his theory of revelation as consisting in a universal history. Man's experience of the individual events of history is of them as

89

fragmentary and incomplete, and his experience of the revelation of God in them is correspondingly indirect and partial. Full understanding can only come when events are seen in their context in history as a whole, but history can only be seen as a whole from the perspective of its end. So the revelation of God lies in the future, in the achieving of, indeed as, the goal of history, for 'history as a whole is the whole revelation of God, and revelation is history'.[6] Pannenberg sees this theological position as having a precedent in that of the late Jewish apocalyptists, who had moved away from the pre-exilic interest in Yahweh's past acts of salvation, and away from the exilic and early post-exilic hope of some act of salvation in the near future, to a vision of the whole of history moving towards its goal. Christianity adds an extra dimension to this, by proclaiming that in the 'event' of Jesus Christ, and especially in his historical resurrection (which must be understood in apocalyptic terms) the goal of history is proleptically present, and the key to understanding given in advance.

Moltmann lays his stress not so much upon history as upon the future, with its connotations of hope and promise. Hope and promise stand over against the present, in dialectic, and proclaim the future as wholly open, unlimited and new. The importance of apocalyptic for Moltmann lies not only in its concentration upon the future, but in its vision of cosmic upheaval. The possibilities of the future are not limited to the frontiers of men and nations, but extend to the whole created order. We are not tied to a self-sufficient mechanistic universe:

> Without apocalyptic a theological eschatology remains bogged down in the ethnic history of men or the existential history of the individual. The New Testament did not close the window which apocalyptic had opened for it towards the wide vistas of the cosmos and beyond the limitations of the given cosmic reality.[7]

Moreover, the radical discontinuity between present and future in apocalyptic provides an appropriate dialectic to express that promise of the future which arises from the resurrection of the crucified Christ, for Moltmann a veritable *creatio ex nihilo*.

Carl Braaten, dependent to a considerable extent upon these two scholars, outlines some categories of apocalyptic thought that can be significant for systematic theology. Its dualism, with a radical disjunction between present and future, may provide support for a real theology of liberation, rather than of development or evolution, and for a hope of freedom expanded to cosmic dimensions. Its vision of a new heaven and earth may awaken a much-needed theology of nature in the present ecological crisis; its picture of world history moving forward into the future may revive the ideal of mission. Finally, its wealth of imagery may lead to a doctrine of mind and of imagination: man can analyse, negate and transcend his world, an achievement for which the ultimate symbol is resurrection, the transcendence of death, the last negation.

Ernst Käsemann, as I have said, may seem to give this adoption of apocalyptic by the systematic theologians a measure of support by according to it a central place in New Testament theology. It is, however, only a measure of support, for he acknowledges that the supremacy of apocalyptic theology did not long outlast either the collapse of the hope of the imminent coming of Christ, or the Gentile mission and the consequent adoption of Hellenistic expressions. However, it did provide the first expression of Christian theology after Easter (for Käsemann does not associate apocalyptic with the message of Jesus) and was 'the appropriate response to the fact that in Jesus the ultimate promise of the world is encountered'.[8] In the apocalyptic scheme, the idea of ultimate authority necessarily carries with it the idea of ultimate in time, and so the hope of the parousia. During its brief, creative reign, apocalyptic instilled in Christianity a number of important concerns, notably an ethical imperative based upon an eschatological *ius talionis* (as in Mark 8.38) and an involvement with history. Apocalyptic, according to Käsemann, conceived of a history of salvation in parallel with a history of damnation, and of a typological relation between epochs ('and as were the days of Noah, so shall be the coming of the Son of Man', Matt. 24.37), which made necessary the formation of a gospel history and the narration of the *kerygma* of Jesus rather than just the proclamation of it. Although this early theological framework collapsed, certain fundamental themes survived the collapse. For Käsemann, the central idea of early Christian apocalyptic was

the hope of the manifestation of the Son of Man on his way to his enthronement; and we have to ask ourselves whether Christian theology can ever survive in any legitimate form without this theme, which sprang from the Easter experience and determined the Easter faith.[9]

Discussion of these various positions has not been slow in forthcoming. Of the systematic theologians, Pannenberg has been the main target for criticism.[10] It is disputed whether he is justified in attributing to apocalyptic so keen an interest in history, both as a unity of past, present and future, and as moving towards its goal. It may be suggested, instead, that apocalyptic springs from a complete pessimism about history, a total disillusion about human possibilities, and an abandoning of any attempt to find meaning in events as they occur. The only hope lies in God's bringing this inexplicable process to an end and establishing a new situation. And if that is so, we cannot really talk about a *goal* of history: history does not reach a consummation, it comes to an end, that the new age may begin. We are talking, as W. R. Murdock expresses it, of *'terminus* not *telos'*.[11] If it be suggested, though, that the characteristic recapitulation of past and present in apocalyptic implies an interest in more than just the totally new age, it may still be questioned whether that interest is really in *history* in any recognizable sense. Apocalyptic is notoriously uninterested in the traditional salvation events of Israel's past; it does not really make events contemporary with the writers come alive; and when the course of past history is systematized into a predetermined scheme of ages, kingdoms or generations it may well be asked whether the past is being taken seriously or whether it has not become, as P. D. Hanson suggests,[12] 'a timetable of cosmic events' and so basically timeless. It may further be asked whether the idea of *universal* history is attributable to apocalyptic, or whether the history of other nations does not rather provide the context of Israel's redemption, if not actually represent that from which she is redeemed. Finally, R. G. Hamerton-Kelly accuses Pannenberg of a one-sided picture of apocalyptic. Certainly it fixed its hope on God's future manifestation of power, but it also asserted the spatial *presence* and pre-existence of God and of the entities which he promises. If Pannenberg chooses to ignore this important feature of apocalyptic thought, so Hamerton-Kelly asserts, he cannot really claim to be basing his theology upon it.[13]

Moltmann and Braaten have not received such explicit criticism as has Pannenberg, but there are features of their approach to apocalyptic, too, that are open to discussion. Both, for instance, lay stress upon the references to the cosmos. But it may be asked, again, whether apocalyptic is really seriously interested in the created order in itself, or whether the elements of the cosmos are not rather seen as symbols for those spiritual forces whose activities give an added dimension to human affairs and ultimately determine their outcome. Both theologians, too, are concerned to stress the openness and unlimited possibilities of the future, but it is doubtful whether this is consistent with two marked features of apocalyptic. First, the future there is certainly limited in terms of time, for the end is imminent. Secondly, the events of the future are quite clearly determined; the apocalyptist can 'predict' them, and it is important for his purpose that he should be able to, for only if he can be definite can he really reassure his readers that there is an end to their present perplexity. It may well be right to say that when the present age is over, the possibilities of the *new age* are limitless, but the use of the term 'the future' seems to obscure a characteristic distinction between these two ages.

Käsemann, predictably, has come under a good deal of fire from his fellow New Testament scholars.[14] He is asked on what grounds he feels that apocalyptic was the inevitable form of expression for early church theology. We need to know more about the currency of apocalyptic: was it the popular literature of first-century Palestine, or the work of learned or sectarian groups? Were its ideas more widespread than the literature? Had it spread beyond Palestine into the Diaspora? (There are many intriguing, and perhaps unanswerable, questions one might ask about the initial production of apocalyptic literature: were the books produced with a parade of antiquity, like Josiah's scroll of the law? Did the pseudonymous authorships convince anyone—and were they meant to?) Käsemann's reconstruction of a unilinear history of early church theology is also criticized: may not apocalyptic have been but one form of expression among several—one of several 'brothers', or, lest we run the risk of identifying form and content, one of the many 'midwives' (the possibilities of playing with Käsemann's familial metaphor are limitless—these two suggestions are Rollins's)? It is difficult, too, to relate Käsemann's argument that it was apocalyptic which made necessary the narration of the *kerygma* of Jesus to the fact that such narration is characteristically given in the form of the gospel rather than of the apocalypse. Again, Käsemann, in the tradition of the 'New Quest', introduces another element of discontinuity between Jesus, his background and his followers, for although John the Baptist and the early Christians were apocalyptists, Jesus, he says, was not.

Ebeling and Fuchs, as the proponents of the 'new hermeneutic' on existentialist principles, might be expected especially to dislike Käsemann's findings. Fuchs claims that Käsemann has disregarded the important element of 'present' or 'realized' eschatology in the New Testament, which he thinks to be central to its theology and its original proclamation—for there seems to him to be little to proclaim in a purely waiting situation. He remarks, too, that even if it were proved that apocalyptic *was* the inevitable initial form of Christian response, it would not thereby be proved that it was the *right* response. Ebeling, congruously, draws attention to what may be called anti-apocalyptic strains in the New Testament, and raises the possibility that the origins of Christian theology may have lain in the overcoming of apocalyptic; and he adds some dark allusions about the stigmatizing of apocalyptic as heresy in the Reformation period.

Clearly, the whole subject is very much open to discussion, and there are a number of basic issues which need, if not to be settled, at least to be aired. One of these is the question of the definition of 'apocalyptic'. It is notable that Pannenberg and Moltmann can isolate wholly different ideas as 'central' to apocalyptic. Käsemann's own definition, when he is pressed to give one, is extremely limited: 'I speak of primitive Christian apocalyptic to denote the expectation of an imminent parousia.'[15] Pannenberg is widely accused of having based his appeal to apocalyptic upon the presentation of one scholar, D. Rössler,[16] whose account of apocalyptic lays the stress upon history which we have seen to be open to dispute, and ignores ideas which other scholars see to be important in it, especially dualism and the imminent expectation of the end. It is probably correct to see emerging in recent work on apocalyptic a broad consensus of opinion about its main characteristics,[17] but the matter cannot be considered to be settled. In particular it is necessary to decide whether a definition of 'apocalyptic' is a definition of ideas, or of literary features, or of a coincidence of the two, and if it should also contain an analysis of the social phenomena which give rise to the ideas and the literature. It is also important to consider possible affinities between Jewish apocalyptic and Persian or Hellenistic ideas: is apocalyptic a specifically Jewish phenomenon? Is it a logical development of earlier Old Testament ideas? Is it so distinctly 'biblical' that a theology based upon it is thereby constituted a 'biblical theology'?

It is also important to be aware that the present interest in the study of apocalyptic may be related to affinities which are felt between apocalyptic and certain contemporary social, political and cultural phenomena. ('Apocalyptic' is, after all, one of the few theological technical terms to find a place in popular parlance.) This is especially clear in the writings of American scholars like P. D. Hanson, who remarks on the way the apocalyptic visions of the corruption of human political structures and of cosmic catastrophe seem to find parallels in the situation of the collapse of the 'American dream' and of the pollution of the environment. The modern dilemmas about finding meaning in history, about the possibility of political solutions, and the theme of meaninglessness in society which characterizes much modern fiction, seem to strike apocalyptic chords.[18] The rediscovery of symbolism, and the delight in extraordinary, even bizarre, imagery that fixes a Bosch, a Blake or a Dali poster upon the undergraduate wall may also suggest a relationship with this most symbolic of literature. But, again, we need to examine whether there is a real relationship: apocalyptic imagery may not have seemed bizarre or extraordinary in its own cultural environment, and we are not certain that we can distinguish absolutely between a symbol, an image, and the description of an entity literally understood in that original context. It is probably true that, as W. A. Beardslee suggests,[19] apocalyptic used to be the point at which the strangeness of the early Christian world-view, and its difference from our own, was most felt, and that this gulf is now (in some quarters, at any rate) felt to be bridged. But this new-felt affinity needs to be treated with considerable reserve. It may be that it is leading to the rediscovery of a highly important but neglected element for theology; it may be that it points only to a superficial and negligible similarity; it may be positively misleading, in that modern ideas and feelings can be anachronistically traced back into the original apocalyptic schemes. We need to ask 'whether it is really historical apocalyptic which is looming up so suddenly at the centre of theological thinking'.[20]

I do not propose now to follow further any of these lines of enquiry, nor to enter into detailed discussion of those words and phrases in the teaching of Jesus and of Paul which may or may not be susceptible of an apocalyptic interpretation. Rather, I intend to suggest another angle of approach to the question which I do not think has yet been explored: namely, to examine those sections of the New Testament which can most readily be described as apocalyptic to see if they exhibit those interests for which it is suggested that 'apocalyptic' is the appropriate expression in Christian theology. I shall, therefore, be discussing Mark 13 and the Revelation of St John. I do not think that questions of date need concern us: even if Revelation is considered one of the latest documents of the New Testament, it is reasonable to suppose that those interests which found early expression in the use of apocalyptic ideas would be retained in a later document which has the apocalyptic form. Nor need questions of place of origin delay us, though the use of apocalyptic in what is often thought to be a *Roman* gospel, and in an address to the churches of *Asia*, might bear some examination.

There have, of course, been attempts to detach both Mark 13 and Revelation from the classification of 'apocalyptic'. It is argued that, strictly speaking, the description 'apocalyptic' only applies to vv. 14–20 and 24–27 of Mark 13; but, whatever may have been the pre-history of this material, the evangelist has chosen to incorporate it in this section of his gospel so that it both affects the interpretation of the material with which it is associated and is in turn conditioned by that material, as it is by its context in the gospel as a whole. It is pointed out that certain motifs characteristic of apocalyptic are absent from Mark 13: holy war, the overthrow of Satan, the last judgment; and that the prediction of calamity for Israel and the temple is inconsistent with the usual theme of their deliverance. However, it is unreasonable to demand that every possible motif be present in every apocalypse; and the changed attitude to Israel may be attributed to the fact that in Mark this is no longer simply a *Jewish* apocalypse. One difference from the usual character of apocalyptic (and I shall be assuming that 'broad consensus' of which I have spoken, bearing in mind that there is no absolute definition of what characterizes apocalyptic) does, however, deserve to be noted. There is, in vv. 7–8, a deliberate drawing away of attention from those events which would, in other apocalyptic litera-ture, be given the character of 'signs of the end'; and the inclusion of the isolated saying of v. 32 has the effect of ruling out the idea of 'signs' altogether.

There have been two recent attempts to devise an apocalyptic litmus test to determine the character of Revelation. J. Kallas finds the decisive criterion to be the attitude to suffering.[21] In apocalyptic, he says, the traditional Old Testament attitude to suffering as retributive is finally abandoned, and suffering becomes a thing which God will crush. However, in Revelation the idea of retribution is re-introduced, for the sufferings of the church are the result of its failings as denounced in the seven letters. In suggesting a changed attitude to suffering in Revelation, Kallas seems to me to draw attention to something important, but his actual analysis seems wholly mistaken. Nor can the *decisive* character of apocalyptic really be said to be something which is as much characteristic of the non-apocalyptic Job and Ecclesiastes. For B. W. Jones, replying to Kallas, the deciding factor is the element of pseudonymity in traditional apocalyptic, and its absence from Revelation.[22] I am not sure how confidently we can make that latter judgment, but in any event it again seems illegitimate to make as an absolute criterion for apocalyptic a feature which is equally marked in the Wisdom literature (as indeed in a number of New Testament epistles). Neither of these objections can stand against the clear overall impression that, formally at least, it is in the category of apocalyptic that Revelation belongs.[23]

I shall therefore proceed to examine the attitude of these two New Testament apocalypses to the three tenses of the past, present and future, which seem to be significant in the current debate about apocalyptic. For Pannenberg it is important that apocalyptic surveys past history, and gathers up past and present into a unity taken on into the future. This is done through the device of setting the visionary in the distant past, so that his recapitulation takes the form of prophecy. It is clear that this is a point at which both Mark 13 and Revelation differ from traditional apocalyptic: neither provides a summary of past events, and the author of Revelation addresses his readers as their contemporary. This contrast needs, of course, some qualification. Inasmuch as the words of Mark 13 are put into the mouth of Jesus before the passion, and inasmuch as vv. 9–13, at least, may reflect something of the experiences of Mark's church, we do have a survey of the present and perhaps of the recent past in the form of prophecy.

Similarly, the letters to the seven churches provide in Revelation some account of the present situation of its readers, and in 2.2–3 and 3.13 some reference to their past. In 11.8, too, the description of the 'great city' as 'Sodom and Egypt, where also their Lord was crucified' (if this verse be not a later interpolation) pulls on the threads of the past to describe the cumulative evil of Rome. But the basic difference remains more striking than the few points of similarity.

This is not to say that the two authors are not interested in the past, in a very particular way. This interest is manifested in Revelation at points where its apocalyptic character is most apparent, but with the effect of transforming the apocalyptic perspective. In 5.1 the seer is shown the sealed book, a familiar symbol of God's plan which he will put into operation. But in 5.9 it is declared that it is the Lamb who is worthy to open the book, precisely because he was slain and is alive. If it be right to assert that, for apocalyptic, hope was vested in the future, in the inauguration by God of his new age, the Revelation, in contrast, asserts that that which determines this hope is an event not of the future, but of the past, in the death of the Lamb. Similarly, in 12.7–11 there is the account of war in heaven, the cosmic battle that traditionally paralleled conflicts on earth and ultimately determined the outcome of those conflicts, since strength in heaven was greater than strength on earth, and therefore, taken together, the forces of good must overcome those of evil. But here, the evil power is cast out of heaven not because of the superior heavenly forces of good, but 'they overcame him because of the blood of the Lamb'. It is an event on earth, and in the past, that is decisive. The figure of the Lamb himself merits examination. Certainly in 14.1 he is the warrior lamb of apocalyptic, the ram who leads his flock, but he is also clearly in 5.6 the lamb of sacrifice. This fusion of the two images of a lamb is, I think, unprecedented, and the catalyst that brings them together must be the appreciation that this Messiah is the Jesus who lived, died and rose again.

Something of the same argument may be made in relation to Mark 13. R. H. Lightfoot originally drew attention to the similarity in language between Mark 13 and the subsequent passion narrative,[24] in particular the use of the verb 'to deliver up' or 'to hand over' in both sections; in the idea of the 'hour' in both; and in the way the division of times in 13.35 tallies with the division of Jesus' last night. The effect of this deliberate parallelism, if it is admitted, may be twofold: prospective and retrospective. Mark 13 prefaces the passion; it therefore provides these forthcoming events with a prior interpretation: this is the light in which they shall be seen. The death of Jesus has its context in the fate and future of the world. In retrospect, the experiences of the later church, to which the chapter may be thought to allude, are to be seen in the light of the passion. To this second point I shall return. If the first point is right, that the apocalypse of Mark 13 serves to provide an interpretation of the passion; and if it is also right that in Revelation the apocalyptic perspective is altered in the light of the cross, then we may conclude that Mark 13 and Revelation are indeed interested in history and in one historical event of the past in particular. But they are interested in history not because they are apocalyptists, but because central to their theology is the incarnation and especially the cross.

It is often said that the attitude of apocalyptists towards their present situation was a negative one; that they took the disillusioned view that human endeavour was meaningless, and that of all incomprehensible things, the sufferings of God's people were the most inexplicable. The only thing to be done was to endure, for the end was not far off. If this is in general true, then I would suggest that we have, again, a change of attitude in Mark 13 and Revelation. In Revelation the martyrs are certainly told to 'wait' till the end of the suffering of their fellows (6.11), but they are also given the title of 'victor' (3.12; cf. 2.11; 15.2) and 'witness' (2.13; cf. 20.4). But, of course, it is characteristic of the Lamb that he has overcome, and that he is the faithful witness, and that he is both of these in relation to his death (5.5–6; 1.5). Clearly we have nothing like a developed theology of martyrdom, but it seems possible that, because the Lamb's victory is seen to be achieved through his death, there is a move towards giving the death of the martyr, too, a positive evaluation in terms of an imitation of or sharing in that victory.

A stronger case for a reinterpretation of the experience of persecution can be made out in an examination of Mark 13. In v. 10 the preaching of the church to the nations is made a pre-condition (though not a sign) of the end. Because this pre-condition is brought into relation with a prediction of persecution (vv.9, 11) it is clear that for Mark that is the situation in which preaching will primarily be effected. The experience of suffering by God's people is given a meaning. (Carl Braaten, as I noted earlier, suggested that an apocalyptic emphasis might give strength to the theology of mission. Here we have a reference to mission in the context of apocalyptic, but I do not think that this has precedent in traditional apocalyptic. It is not *apocalyptic* that suggests mission.) A further dimension to this may be added by that parallel between Mark 13 and the passion narrative. It is in the context of accusation that Jesus himself makes his self-declaration (14.62), and it is at the point of his death that he is seen for what he is (15.39), in a confession about which the evangelist shows no reservation. Finally, J. M. Robinson draws attention to the fact that in v.11 we have one of Mark's rare references to the Spirit, and suggests that in its experience of persecution the church is shown to continue that conflict between the Spirit and Satan that characterized the mission of Jesus.[25] Again, therefore, the present events of the church's life are given meaning, in the light of the understanding of Jesus' life.

It is in their view of the future that Mark 13 and Revelation stand closest to apocalyptic. Both see the end as imminent (Mark 13.13 and 20 imply as much; Rev. 1.1–3 and 22.6 are explicit); and the course of its coming as determined (here Mark 13.23 is explicit, and the idea of the recorded vision in Rev. 1.3; 22.7, 9f., and 18f. seems to imply the same). I have already indicated the difficulty in harmonizing these ideas with Moltmann's and Braaten's theory of the 'open future' in apocalyptic. Both, too, look for the coming of the Son of Man, which Käsemann sees to be central to early Christian apocalyptic theology (Mark 13.26; Rev. 22.20). But here again a qualification needs to be made. The Son of Man who is to come is not just a heavenly figure of the future. For Revelation the Lamb has already died and he lives again, and the one like a son of man walks now among the candlesticks (1.13). He holds the seven stars in his hand (1.16, 20f.), but he is not located among the angels, but among the candlesticks, the churches, comforting and disciplining them. For Mark, too, the Son of Man is distinctively the one who must, and does, suffer (8.31; 9.12); and Jesus has both declared himself to be Christ and been declared to be Son of God. It would seem inadequate to qualify this appreciation of the past and present activity of Jesus by use of the adjective 'proleptic'.

I have been suggesting that the evidence of Mark 13 and Revelation may be used to test some of the appeals currently made to apocalyptic in Christian theology. It may be that I have stretched the evidence, and that my interpretation of these two sections of the New Testament is incorrect; it may be that the test itself is not a valid one. Certainly the contrasts I have drawn between these two and 'traditional apocalyptic' are subject to that further necessary definition of the characteristics of apocalyptic. But it seems to me that the apocalyptic mould broke in the hands of those who most obviously tried to use it, and that they broke it deliberately because of their Christian presuppositions. And if that is so, then it must raise a doubt about the value of appealing to apocalyptic *per se* in subsequent Christian theology.

Many questions remain open. There is the historical question: if the form was inadequate, why did they use it? Was it, as Käsemann assumes, the inevitable form of expression? Or did they adopt this form from among others because it expressed some things which *were* of importance—the coming of the end, the vision of glory and majesty in which they thought it appropriate to express their understanding of Jesus? And there is the question of the subsequent use of this material— what do we do with it? Do we keep it, knowing that from time to time and in certain situations it will spring to life for those who read it—bearing in mind the dangers of misinterpretation that may lie in facile feelings of affinity? Do we, like H. H. Rowley, mentally distinguish those features which may appeal to us (a belief that God is in ultimate control of history; an appreciation of the cumulative power of personal evil; the hope of the hereafter), and suppress those which do not (the imminent end, perhaps; the cries of vengeance; the absence of a feeling of the love of God for sinners)? Or do we retain it as a particular example of the transcendence of content over form, of the capacity of their Christian faith to expand the normal framework of men's conceptions? It may be that we have here some data for a 'theology of the imagination'.

NOTES

1. H. D. Betz, 'The Concept of Apocalyptic in the Theology of the Pannenberg Group', *JTC* 6, 1969, p. 206.

2. See especially W. Pannenberg, *Basic Questions in Theology*, SCM Press 1970, chs. 1 and 2, and *Revelation as History*, Macmillan 1968, chs. 1 and 4.

3. J. Moltmann, *Theology of Hope*, SCM Press 1967, especially pp. 133–8.

4. C. Braaten, 'The Significance of Apocalypticism for Systematic Theology', *Interpretation* 25, October 1971, pp. 480–99.

5. E. Käsemann, *New Testament Questions for Today*, SCM Press 1969, p. 102.

6. W. R. Murdock, summarizing Pannenberg's position, in 'History and Revelation in Jewish Apocalypticism', *Interpretation* 21, April 1967, p. 168.

7. Moltmann, op. cit., p. 138.

8. Käsemann, op. cit., p. 124.

9. Ibid., p. 107.

10. Especially from Betz, art. cit., and Murdock, art cit.

11. Murdock, art. cit., p. 176.

12. P. D. Hanson, 'Old Testament Apocalyptic Re-examined', *Interpretation* 25, October 1971, p. 479.

13. R. G. Hamerton-Kelly, *Pre-existence, Wisdom, and the Son of Man*, Cambridge University Press 1973, pp. 276–9.

14. Notably by G. Ebeling, 'The Ground of Christian Theology', and E. Fuchs, 'On the Task of a Christian Theology', *JTC* 6, 1969, pp. 47–68 and 69–98 respectively, and, commenting on this discussion, W. G. Rollins, 'The New Testament and Apocalyptic', *NTS* 17, 1970–71, pp. 454–76.

15. Käsemann, op. cit., p. 109 n. 1.

16. D. Rössler, *Gesetz und Geschichte*, Neukirchen 1960.

17. There is a large measure of agreement among major recent studies of apocalyptic, e.g. K. Koch, *The Rediscovery of Apocalyptic*, ET SCM Press 1972; D. S. Russell, *The Method and Message of Jewish Apocalyptic*, SCM Press 1964; P. Vielhauer, in E. Hennecke and W. Schneemelcher, *New Testament Apocrypha* II, ET Lutterworth 1965, pp. 581–600 (Vielhauer refers contemptuously to Rössler's 'pretentious little book', p. 593); and H. H. Rowley, *The Relevance of Apocalyptic*, revised edn. Lutterworth 1963 (first edn. 1944), as also in the briefer accounts of L. Morris, *Apocalyptic*, Inter-Varsity Press 1973, and P. D. Hanson, art. cit.

18. Cf. the discussion by A. N. Wilder, 'The Rhetoric of Ancient and Modern Apocalyptic', *Interpretation* 25, October 1971, pp. 436–53.

19. W. A. Beardslee, 'New Testament Apocalyptic in Recent Interpretation', *Interpretation* 25, October 1971, p. 423.

20. K. Koch, op. cit., p. 15.

21. J. Kallas, 'The Apocalypse—An Apocalyptic book?', *JBL* 86, March 1967, pp. 69–80.

22. B. W. Jones, 'More about the Apocalypse as Apocalyptic', *JBL* 87, September 1968, pp. 325–7.

23. This is argued in detail by P. Prigent, 'Apocalypse et Apocalyptique', in *Exégèse Biblique et Judaïsme*, ed. J.-E. Ménard, Strasbourg 1973, pp. 126–45.

24. R. H. Lightfoot, *The Gospel Message of St Mark*, Oxford University Press 1950, chapter 4.

25. J. M. Robinson, *The Problem of History in Mark* (SBT 21), 1957, p. 63.

8

The Place of Jesus

LESLIE HOULDEN

GOD broods over the New Testament, but Jesus fills the foreground. If we transfer its reference from the New Testament to the world, that sentence could almost be a summary of the prologue of the fourth gospel. But whatever the reference, does it not present us with a theological picture whose measure we are reluctant to take? The pattern it reflects is surely bound to be problematic for us, in two respects.

First, there is the question of the proper direction of thrust in expounding the Christian faith in our society. Should we start with God or with Jesus? Some of those who choose the latter do so because they are sceptical of God's existence, at least in the traditional senses, but find in Jesus the focus of faith, devotion and inspiration. More do so because they share the New Testament's perspective and, taking God without question, let Jesus fill the foreground of their attention and discourse. Sometimes of course the doctrinal backing is traditional and orthodox, that is, it is thoroughly theistic, and the reason for what may appear an over-emphasis on Jesus is mainly tactical: here is the most attractive and convenient point of entry to a faith which can be expounded later in more systematic fashion. Sometimes, however, the effect is *as if* God did not exist, and the links with traditional Christianity become tenuous. There is then at least a possibility of distortion or imbalance when, in presenting the Christian faith in our society, we follow the recipe stated in our opening sentence, letting Jesus fill the foreground and leaving God, implicitly and at least in certain respects, in the background.

It will of course be replied that for a Christian, to speak of Jesus is to speak of God, to expound christology is to expound theism. But even the most devoted adherent of Nicene orthodoxy will admit a certain priority to the question of God over the question of Jesus, will see the latter in the setting of the former, and will recognize the dangers of anything that looks at all like a foot-loose 'Christ-religion'.

Unless we are to adopt a most extreme doctrine of development or an extreme degree of demythologizing (as for example Alistair Kee in *The Way of Transcendence*[1]), any exposition of what can purport to be New Testament faith must penetrate behind the appearances and place God before Jesus. The situation in which that exposition now takes place fortifies this policy. For while the New Testament was written in a world where belief in the divine was normal and lively, our society presents a quite different face; and where there is any serious enquiry into religious questions it is likely to be at the level of wondering whether there is anything at all in 'the divine dimension'. Tactically or emotionally prior in certain circumstances perhaps, the place of Jesus is logically secondary; it is also secondary from the point of view of the demands of our current religious situation. God needs to have a more active role in our theological picture than to brood over it.

If we now take the matter away from apologetic, we encounter a theological problem which stands in its own right. *God broods over the New Testament, but Jesus fills the foreground.* Does the New Testament give to us, as we read it today, a fair impression of the shape of the theology which its writers held? And even if it does, were they possibly carried away, beyond what could properly be affirmed, by the novelty and force of their experience of Jesus? For reasons which are not wholly theological, does the New Testament give an exaggerated place to Jesus, which needs to be corrected not only because of certain apologetic needs but at the level of theology itself?

The questions are posed from the point of view of the modern reader looking back at the New Testament. But another aspect of the matter is this: did the patristic builders of classical Christian doctrine, in taking New Testament texts at their face value without attempting to penetrate into their pedigree or the living circumstances of the first century, find themselves impelled into a view of Jesus which not only failed to grasp the 'real shape' of the New Testament writers' theology but also accorded him a place unwarranted by a 'proper' understanding of those documents? This question goes beyond our present scope. It is much more complex because it involves the whole question of the conditions under which concepts may be re-expressed in fresh philosophical contexts. But in so far as the patristic formulations retain a place in church language, the question imposes itself. We turn, however, to the New Testament.

To sharpen our focus, let us put up a hypothesis which may be fit only to go the way of many predecessors; and then let us unravel a story which expounds it.

The hypothesis is this: that the first Christians found their attitude on all fundamental questions so transformed as a result of Jesus that they could only speak of him in language which was hyperbolic rather than sober, evaluative rather than factual, and riotously diverse rather than carefully consistent. This is the first step in a particular kind of christology. This christology rests on certain convictions: that experience of Jesus, direct or indirect, is at the heart of the matter; that the words in which the experience was expressed must, for their proper understanding, be traced to their roots in that experience; and that these words (e.g. the titles of Jesus) are attempts to objectify that experience, to transfer it from the heart of the believer and place it 'out there' in the world of external 'facts'.

Still further back lies this belief which must be left for the moment in the form of assertion: that doctrinally speaking christology is, in the New Testament, despite all appearances, wholly secondary. It is a disguised way of speaking about God. This is true not in the sense that the early Christians did not really believe they were making statements about Jesus, but in the sense that the experience those statements reflect was in fact concerned primarily and ultimately with God. The attitudes which were transformed were, at the deepest level, attitudes to God, then, secondarily and dependently, attitudes to the world, to oneself, to human relationships and society, and indeed to Jesus himself.

There is of course a half-concealed empiricism in all this which had better come into the open. Theology is subjective human language, it is not objectively descriptive language about God. It suffers (or benefits!) therefore, like all other language, especially that which goes beyond the most direct account of sense-data, from fragility and mobility. While it often represents a consensus of agreement (and therefore is not subjective in the purely individual sense), it is nevertheless deceptive when it appears to be giving a 'solid' account of God. It is not merely that it is analogical (that when God is described as 'loving' or addressed as 'father', our use of these terms in ordinary life applies only so far and in certain respects); it is also that the words themselves shift in meaning from one speaker or culture to another (my father colours my use of the word as your father colours yours, and a thirteenth-century Polish father is not wholly like a twentieth-century American one). Shifts may be small, but they are constant, and variety of experience lies behind them.

While it is controlled by formulation and tradition (working at least implicitly on a more optimistic view of the solidity of language), talk about God is peculiarly open to this fragility and mobility, for its subject is not exposed to sight or touch. In this sense he is at the mercy of the human imagination. At the same time theological language is peculiarly prone to arouse claims for its solidity. The investment of allegiance and devotion in God transfers itself, inevitably it appears, to language about him: if he is rock-like and eternal, so are the propositions concerning him. In an area where mobility of language is high, willingness to recognize it is low.

We wish to give that mobility full recognition. We wish also to give full value to the change that comes over language when it moves from the factual to the evaluative. It becomes less controllable, more mobile. It becomes more a matter of impression and opinion. It becomes more expressive of shallowness or depth of feeling and conviction. All language about God, in the end, bears this character, and the closer it is to roots in experience and the further away from purely intellectual formulation, the more this is so.

This is no comment on the question of the 'truth' or 'falsity' of the language in question. It is comment on the conditions under which language concerning God can point to truth: on its limitations and its possibilities. For the mobility and fragility of language are not matters for regret or for 'getting round'. They alone make it possible for the language to reflect rather than suppress the ever-changing variety of experience. They are the conditions by which spontaneity and immediacy can play a part in religious discourse and by which it can respond to developments in other spheres of thought.

The period of the early church was one in which these qualities were abundantly present. It is therefore not surprising that, according to our hypothesis, the language was hyperbolic rather than sober, evaluative rather than factual, and riotously diverse rather than carefully consistent. And the language of christology was disguised language about God because it reflected transformed attitudes to God. How does this work?

We do not know the precise nature of Jesus' personality and if we met him we should differ about it; nor do we know the exact content of his message. However, we do know a considerable amount about the effects of both his teaching and his career. It may not be possible to argue very accurately from the observable effects to a description of the causes, that is to a description of Jesus' person and teaching. But certain probabilities will emerge and we shall at least feel confident in asserting the intensity of his influence in certain directions. Nevertheless the nature of the experience to which the historical Jesus gave rise (indirectly in all cases that are observable to us, but in some ways all the more impressive for that) is our firm starting-point. It is the beginning of Christian theology.

Experience gives rise to formulation, and, especially when words are being given new applications, is very close to it. In such cases, the words explode into existence from the interior force of the experience: so a poet may coin words only intelligible to those able to some degree to share his mind, and the man seized by religious ecstasy may utter sounds which strike others as pure nonsense. The words are selected not for their coherence with each other, but for their appropriateness as expressions of some aspect of the experience. The more vivid the experience, the more likely it is that the words chosen will have an impressionistic quality. Not all sides of their existing sense will necessarily apply, rather they will catch, in some striking way and perhaps with only one facet of their significance, the sense of the experience. This facet may be so isolated and exaggerated that, effectively, the word receives a new meaning—merits a new entry in the dictionary.

The process can be most neatly demonstrated with regard to some of the titles of Jesus. For this purpose it does not matter whether they were claimed by Jesus himself or accorded to him by early Christians. In the former case, they arose from Jesus' own understanding of his role or, in our terms, from his own 'experience of himself'. It is easier, however, if we consider them as they were used by his followers. Then we can see how they arose from attitudes transformed as a result of Jesus.

Moreover we can see something of the process at work in the pages of the New Testament.

Let us examine cases. First, one which does not have the complication of having led to later dogmatic formulation. It retains therefore for us something of the informal character which it has in the New Testament. Paul sees Jesus as parallel to Adam—a second Adam, reproducing his role as head and fount of the race but reversing his dreadful inheritance (Rom. 5.12ff.; I Cor. 15.21f., 45ff.). The relatively informal character of this language means that we scarcely think of 'last Adam' (I Cor. 15.45) as a *title* for Jesus or as an 'objective' description. We do not immediately range it with Messiah, Son of God, or Son of man. We might instead speak of it as an image, or, more technically, a piece of typology.

But prior to that, it is the expression of a certain quality of conviction about Jesus, and, more deeply, the expression of experience brought about by him. Can we be precise about the character of that experience? It found appropriate expression in language about Adam, the father of the race. It must therefore have represented experience which we might express, in rather pretentious jargon, as 'a rejuvenation of a sense of being human'. That is, the experience was individual, but it related to one's awareness of solidarity with one's fellows. We may suppose that for Paul the experience at this level was both profound and crucial: how else may we explain his vital (and original?) sense of the universality of Christ's significance and of the abolition of the distinction of value between Gentile and Jew?

Now it is usual to suppose that Paul's language concerning Adam and Christ arose from reflection upon scripture and from quasi-dogmatic convictions about its fulfilment. But on any showing Paul is highly selective in his use of the Old Testament, and we have to enquire what led to the selection he made. The answer lies, we suggest, at least with regard to this example, in an experience, brought about as a result of Jesus and giving rise to a conviction about man's new potentialities.

If we go on to ask how Jesus brought about such an experience, so giving rise to such a conviction, we are immediately on uncertain ground. Was it an overwhelming sense of the simplicity and directness of Jesus' teaching about God which evoked the feeling that this was of universal human import? Or was it derived from other features of the experience of which he was the cause? Thus: as a result of him, there was a sense of forgiveness and release so profound that it could not but be available equally to all men. Was it, that is, Jesus' effect upon his followers' sense of their relationship with God rather than their apprehension of God that spread into a sense of its universality? The route by which Jesus impelled Paul to the conviction that he could be described as (or even *was*) the last Adam is not clear to us—Paul does not show his working and was quite probably unaware of it. What we can say is that as a result of Jesus (whether his teaching or his whole career or some elements within it), Paul's sense of what it meant to belong to the human race was so transformed that this startling language arose as alone adequate to the need.

Other titles given to Jesus function by comparable but quite distinct lines of working. For example, he is God's creative and pre-existent Word (John 1.1–14; I Cor. 8.6; Heb. 1.3). In this case, a factor absent from our previous case enters the discussion. That Jesus was the Word was to become a matter not merely of isolable or occasional scriptural exegesis but of coherent dogmatic statement. Moreover it led to convictions about his biography: he had existed from all eternity. To all appearances, that is, it added to the stock of facts about him.

But what could possibly lead to the according of such a status and the attribution of such a 'fact' to a man of flesh and blood? The usual answer of historical criticism is familiar: whatever its later development in a Greek milieu, the idea has its roots in Judaism, and on that basis is perfectly explicable. The Jews were accustomed to attribute pre-existence to those features of their religion to which they gave special value as mediators of the knowledge and activity of God, supremely but not exclusively the law. This tendency to hypostatize or make 'solid' realities in the divine sphere out of earthly concepts (e.g. wisdom) or religiously valuable objects (e.g. the law) was of long standing in Judaism and was not surprisingly transferred to Jesus by Jewish Christians who ascribed to him the supreme religious value which they had formerly discerned elsewhere. Indeed they saw him as unique in this respect and so in the New Testament writings he steps into the place of all the great mediators of Judaism—God's wisdom, his word, the law, the temple. Not all writers worked this out over the same range of ideas and some never took the step of putting Jesus into the place of any of the entities regarded by Jews as pre-existent. So while the gospel of John attributes pre-existence to him (as it works with the idea of the Word), neither Matthew nor Luke has any clear trace of it.[2]

So the answer runs, and it is of course accurate—as far as it goes. But it scarcely explores to the full how there came to be ascribed to Jesus a title which signified not only pre-existence but also creativity. Was it just a matter of reflecting a sense of his supreme significance? The question remains: what could possibly lead to the according of such a role, that of God's agent in creation, to a man?

The Johannine tradition reached the point of ascribing it to Jesus' own claim for himself (8.58; 12.41): he himself was the source of this belief. But even if we were to accept these sayings as authentic and even if we were to see them in the setting of classical Chalcedonian teaching, we are still concerned to ask how a human self-consciousness could arrive at such a formulation of its understanding of itself.

If instead we adopt the assumption that the sayings are not authentic and that we cannot look to Jesus as the source of this belief, we turn instead to Christian experience. Taking the same path of argument as in our earlier example, must we not say that the understanding of Jesus as the pre-existent agent in creation was rooted in an experience, as a result of him, of freshness in relation to *everything*? The first Christians (we may express it thus) looked out on a new world, a universe transfigured. We can even lay our hands on an early stage in the process: 'When anyone is united to Christ, there is a new world; the old order has gone, and a new order has already begun' (II Cor. 5.17 NEB). Of course this is rooted in current eschatological hope: but the question is, what brought that hope into play in this particular form? To answer that we must penetrate deeper than the examination of the Jewish background to Paul's ideas and ask about the experience which led him to draw upon certain areas of language and imagery rather than others.

Two questions and one conclusion follow. We raise the questions rather than answer them.

First, how did Jesus give rise to an experience of such wide and deep ramifications? We cannot tell how far it was the effect of his teaching, how far the impact of his whole career, how far the force of his person expressed first by direct contact and then by reputation.

Second, how far was it a genuinely theological experience and how far emotional? That is, were the early Christians who reacted thus to Jesus in any way justified in drawing theological inferences from their experience or should they have stopped at the simple conclusion: 'Jesus is wonderful. He makes the world feel different to me.' Was that what they *really* meant, or was there sense in moving on from that expression of *feeling* to statements about the true nature of the world's relationship with God and Jesus' crucial role in that relationship?

Again, the evidence is not wholly lacking. The experience was not one of enthusiasm merely for Jesus' person, still less one of undirected euphoria, but seems to have *involved* a renewed apprehension of the world's nature and destiny. So Paul saw the natural order itself as destined for salvation (Rom. 8.19ff.).

It is arguable of course that Paul arrived at this doctrine by a process of argument, or rather that it was part and parcel of his eschatological beliefs. But there was nothing in these beliefs to compel him to see Jesus, even if he was the central actor in the eschatological drama, as the pre-existent agent of creation. At this early stage, when there was still a struggle to arrive at appropriate words, the experience is dominant. The universe had been made through Jesus at the start (I Cor. 8.6) because for Paul it had been remade through Jesus in his own unmistakable experience.

A parallel will shed some light. Edwin Muir's poem 'The Transfiguration'[3] and G. M. Hopkins's 'The world is charged with the grandeur of God'[4] express a comparable vision of the world's true nature. If the vision were to be translated into a message, it would be that we must look beneath the surface of things if we would see their real value and that the world in all its parts is the beloved creation of the living God. We must cast off our customary dullness and flatness of vision, for the world is full of beauty, vitality and hope. The sense of near ecstasy which the poems reflect extends to and is of a piece with a genuine apprehension of the world as related to God which is capable of propositional statement.

So for the early Christians, the experience of Jesus seems to have carried with it a transformed attitude to the world. This meant not so much new beliefs about it as an intensified and heightened awareness of its status as the creature of God. And deeper still and prior to it lay a renewed awareness of God himself. That, we may suppose, was the main thrust of Jesus' impact upon his followers.

The conclusion is this: that the description of Jesus as the pre-existent and creative Word was a projection into 'objective' language, by a process wholly intelligible on the Jewish background, of a transformed awareness of the world, which was in turn derived from the understanding of God and the form of relationship with him which Jesus had so compellingly conveyed.

The remaining point of obscurity is the nature of the force which clearly came from Jesus to produce effects so deep and comprehensive in the attitudes of his first adherents. The obscurity has two dimensions. There is the historical problem, for the solution of which the evidence is simply insufficient. And there is the question of faith involving the theological problem concerning God's action here as anywhere. It is important to identify the point of obscurity as exactly as possible, or else we shall see mystery where there is only muddle.

The other titles of Jesus, and indeed more complex statements about him, are equally open to treatment along these lines.[5] We have chosen for detailed examination two claims made for him which from the point of view of plain statement seem peculiarly extravagant. Other titles are often taken to be in some sense more 'literal' or 'objective': Jesus *was* Son of God or Son of man, Jesus *is* Lord. The understanding of all these titles is complicated at the purely historical level by the likelihood that they had meant a number of different things by the time they reached written expression in the New Testament. But each of them reflects a certain facet of experience of Jesus leading to a particular strand of conviction. The title is earthed in the experience; whether the experience be one of a new immediacy of relationship with God, as a result of Jesus (so Jesus is Son of God), or one of absolute confidence in God for the future (so Jesus is the Son of man of apocalyptic hope).

Messiah, which we are often inclined to see as the simplest title of all, is in some ways the most surprising. It must have burst from the experience with the peculiar power of paradox. For Jesus betrayed few of the stock messianic characteristics: military leadership, this-worldly rule and victory, and fervent patriotism. How then did the title emerge? It must have sprung from an overwhelming sense that he was God's agent for the satisfying of his people's deepest needs; and behind that from an experience, occasioned by him, of certainty that God's cause, now widened in scope, was moving towards its triumphant vindication.

This approach to the teaching of the New Testament about Jesus yields a simple, even at first sight platitudinous result. People turned to Christianity because they experienced, as a result of Jesus, a transformation of their attitudes to God and to everything. This is a statement of plain history. Put as a christological proposition, it goes: Jesus is the one who, as a matter of fact, produced this transformation of attitudes to God and to everything. Or in theistic terms: God, and everything as depending upon him, is best understood in the manner which results from the impulse derived from Jesus.

An interesting line of enquiry would be: in what sense, if any, is such a set of statements a fair re-expression, in fairly severely empirical terms, of Nicene orthodoxy, whose philosophical assumptions are so different and whose claims appear at first sight so much higher? Meanwhile, our statements can claim certain advantages. First, they place the point of Christian distinctiveness and so decision where it ought to be placed: do you believe in God in the manner which results from the impulse derived from Jesus? That is, theism is the beginning and end of the matter. Second, it takes seriously the necessarily negative nature of discourse about the 'inner workings' of God. We can make no strictly descriptive statements about the divine—but we are continually reluctant to accept the fact! We can speak only of our experience of him and we can *believe* that the experience is not misleading. A Christian is one who finds the source of that experience (by whatever long route it came to him) in Jesus, and he is a Christian because he judges that experience to be uniquely illuminating and fundamentally significant.

Our approach does not only claim advantages, it also points a finger of warning.

We have held that the christological statements of the New Testament are 'projections' in ostensibly descriptive and literal language of experience concerning God and the world to which Jesus gave rise or to which he at least gave decisively new shape. We have suggested that the experience and the statements are utterly bound together: the latter spring straight out of the former. We have suggested too that the experience is the point of primary interest and importance, theologically and religiously, and that it is in principle capable of quite different verbal expression. Moreover, its bearing is clarified if it does receive a variety of verbal expression, for it can then be shown to be concerned above all with a strong and sharp awareness of God and of relationship with him: such awareness is bound to result in constantly fresh verbal formulation. We judge too that this approach not only uncovers the workings of the New Testament propositions about Jesus but also makes possible the use in speech about him of our present, ordinary language, by relating all formulations to the experience, which is nearer the centre. In the experience the lines converge more clearly than in the language. So this method removes certain strains—or rather places the strain where it ought to be, in the issue of theistic faith.

It follows that the whole matter is put in jeopardy when the statements which in New Testament days fittingly expressed Christian experience (but have now become technical terms and no longer current speech) are divorced from it, and used by those who, whatever their stated beliefs, do not share it. Thus, when Jesus is referred to as the Word, the agent in creation, simply as a description of his place in the divine sphere, and there is no longer any sense of a world transformed; or when Jesus is called Son of man, but his followers no longer have any vivid assurance or hope; or when he is called Son of God, but Christians lack any strong sense of God's immediacy; then the fatal divorce has taken place and the structure of the earliest Christian theologies observable in the New Testament has begun to collapse. Over large tracts of Christian history and life the divorce between experience and statement has been endemic and Christians have lived in 'the old world' on a theistic belief which includes a seat for Jesus in the heavenly places. The framing of creeds and articles as tests of belief has, whatever its merits, been the danger signal that the divorce is on the way, for then the literally descriptive element is likely to be winning independent life.

A final remark. While many Christians still hold to the New Testament in an uncritical way which does little credit to belief in a living creator God, others have virtually abandoned it as an effective guide, and the question of the use of the Bible imposes itself on the church.

One important and necessary use of the New Testament, and particularly its earlier writings produced when the struggle for formulation was still visibly in progress, is to show both that experience is properly anterior to statement and that the two must be indissoluble if distinctively Christian faith is to persist. If the experience is authentic and valid, the statement may be trusted to find its own proper form. Renewal must still find its source in the New Testament. The common error is to think that it should stop there.

NOTES

1. Alistair Kee, *The Way of Transcendence*, Penguin 1971.
2. But see R. G. Hamerton-Kelly, *Pre-existence, Wisdom, and the Son of Man*, Cambridge University Press 1973, ch. 2.
3. Edwin Muir, *Collected Poems*, Faber 1960, p. 198.
4. G. Manley Hopkins, *Poems*, Oxford University Press 1948, p. 70.
5. For an examination of the language of atonement in the New Testament from this standpoint, see John Knox, *The Death of Christ*, Collins 1959, pp. 146ff.

9

The Multidimensional Picture of Jesus

ULRICH SIMON

'Die Dichter müssen, auch
Die geistigen, weltlich sein.'
Hölderlin[1]

IT may well be questioned whether the endless production of New Testament commentaries and related monographs has added anything substantial to our knowledge of Jesus. As one surveys the entries in catalogues, indices, abstracts, dictionaries, one may either laugh mockingly that the mountain has brought forth so many mice, or lament that we do not know, and never shall know, the answer to so many questions. There is certainly something ridiculous in the fact that a fairly small collection of writings evokes so much learned comment with so little result.

A comparison of the articles 'Jesus Christus' in *Die Religion in Geschichte und Gegenwart*[2] 1929 and the third edition of 1959 shows the heights of scholarly ambition and its diminishing returns. In the former, Karl Ludwig Schmidt gave his magisterial summary under the headings of the tradition and the historical framework. He emphasized the basic tension between an individualistic and collectivist approach, between Jesus the hero and the community, between history and super-history. Schmidt talks of colourful multiplicity and strata of material, held together by the passion narrative. But the factual residuum remains unimpressive, whereas the abundance of floating ideas yields an embarrassment of riches. Messianic expectations, cosmic catastrophes, the law, ethical demands, miracles and exorcisms feed into the pattern of the present secret and the future disclosure.

Conzelmann's spectrum in 1959 is even vaster, but more directly controlled by the task of reasonable verification. Form criticism must not serve as an excuse to evade the question of historicity. Even such problematic topics as Jesus' awareness of himself as Messiah, and his use of titles—Son of man, Servant of God, Son of God—must be caught in the net of historicity. Similarly Conzelmann wants to 'get at' the teaching of Jesus from the historical angle and is thereby forced to deal with the break between Jesus and the subsequent history of the community. His continuing influence affects not only the development of the church but also the making of the New Testament itself. Conzelmann demonstrates the deadliness of the trap of historicity, though this is hardly his intention. The human continuum simply disallows the existence of a Jesus in history who is also a Christ beyond history.

Our comparison suggests that, as one might expect, the second world war sharpened the sceptical evaluation of the material. Even the finds from Qumran and the ever-increasing stream of archaeological data failed to dictate a noticeable change of tone. Nor has this flood since 1959 altered the perspective in Germany. Whereas the weight of American research,[3] approaches such as that of Daniélou,[4] and Israeli reappraisal of Jesus[5] favour a solution of the problem of the Jesus of history within the historical-geographical givenness of an accessible background, these empirical noises evoke but the faintest echo elsewhere.

The problem is a real one; some would say with Karl Barth, perhaps the only one. How can this man be what the New Testament claims him to be? The 'Jesus the Jew' school disposes of the problem coolly. Whether Jesus is Brandon's freedom-fighter, later grossly betrayed (Mark's gospel being perhaps the worst type of forgery in the history of literature),[6] or Vermes' *ḥasid*,[7] or indeed Allegro's righteous teacher, Essene[8], or perhaps anti-Essene (the computations are endless), he cannot—even if called *Meshiah*—stand above, outside, beyond the historical drama, except as an example and influence. The Jesus-the-Jew style of apprehension of the New Testament founders upon Jesus the Lord.

We are back again with the Christ-of-faith dialectic and the fruitless search for a synthesis. Here the two *RGG* editions of 1929 and 1959 also prove revealing, in that they supplement the article on Jesus with a sketch of the picture 'at present'. We are made to run the whole gamut of imaginative and selective models—variations of the romantic Jesus, the sentimentalized Nazarene, naive, pious, sweet, sectarian, and opposed notions of the enlightened philosopher, modern, progressive, psychologically self-aware. Jesus ranks as the depressive, the embodiment of every pathological and destructive urge, as well as the great artist who affirms life and creates cultural beauty. He must be fitted into every political calendar, racist (anti-semitic!), pacifist, socialist, anti-clerical. Mythology, theosophy, and even eroticism claim him. It is against this welter of nonsense that *RGG* of 1929[9] hails the work of Bultmann, Barth, and Brunner (no non-German-speaking writer is even mentioned).

Bultmann's treatment has become normative in the generation after the second world war, and his success almost obscures the extraordinary twists of interpretation. Bultmann's Jesus is in essence *not* the Jesus of history, in consequence of the historical methods now employed. He triggers off encounter in proclamation and decision in the existential predicament of man. The word 'Jesus' must stand between inverted commas. It is an abstract counter, perhaps a code, but not a picture. Dibelius, Büchsel, of the older generation, and Bornkamm, Käsemann, among the successors, try to advance on the steep and vertiginous ridge of a unique and original 'I figure', in pursuit of the 'Sign' which can never be the thing itself.

The writer of the corresponding article in *RGG* 1959[10] does not consider that the christologies of our era contribute to, or even profit from, the *Jesusbild*—the portrait which we try to form of Jesus—such as it is. Karl Barth, for example, is given unstinted praise, but the pre-existent, eternal Son, even if associated with man, made man, a servant learning obedience, etc., falls outside the *Jesusbild*. The picture of Jesus merely serves in an illustrative way, claims the writer, however much Barth himself may protest against such a method on hundreds of pages on the Word, proclaimed, written, revealed as One.

This impasse, reached by 1959, has become more solid and daunting during the last decade. The decline of Western Christianity and the surge of sub-Christian cults, with their charismatic offers and intimidations, is seen by most to stem from an academic defeatism, which spills over into every area of private and public concern. If we cannot 'have' Jesus, what can Christianity remain except one of the many options in Religious Studies, i.e. a subject in the sociology of the past? In reply to this crisis the fundamentalist cry of 'Back to the Bible!' is loud, but on closer inspection often invokes no more than the repetition of a number of slogans. The capitulation to the 'Death of God', on the other hand, is already too dated to entice a dog to leave the fire.

Yet the intellectual solution seems to me fully stated in the multi-dimensionalism of Tillich's writings. Once it is grasped that the Testaments not only suggest, but demand, a method which contrasts with the unilateral, univocal, and uniformal approaches of the past, we do not even have to penetrate the subtler points of Tillich's epistemology. After all, Maritain made a very similar thesis popular and acceptable in his book *The Degrees of Knowledge*.[11] Theirs is not a plea for a vague pluralism, translated from the contemporary sciences and culture into theological thinking, but a clear recognition of the way things work. Indeed, how can prose narratives, legal documents, lamentations, curses, blessings, genealogies, letters, fantasies, indictments, protestations (to name but a few *Gattungen*) be reduced to a monolithic structure, when the centre of gravity in each defies such a bending towards uniformity?

The application of multidimensional hermeneutics does not, as is often supposed, jump the gun of historical criticism. The allegation to the contrary, namely that all theologians, such as Barth and Tillich, use and abuse the New Testament by paying scant attention to the Jesus of history, rests upon a misunderstanding. There is, perhaps, a gnostic ring about Tillich's phrase 'Jesus the Christ', but in the context it vindicates his understanding of the dimension of history. Human existence *suffers* in and through history. We lose our identity in the collectivism and anonymity of the social continuum. The incontrovertible experience of alienation derives from our being thrown into events. The historical plane, therefore, is real enough, but it is essentially negative and hostile. Now Jesus the Christ certainly cannot be divorced from this plane. Indeed, the historical dimension, from start to finish, shapes his life, but it is the antithesis to his, and thus God's, real being, which is the new being, the spiritual self which endures the historical ferment and conquers its fragmentation. The historical framework, seen in this light, is the necessary but accidental, even trivial, factor in the soteriological and eschatological disclosure of the new being. There could be no such disclosure apart from Galilee, Jerusalem and the Mediterranean world, but its contribution to our apprehension of Jesus is dialectical through and through.

This approach has many advantages which cannot be articulated here.

The most important one, it seems to me, lies in the implicit recognition that the New Testament is more likely to be polemical than not. If historical existence is to be overcome it follows that most of the writers will adopt a *contra mundum* stance, though they may modify their utopian otherworldliness by short-term compromises with the state. In fact, the political conundrum becomes as acute as it does, for example in Acts and Romans, because the polemic of the kingdom of God is forced into reorientation. The missionary fervour is dialectically at odds with the straightforward indictment of society, though the goal of the redemption of historical existence cannot be rescinded. The multidimensional method enjoins on the reader an awareness of the constantly changing climate of power and opinion in the first century. Thus even short segments of the gospels should never be given a univocal interpretation, since they display differing polemical purposes. It is a matter of unceasing bewilderment that this key demand of interpretation is so often ignored, as if any gospel passage could have meant the same thing in AD 30, 40, 50, 60, 70 and after 70. Raymond Brown's five stages in the making of the fourth gospel should be considered a minimum in the articulation of the historical dimensions and the polemic arising out of them.

Looking at the historical dimension in this way it turns out to be both trivial, for example from the cosmic standpoint, and decisive for hermeneutics. A Jesus who preaches love for enemies cannot be hidden under a general umbrella of non-violence, but his counsel of utopian perfection must be spelt out in terms of different governors and policies. Similarly, and I think even more important, the different linguistic channels of polemic must be investigated at every stage, so that we do not merely have Jesus denouncing hypocrites in a general way, but at least in Aramaic, Greek and perhaps Latin. Every word undergoes a sea-change as it is spoken in a different dialect. A good example of the pertinence of such a fine, almost pedantic, approach to the words of Jesus can be seen in the contemporary problems of translation, as they affect such prayers as μὴ εἰσενέγκῃς ἡμᾶς εἰς πειρασμόν (Matt 6.13) or μαραναθα (I Cor. 16.22). The latter is at least in undisputed Aramaic, even if the word division remains in doubt (and was perhaps meant to be ambiguous). The former demands a retranslation into either Hebrew or Aramaic, in which the verb-noun stem *nsh* must figure and thus restore and maintain a semantic fact in the area of temptation-trial-test-ordeal (cf. Gen. 22.1).[12] Only when the linguistic provenance is known or postulated can the polemical thrust be evaluated against the constantly changing scene. The fight against historical existence is thus seen to be very historical indeed, even though history is a flexible, fluid dimension.

This stress on the details of history can, but need not, lead to the death of historicism and the concomitant death of a thousand qualifications (which makes so much of the discussions around the topic of the trial of Jesus almost unreadable). The historical dimension cannot be freed from its atomistic structure. Endless molecules go chasing around, and only we, the observers, impart order and meaning to the process of fragmentation. The nature of historical atomism is such that it vetoes too rigid a systematization. Tillich is often accused of 'system building'; if you remove one brick the whole multidimensional edifice must collapse. The same charge, *a fortiori*, is brought against Barth's *Church Dogmatics*. But although both theologians profess openly to write 'systematic' theology, the admixture of the historical chaos prevents the making of a purely formalistic build-up. Tillich, for example, resists the temptation of saying how the varying dimensions are to be arranged. It would be inviting to try afresh to make theological models, in which, say, history occupies the lowest stratum and supports further layers of science, sociology, psychology and the arts. But such a model would be manifestly absurd. Barth eschews it altogether with his *Nein!* to natural theology, but Tillich, too, refrains from sketching an objective hermeneutic model, though he deliberately relates the speech of theological claims to that of the historical-cultural deposit.

The result of all this intellectual manipulation may at first look disappointing, for we cannot (to resume our previous quest) claim to obtain anything resembling a *Jesusbild*. It would be better to acknowledge candidly the harvest of a whole series of *Jesusbilder*, the plural replacing the singular. But what is wrong with these pictures? Even traditional Christianity has never shirked, but rather encouraged, the fondness for pictures of Jesus, if not so much in literary as in iconographical form. Recently there has also been a revival of interest in these 'faces of Jesus'. The line of development from the Semitic to the Hellenistic, the Apollonian to the Byzantine, the Renaissance to the Baroque, the Flemish to the pre-Raphaelite, is so rich a quarry that even now it is far from exhausted. These cultic and non-cultic pictures of Jesus give their own answer to the spurious quest after the one *Jesusbild* and affirm the multidimensional realism in which theology and popular feeling blend.

Nevertheless, these very pictures also underline the seriousness of the problem of the genuine *Jesusbild*. There is no harm in seeing and making differing pictures, for even in our common experience of human beings we do in fact apprehend different faces in one and the same person. Even vagueness of representation need not worry us, for we have the least stable impression of those we know best (parents, spouse, children). But some of the *Jesusbilder* are simply bad and cannot conceivably claim kinship with the scriptural tradition. For example, the Sunday School, chocolate-box good shepherd is a flagrant offence, not made less offensive by the plea that it is a product of the imagination.

Here multidimensionalism runs into real trouble, and it is not an isolated and rare one. All the statues of the Sacred Heart come under the indictment. Their place and use in the cultic tradition shows that ecclesiastical or community sanction gives no protection against distortion and theological forgery. It is, therefore, not surprising that one looks to aesthetic norms in the portrayal of Jesus, unless one prefers total censorship and a bridle on imaginative creations, as provided in Orthodox iconography.

Films and musicals create a wider market and even more confusion, and aesthetic norms are notoriously difficult to establish. The work of H. U. v. Balthasar may one day be called epoch-making, because in the as yet untranslated *Herrlichkeit*[13] he attempts nothing less than an aesthetic of the Christian Spirit. It would be a simplistic summary of this great work to conclude that Glory-Majesty-Splendour-Edification alone pertain to the legitimate portrayal of God, but such a criterion is urgently needed in our assessment of the immensely large crop of *Jesusbilder* in European literature. The making of non-scriptural portrayals sprouted and increased as the lives of Jesus foundered under the hammer of Albert Schweitzer. For over a hundred years the Western world and especially the English-speaking public have received a flood of Jesus novels, in which Jesus either appears himself or is thinly disguised in a hero under another name. As Balthasar notes, with approbation, the English tradition welcomes images without offering too much theological opposition.[14]

Unfortunately, however, one really cannot swallow every Jesus-motif uncritically. There is too much sheer rubbish about (often disguised by sincerity!), and even a judicious selection of modern *Jesus-bilder* in fiction cries out for some minimum criteria of validity. Ziolkowski has performed a masterly task in assembling a representative gallery of literary portrayals over the last two centuries. In his *Fictional Transfigurations of Jesus*,[15] distinguished works share the company of less worthy products. Ziolkowski groups these novels under five headings: the Christian Socialist Jesus, the Christomaniacs, the Mythic Jesus, 'Comrade Jesus', the 'Fifth Gospels'. Though these divisions overlap they mark the progress (or regress) engendered by the de-Christianizing of Jesus, begun with Reimarus as early as 1778, and brought to a climax by Strauss in 1835. The 'transfigurations' take some element of the original gospel story—such as the miracles, or the common meal, or the passion—and harness it to a purpose alien to the by now antiquated *kerygma*. The pious tracts in the nineteenth century lead up to the great break and culminate in the open parody of Jesus in the second half of our own. The authors operate a 'principle of incongruity' and no longer even profess to interpret the gospels. The way is thus open to a return to the myth, and in a sense all modern writers, especially of the political left, indulge in a technique of transcribing Jesus into a different framework, such as the Vietnam war or post-Victorian flashbacks. The bitter and often obscene pictures from the pens of the ephemerally famous (Vidal, Grass, John Barth), who may claim Hesse as a parent, may shock us less than the preposterous horrors of Victorian baby-Jesus or boy-Jesus stories. Their atheistic intent differs only in its explicit tone from the implicit ungodliness of the latter. All of them share the strange obsession with Jesus, whom they discredit by their imagery.

Literary criticism can sift the wheat from the chaff. Thus, as in art, we are led to approximate to certain standards of form and content which enable us at least to disqualify the pastiche. But a purely negative procedure must be coupled with a positive theological method of the recognition of the genuine. Clearly, it is not enough to bandy around religious language, nor should we be over-impressed with replicas of gospel events. Anyone can, for example, cite the raising of Lazarus or the exorcism of Legion, but not everyone can do so in the inspired context in which Doestoevsky uses these texts in *Crime and Punishment* and *The Possessed*. Similarly, we know that most hymns written during the last hundred years are poor and to be rejected, if we have once grasped the texture, rhythm and 'pitch' of Hopkins' anti-mythical, anti-sentimental, 'sprung' verse. But we apprehend the genuine *Jesusbild*, in prose and in poetry, not only through the achievement of genius, but also because this genius obeys the orders of Christian discipline. Hopkins' *Windhover* and *Heraclitean Fire* throw the whole Victorian concept of aesthetic beauty into the dustbin, not because Hopkins just writes good poetry, but because his *Jesusbild* rejects the false dimensions on the grounds of an ascetic, sacrificial, sacramentally ubiquitous, eternal Christ, who brings resurrection, not after, but in death.[16]

Many modern poets achieve what theologians would like to claim for themselves: the making of a valid *Jesusbild*, compounded of, and appealing to, many dimensions of experience. Prose lacks the 'single eye' which discerns the Christ in strictly formal diction. The narrator mixes description with dialogue and depends upon inventing characterization to be successful. There is, therefore, much to be said for C. S Lewis' restraint which placed prose as distant commentary only, whereas Dante and Milton verge upon sharing in the disclosure of the divine. The author of the *Screwtape Letters* and much Christian apologetic had no qualms about the revelatory and cultic uniqueness of the New Testament and he even vetoed the evaluation of the Authorized Version as 'literature'.[17] Our experience of literary fiction since his day can only confirm his insistence on clean distinctions.

The poet, by way of contrast, stands in the dimension of Christ. He is at home in the Jobian tradition of the night of chaos and longs for light of day. Poets are themselves inspired, or as Hölderlin puts it:

> An das Göttliche glauben
> Die allein, die es selber sind.

Hence they are at one with the Christ, captive eagle:

> Denn wie der Meister
> Gewandelt auf Erden
> Ein gefangener Aar[18]

they also long to soar in the air towards the heavens.

Our disappointment that so much scientifically accurate labour has yielded meagre or no harvests in the transcendental-eschatological field cannot really surprise us any longer. This dimension of the *Jesusbild* must confound historians and theologians alike, since propositions about Jesus cannot evoke the *Herrlichkeit* of poetry and music. We suffer linguistic, and thus total, shipwreck until we are prepared to meet this dimension in its own language.[19] Nor is this task an optional extra, for we must be threatened by the Scylla of a secularized hope— Ernst Bloch's *Das Prinzip Hoffnung*[20] having sired, by way of return, most so-called theologies of hope—and the Charybdis of sick and destructive fantasies. Secular utopianism feeds the fanaticism which dispenses with the *Jesusbild* altogether and replaces it with the idol of the Beast.

In this context of an eschatological menace in the world the poetical *Jesusbild*, far from being lost in its own lyricism, regains its polemical thrust. Being beyond history it re-enters the arena, and the eternal There and Then becomes our eschatological Here and Now, not as a faceless principle but as the One who is addressed *Maranatha*. Here poetry indwells the practical need and transforms it. Hopkins may well be our guide, as he enunciates the 'Come quickly' (*The Wreck of the Deutschland*, st. 24) to celebrate the death of the nun who drowned on 7 December 1875. In this evocation he symbolized both the dying and the liberation of generations to come. He united the dimensions of the Jesus of history and the Christ of faith:

> She to the black-out air, to the breaker, the thickly
> Falling flakes, to the throng that catches and quails
> Was calling 'O Christ, Christ, come quickly':
> The Cross to her she calls Christ to her, christens
> her wild-worst
> Best.

Here eschatology ceases to be a problem, but in the context of Gennesareth and the Milky Way we attain to Him, *Ipse, the only one Christ, King, Head.*

NOTES

1. 'The poets, even the spiritual ones, must also be worldly', from *Der Einzige* ('The Only One'), written between 1799 and 1803. See the fine edition and translation of Hölderlin's works by M. Hamburger, Routledge & Kegan Paul 1966.

2. The first by K. L. Schmidt, *RGG* III, 2nd ed., Tübingen 1929, cols. 110–51; the second by H. Conzelmann, *RGG* III, 3rd ed., 1959, cols. 619–53. (The latter article has been translated and brought up to date, with an introduction by J. Reumann, as H. Conzelmann, *Jesus*, Fortress Press 1973.)

3. E.g. the Albright 'school'.

4. E.g. Daniélou's chapters 'That the Scripture might be Fulfilled' and 'The Word Goes Forth' in *The Crucible of Christianity*, ed. Arnold Toynbee, Thames and Hudson 1969, pp. 261–98.

5. D. Flusser, *Jesus*, ET Herder and Herder 1969.

6. S. G. F. Brandon, *Jesus and the Zealots*, Manchester University Press 1967; *The Trial of Jesus*, Batsford 1968.

7. G. Vermes, *Jesus the Jew*, Collins 1973.

8. J. M. Allegro, *The Dead Sea Scrolls: A Reappraisal*, Penguin Books 1964, pp. 173–6.

9. H. Weinel, 'Jesusbild der Gegenwart', *RGG* III, 2nd ed., 1929, cols. 151–69.

10. C. H. Ratschow, *RGG* III, 3rd ed., 1959, cols. 655–63.

11. J. Maritain, *The Degrees of Knowledge*, ET Bles 1937.

12. For Jesus himself the 'temptation' refers to the demonic, for the early church to the *Aqeda* (Abraham's test), for the missionary church to the danger of apostasy, for the persecuted church to the ordeal of martyrdom, for the established church to immorality.

13. H. U. von Balthasar, *Herrlichkeit*, vol. II, Einsiedeln 1967.

14. Ibid., pp. 719ff.

15. T. Ziolkowski, *Fictional Transfigurations of Jesus*, Princeton University Press 1972.

16. Cf. H. U. von Balthasar, op. cit., pp. 749ff., 766.

17. C. S. Lewis, 'The Literary Impact of the Authorized Version', Athlone Press 1950, now in *Selected Literary Essays*, ed. W. Hooper, Cambridge University Press 1969. I remember the cold fury with which the platform greeted the original Ethel M. Wood Lecture.

18. 'Only those believe in the divine who are themselves divine . . . For just as the master walked on earth, a captive eagle, . . . ' (from *Der Einzige*).

19. Cf. A. N. Wilder, *Early Christian Rhetoric*, SCM Press 1964.

20. Ernst Bloch, *Das Prinzip Hoffnung*, Berlin 1954.

10

Meanings

GERALD DOWNING

IT might be easier to decide 'what Paul means for us today', or what a resurrection story means to a nine-year-old, or what the fourth gospel meant by 'life', if we were clearer as to what 'mean' means (or perhaps, what we mean by 'mean'). In a sense we take some sort of answer for granted in all our use of language; we presuppose meaningfulness. But that does not guarantee a clear or easy answer when we try to sort out just what it is we are presupposing. Questions may even make matters worse. Yet we seem bound to ask them, especially when we are trying to judge whether a translation for instance captures 'the meaning of the original'. How do you tell what constitutes 'the same meaning'?

The question is inescapably circular. Asking the meaning of words and sentences presupposes (as we have noted) the meaning of words and sentences. We can try to make it appear a little less introverted by asking what we understand by 'mean' (or mean by 'understand'). But we remain in a circle; and it is important to realize that, and make the best of it. We can do worse than muddle along unreflectively: we can try to orbit outside the circle (and find ourselves trapped in a tiny speech-craft with even less chance to manoeuvre). And we can do better: noting, avoiding or even removing the stumbling-blocks and pitfalls in our way, allowing ourselves a freer run within language as we more or less creatively receive and use it.[1]

What are we up to, then, when we ask about meanings, translate, do exegesis, interpret, practise our hermeneutical principles; how do we assess a better or worse attempt; and how do we assess our standards of assessment? The questions are important, if only in face of recent arguments which try to show that the translation of anything as ancient and foreign as the New Testament documents for us to understand is an impossibility. Either we have to step out of our cultural selves and be re-incarnated in the first century (Winch, Malcolm, Hudson[2]) or the first-century ideas remain so foreign as never to be credible, and we are left simply to clothe our own thoughts in the fancy dress of a mock-antique jargon (Bambrough, MacIntyre, Luckmann[3]).

We have quite a useful terminology, but I shall suggest that we too readily misunderstand and abuse it. We distinguish 'what he said' from 'what he meant' (and that perhaps from 'what it means to me, to us, to you, to them'). We talk of 'form and content' (or 'matter' or 'substance'); of 'letter and spirit', of 'sign and signification', of 'sentence and proposition', of 'symbol and its reference', and so on. These are useful when they help us to attend to the other person, remind us to check whether we have grasped much or anything of what he has been saying or has written. But these distinctions can be very misleading if they persuade us that we are trying to unwrap the thought from the words that seem to surround it, and then re-package it for 'translation'[4] to another cultural shore. No 'beetle-in-a-box' model of the relation of meaning and language fits the facts, as I shall try to show.

On the other hand, I am not suggesting that we join McLuhan[5] and simply coalesce 'message and medium'. Just to squash beetle and box together only makes a nasty mess of what is still precisely the same paradigm.

'The new hermeneutic',[6] with its stress on language as such, on 'the linguistic character of existence', is also, but more restrainedly, pressing us to reconsider the relation of language and what we mean. Yet its proponents too seem to retain a traditional 'form-and-content' terminology with few if any overt reservations. Words (and sometimes sentences), it is suggested, are the outer husk for the inner kernel of meaning.

I

Consider by way of contrast how we in fact sort out what we mean in our conversations with one another. Often, of course, rightly or wrongly we take it that we have understood perfectly. We may indeed have understood completely, or well enough for the purpose in hand.

It will depend very largely on how large an appropriate context of meaning we share together. In military training, for example, recruits are forced to concentrate on a very limited context, to the exclusion of other normal concerns, so that commands may be few, brief, and unambiguous. Family life provides a wider and more flexible context for its members, yet there, too, the frequent sharing of verbal, non-verbal and mixed purposeful activity allows very brief utterances and small gestures to be quite clearly understood, however enigmatic to outsiders. In less settled situations, we explore and create a common context with a large amount of repetition in the same and other words on both or all sides of the conversation, along with making and noting voluntary and automatic gestures, facial expressions, changes in intonation. We check whether we have understood the other(s) by offering back perhaps the same set of words, or another set that we think would work as well, or better, in the situation; perhaps one we would ourselves normally use. The other person perhaps allows ours, or reiterates his own, or offers yet another; or produces any combination of those possibilities.

'I think the glass is falling,' said conversationally suggests that the barometer is registering a lower pressure; but it might express an affected casualness as a drinking-glass teeters; or a hapless resignation from the far end of the room. But said by someone jerking forward with hand outstretched it is concerned with a tumbling tumbler, in explanation or warning. We understand what was meant. But someone understanding the remark in the first way might go on, 'You mean you don't want to come out with me?' and the original speaker says, 'No, I didn't mean quite that; but I have got lots to do this evening, and the small chance of a pleasant stroll doesn't make it seem worth the effort.' 'It's only that you'd rather watch Match of the Day than chat with me on a walk.' 'Well, put it this way, if you clean your room yourself, I may have time to do my other jobs and give you some time with me on your own.'

You could mean all that, and be understood too, when you said 'the glass is falling'; you (and your listener) could have thought all those sentences to yourselves (but did not have to); you could between you utter them (or others near enough like them). That is how we sort out meanings, what we meant, what 'it' (an utterance or action) meant.

If we are asked, or ask ourselves, what we mean by words or actions or actions and words together, we respond with more words (and perhaps with other actions that we take to be significant). Usually it is words in the main. Never does a naked 'meaning' appear: only more words. Even for ourselves, we don't in fact look at some inner meaning or intention of our own (some private beetle) and check the words against it, to see if they are a proper clothing for our thoughts' public appearance. We compare words with words, we choose, issue, give backing to, withdraw, put it in a nutshell, elaborate, complement, qualify words with words. This is how we communicate, whenever we try to communicate. We paraphrase, we overlap a sentence with another, a sequence with another.

And this too is precisely what those do who profess a belief in an inner content, matter, substance, spirit, proposition or whatever. However much they purport to be getting under or behind or down into the words (or words-in-sentences) they still emerge with words, just words, often quite a lot more words. And if we ask the meaning of these that are meant to give us the meaning of those, then we still receive more words. '*The* meaning', 'the substance' never emerges.

For classical instances of ideas and images being piled up to reinforce and qualify each other one need turn only to Paul in Romans, our chapters five to eight, as he tries to find common contexts of meaning that will not only make sense of what we can express as a 'theme' (a new life as a gift that is only enjoyed in living it) but will also qualify each other and will build up the total picture of what he wants to say. There are other examples: the meat-and-idols discussions in Romans and I Corinthians; the building up of imagery in the Revelation to John; the attempts of the second-century apologists.

For any important namable topic there may well be quite a wide vocabulary and stock of metaphors and so on, as well as a variety of sentence-structures. A number of sequences can be produced that overlap in detail or in large, more or less well; sentences and even paragraphs that would function with similar results on their own, given a cohesive social unit. It does no harm to say that they express much the same 'idea' or 'meaning', to draw attention to the overlap, the interlock, the fit, the similarity. But we can no more observe 'the meaning' or 'the idea' on its own than we can 'the fit' or 'the similarity'.

Put this way, what I am saying is perhaps very obvious. We cannot get outside language to look at what we use language for, not even when we want to concentrate very hard on what another person or what we ourselves are saying. But before I go on to suggest ways in which we can help ourselves in such concentration I want to point out some of the dangers involved in failing to take this seriously, however obvious they may be.

Norman Perrin, for instance, insists that we cannot understand Jesus himself (as opposed to projecting onto him nineteenth-century liberalism or twentieth-century existentialism) unless we interpret him in categories from his original setting. That seems unexceptionable. Perrin goes on to talk of the 'intrinsic difficulty' in comprehending the meaning these categories had for the men of first-century Judaism; though we must try.[7] But if we take the logic of both these theses together seriously, it is not difficult, it is impossible. We have to understand Jesus only against the setting of his time; we have to understand the setting of his time against the context of—what? Against itself? Or against some wider context still? If we say, against itself (as Perrin seems to intimate), then it must be as impossible as he says understanding Jesus on his own is. Or at best, it is something we might hit on by chance, but never know or be able to show we had achieved. We, the people we are, would have no criteria by which to judge a better or worse shot, no way of telling synonyms from contrasts and antitheses, creative juxtaposition from confusion and incoherence; and obviously no way of relating any beliefs expressed in those ways with beliefs of our own.

And if we take the fideist line, insist on repeating first-century talk simply in its own terms, still we as twentieth-century people have no way of telling whether we have in fact succeeded. We might still be using these words to express a systematically other complex of meaning, self-consistent, but still quite other.

Yet another, and in fact a classical approach, is to suppose that eternally constant truths are enshrined in all serious human literature, identical under their diverse cultural guises—a sort of embalmed super-beetle in a sarcophagus.

No view of meaning as some 'thing' dressed in words (whether revealing, misleading, or concealing) makes sense of how we in fact use words, and in fact learn from each other.

The process of conversing that I have briefly described and instanced allows us to grow, to enlarge understanding, to increase our context of meaning temporarily or for longer. Of course when we read a modern or an ancient text we do not have the same feed-back from the source, monitoring our understanding, rephrasing for us. On the other hand, we are better placed to check back for ourselves. But fundamentally we are engaged in the same procedure, interpreting on the basis of what we have already acquired and learned (and all that is presupposed in what we have learned and simply acquired) and at the same time gaining a wider basis for understanding.[8] As we try to put the New Testament writings (for instance) into our own words-in-sentences, and compare possible sequences, we find we are supplied with new words and phrases. We gain slowly, or even rapidly, new criteria of meaning. We include fresh fields in our language world.

Of course, we do not always accept or agree with what we learn. We are not persuaded by first-century Jewish apocalyptic, nor by Hellenistic gnosis, nor by Neoplatonism; nor by Paul nor Jesus, necessarily. In a proper sense we still do not understand what was being said, we are not able to use even our own version. But the same holds for any communication. We learn to entertain ideas which may seem seriously objectionable, find what it means to reject them carefully, understand their similarities (if any) to traits in ourselves and those around us and their contrasts. Conversation is not always agreeing, but it is always in some measure self-involving, even in denial (or else we call it something like parroting).

These new fields then may fit better or worse in our current state of mind, they may be very independent ghettos or depressed slave-settlements. But there is always more to acquire, and the acquisition is always possible. We can import, even if assimilation of the imports is sometimes more difficult than others. And the process is never different in kind from the ways in which we understand a close contemporary talking with us, and *pari passu* learn from him how to understand more. Often this is, and has to be, at the time unreflective. With a text, modern or ancient, we have ways of sifting the questions of meaning. To these we now turn.

II

In some of the philosophical discussions of meaning of forty and fifty years ago (which linger on, if only as straw bogeys) the possibilities of meaningful communication seemed to be pared down to vanishing point (early Wittgenstein; Ogden and Richards; Ayer[9]). Factual, verifiable (scientifically), testable discourse alone could be said to be meaningful, and we learned it as a response to repeated sensuous stimulus. Perhaps closed logical systems (like mathematics) made sense, too, but only by referring to nothing but their own workings. All the rest was 'emotive', 'non-sense', and we had best keep silence.

The arbitrariness of this (even in its own terms) and its inability to account for the complex ways in which we do (seemingly with success) converse ought not to blind us to its importance. It is very much easier to communicate on matters of recognizable and more or less repeatable 'fact' (though that too is circular, part of our criterion for 'fact'). We can talk of cabbages and king-pins, and fairly readily check whether we have understood each other. And even though a great deal of what we say goes beyond the simply factual (perhaps 'the simply factual' is an ideal construct), yet a large part of what we say certainly includes a measure of commonly acceptable factual reference. And that provides a firm base from which to create a common context of meaning. The wider the shared factual base, the better chance there is of coming to understand what the other means. If such facts are not available, or are mishandled, the task is very much harder.

The question of natural regularities cannot be fudged; if some of it goes, how much goes, and how much are we still to presuppose, and why? Accounts of miracles, demon-possession, warring angels and the like reduce the potential common ground, and arouse suspicions as to the soundness of the rest. Dates and mapped journeys may give a spurious sense of verisimilitude, and distract from the points really at issue. But where they are relevant it is worth taking them seriously. Assertions about the distant past are usually (but not always) harder to check than those about very recent times or about the near future. But there are ways to verify '*Asia* is the name of a Roman province'; the meaning is pretty clear; the two go together. It is much harder to check, and, at the same time, much harder to give 'the meaning of' 'God is love', ὁ Θεὸς ἀγάπη ἐστίν (I John 4.8). If we cannot test even our standard English version, nor the Greek, how do we tell what either really means, and so whether the standard English fits at all? However, in this instance John goes on to tell us that loving God involves loving your brother, and that involves sharing your livelihood with your brother in need; and this has the immediate effect of 'earthing' what he writes, even though it may leave much else unclear.[10]

The importance (theological importance and more) of historical research into early Christian origins is not (mainly) to prove whether 'it' happened (say, the resurrection of Jesus in some sense) nor how. The importance (for Christians) is to provide as wide a relevant context of acceptably factual reference as can be achieved. But it has to be done with full rigour.[11] The worst apologetic is the special pleading that would confound fact and fiction (e.g. taking as they stand the journeys of Paul in Acts, despite the letters) and so destroy a promising base from which to expand understanding.

One of the most tempting but one of the most difficult fields for supposedly 'factual' talk is that of our own 'inner experience' or 'self-understanding' (even if these are held to be distinct). The issues between behaviourists who would abandon such talk and those who would maintain it in some form are not settled. But if this is something 'inner', something beyond scientific observation (Bultmann[12]), we have no way of sharing it, no way of relating it as 'fact', and it in fact provides no sure basis at all for interpreting a text. Only if we can give some account of the standard symptoms, overt manifestations, have we any chance of latching on.

The 'new hermeneutic' way of seeing 'self-understanding' as 'language-event' (where it does not revert to talk of inner meanings and outer forms) is again more promising. Exegesis then consists in allowing us to share new language games (by showing how they overlap with, and how they go beyond, the language games we already play). The question whether we also share some early Christian experience or meaning behind the talk is then secondary (and may have to remain largely unsettled). It cannot provide the starting point for exegesis.

Ogden and Richards went on to suggest that all non-factual talk was indeed simply 'emotive', if in varying ways. Further philosophical work has suggested that much more needs to be said. Certainly emotive effect is very diverse among different people at different times; but we can ask them what they feel, and still go on to discuss none the less 'what it means', or (better), 'What are the words being used for?'

The slogan, 'Don't ask for the meaning, ask for the use', gained currency for a while. J. L. Austin (whose work has been sadly neglected by exegetes, even English-speaking ones, despite the efforts of Donald Evans[13]) suggested that there are all sorts of meaningful things that we can *do* with words. We can simply assert statements of fact (even if that turns out to be not so simple after all; assertion—and silence—can be strongly purposive). But we can express commitments, we can utter intentions, make promises, issue commands and warnings, absolve, pass sentence, give verdicts; we can commend, disparage, make ethical pronouncements. All of these will have some more or less explicit factual reference or context; while the degrees and sorts of emotion expressed or sought may differ considerably. (This, to use Austin's coined term, is 'illocutionary' language—or use of language—we *do* something *in* speaking.)

Austin also distinguished what we might achieve *by* speaking (perlocution). We might effectively warn, persuade, arouse, convince.

When we are trying to translate or interpret, when we are trying to make our fields of language overlap with those of, say, the New Testament collection of writings (and allow theirs to lap into ours) we must have as wide a range of questions in mind. Austin lets us see that there are many areas where overlap may occur, lots of questions of meaning (or like questions of meaning), many more than one or two ways to make sense.

We can ask what sorts of assertions of fact seem to be in question, what ethical commitments are being made, what programmes of action are implicit or announced, what attitudes expressed, what 'on-looks' (D. Evans' term)—how does this writer 'look on' other groups, individuals, events, ideas, and so on? And was he thanking, praising, confessing . . .? In a hundred words or so, he may have been doing any or all of these or more. The wider the range of meaning—or use—detected, the more the chance of finding some point of contact or overlap with what we ourselves talk about, some point of attraction that may draw us into this field of discourse.

III

This may by now seem a long, and not necessarily engaging, way from standard practice. Usually when we ask about meaning we start by consulting a standard dictionary. The lexicographer gives us lists of uses in terms of synonyms and contrasts, the main uses in contexts that make the uses in some way logically distinct. But even if he has done his work well, we shall at most be able to sort out the range of possible subject matter and treatment of a sentence or paragraph.

Unless we know something of at least the superficial grammar (syntax) of the language, we shan't know in what ways the words may be modifying each other. Noam Chomsky[14] would say that unless we at least implicitly detect the underlying 'deep' structure, we still will not understand. We need to be able to discern the passivity and potential activity underlying the seemingly identical forms, 'John is easy to please' and 'John is eager to please' (compare the point that is often made about impersonal passives and the possible meanings of the words δεῖ παθεῖν).

A dictionary, then, will give us some possible and general meanings of units (words) that might be spoken or written on their own, and some indication of related forms (*Je, me, moi*; go, goes, went; run, ran). The dictionary does not tell you what the word in the context before you must or does contribute to the meaning of the sentence. There is no guarantee that your writer or speaker was not idiosyncratic, or that the lexicographer has covered all the possibilities. And even if he has supplied one that is relevant here, that will still not give you the precise contribution of that unit to the whole. What we call (disparagingly) a 'literal' translation is one in which the dictionary units are taken as frozen entities, and not allowed to modify each other beyond the precise synonyms and definitions the dictionary provides.

Of course a word cannot on its own be made to mean whatever Humpty Dumpty decides to make it mean. What he meant by it is not necessarily what it meant (any more than what we understood by it is what it meant). Intentions are not enough. But, given enough context (verbal and wider), we may accept quite readily a new meaning for a word, realize without more ado the part it plays in his utterance. In the actual situation (armchairs; building a house) we know enough of what the user is likely to want to convey, enough of what other words he is using normally mean, and so gather enough of what he does mean by his utterances, for the purpose in hand.

We have to take full note of creativity, change, adaptability. In his controversy with behaviourist accounts of language (the associative acquisition and repetition of sounds, 'dog' when a dog is around), Chomsky points out that we understand and use sentence-patterns that we have never met before, and that it is in them that creativity lies, in the structure. I would suggest that it is the choice of units to build up the structure that is creative and novel. New words can be fitted into a very simple and repetitive pattern, in fresh situations. Words modify each other and the situation and are modified by it in ways for which there is no exact precedent. Creativity is normal, in accepting and responding to new patterns, new words in new or old orders, even clichés in fresh circumstances; and the hearer has a creative role, as well as the speaker.

It becomes very difficult to make clear distinctions between literal translation, paraphrase and exposition. We have noted that a literal version tries to ensure that every word or phrase in the original is paralleled by one given in the dictionary. The result is that our own fields of language may overlap very little with this supposed 'translation'. On the other hand, overlaps there are, and we can *learn* the Authorized Version, and its vocabulary has been modified by being used. (I may perhaps be permitted an autobiographical note: the *New English Bible* New Testament was published when I was lecturing on Christian origins at an Anglican theological college. I estimated then that between a third and a half of my lecture material became superfluous. I no longer had to translate the translation.) An intentionally archaic, 'faithful', literal translation is only another form of paraphrase: paraphrase into yet another tongue which people have to learn. (That they enjoy this esoteric experience, and take pride in appreciating its beauty is not relevant to this discussion.)

This does make translation seem harder. There is nothing settled, nothing finally correct (however much we may desiderate the examinable 'right' answer). On the other hand, it is precisely the conviction that only 'the right answer' is good enough which allows the sceptic to argue that translation is impossible, when—as is inevitable—he fails to achieve absolute accuracy.

If I am correct when I say that creativity in language is normal in listening as well as in speaking, then trying to make sense of texts that are foreign or ancient or both, 'new' to you in some sense, is only a variant (perhaps harder, but only perhaps) of what we are (more or less successfully) doing in all communication. We are used to making better or worse shots, and risking misunderstanding, and coping with our mistakes.

Despite the experience of two Christian millennia, we still seem to hope for clarity and certainty, an unambiguous declaration of God's meaning and purpose; even, in the last two hundred years, a revelation of God himself, in the words or 'the meaning of the words' of Scripture; or in the distinctive 'concepts' that we hope the words enshrine. Words just do not work like that (nor does God, but that too is another question). Nor do 'concepts', however convenient a closed and static concept of 'concept' may seem. Even so socially limited a one as 'the north-west European concept of "God" ' is diverse at any one time, and the variants change in time. It is always worthwhile taking a word, meaning, concept, as continuous; but it is only continuous through change. 'The concept' again, only denotes something of the range of possibilities at the time; and the range changes. It is worth insisting on 'the meaning', the imaginary ideal, like a geometric point or circle; but only to remind you to keep modifying your own attempt to match it, lest it drift further out of theoretical true. Beware of assuming you have it captured and caged.

IV

This is far from suggesting that in the translation or interpretation of the New Testament collection (or any other ancient texts) 'anything goes'. Certainly, if we suppose there is a great gap, a total otherness, then almost inevitably, as we have suggested, anything may go, there is no way to restrain it. If we suppose that our current concerns are perennials that must have been anticipated, then of course any current concern of ours will recur. But if we suppose there are lots of possibilities of overlap, more or less extensive, lots of chances to see if a fit of one kind marries with a match of another sort—then there is always a chance of obtaining, and demonstrating, a clearer representation of 'the meaning'.

But how do we know if we are right? How do we in any field? Surely only in the ways I have outlined, dealing with detailed doubts as they arise, on the basis of what we feel no need to question. If the question is 'How can we know at all?' it is unanswerable—because it is impossible to specify what is really being asked (Wittgenstein).

Certainly, writings composed a long while back may be more difficult to translate/interpret than recent ones; of course, with any writings of the dead there is no chance of feedback from the author (not that authors are infallible authorities on their own works). But there is a long tradition of interpretation of the New Testament documents, and of others from around the same time and places. Many of the possibilities are already mapped, many blind alleys marked (though they too may be re-explored the more easily). We have lots of ways to enlarge our own contexts of understanding in promising directions.

I venture the opinion that the New Testament documents are also extremely engaging in themselves, and not just as 'the canon'. They are so occasional, so intense, so open, so *lacking* in clearly defined concepts, that we are very readily invited in (and as readily taken in, too). We can easily find our thoughts seemingly mirrored, anticipated. It is then possible (but by no means inevitable) to move on to check how good the reflection is, to find ourselves admitting perhaps peripheral distortions, widening our understanding almost imperceptibly, taking note of what others find, asking why we differ; and so, perhaps, approximating a little more closely to 'the meaning'.[15]

It is perhaps even worth setting out with a table of questions of meaning(s). At some point you will have to decide how many authors' or editors' successive contributions to the meaning of a text you are going to consider (i.e. how many times the set of questions is to be asked); but that may have to wait for a preliminary run through the list:

1. What the words meant (range of main known uses then).
2. What the phrase/sentence/paragraph etc. meant (range of understanding for that sequence at that time). This includes questions of the meaning of the medium, spoken or written words, the sort of style ('down to earth', narrative, gnostic, &c.), the sort of social setting where such a text would be most readily appreciated.
3. What the author meant in saying it (e.g. 'we can tell what he meant here by what he says at greater length elsewhere').
4. What he meant to achieve by saying it (of which we may have no record).
5. What it meant to him emotionally 'interiorly' (probably unrecorded).
6. What it in fact meant to intended and other hearers/readers then (probably unrecorded) as evinced in verbal and other response.

7. Their emotional response.
8. Understanding these 'meanings' in words that are meaningful to us (the slow 'more-or-less' process I've been discussing; *not* 'all-or-nothing').
9. The implications, *if any*, we find or that find us or that we choose to accept, for ourselves: intellectual, ethical, aesthetic, and often emotional.
10. The Austinian illocutionary analysis at many points, especially 1–4. (5–7 I have included as marginal and insecure.)

Conventionally, 'translation' tries to give something of the *range* in (1) and (2), to give briefly something of what it may have meant, but may do it badly if it tries to ignore the other questions. 'Exegesis' conventionally attempts to restrict itself to (3), (4), and sometimes tries to cover (5), with (6) and perhaps (7); again, it may hope to avoid (8) and (9), but is likely to include them by accident, badly. Exegesis in particular demands (10), the Austinian analysis. (8) and (9), too, in fact have to happen all the while; if the exegete or translator attempts to leave them until later or to another interpreter, they are likely to be included uncritically. I think it is important to make stages such as these, and to mark them with terms like 'translation', 'exegesis' and 'interpretation' (even 'hermeneutics'); but to realize that they are arbitrary divisions, for convenience; and that the matter is more complex still.[16]

The idea of a 'holy scripture' as an authoritative book,[17] then, is patently self-defeating in practice if not self-contradictory in theory (along with its wider disadvantages). The clearer its supposed authority, the more pressing the demand to find in it what is convenient or orthodox, and the less real notice is taken of it itself; the readier we are to canonize some imagined changeless version in its place. The only appropriate respect for the collection, for Christian origins, for the God we hope to be drawn to know, is a critical sceptical painstaking and endless investigation.

The understanding of language, of interpretation, translation and meaning that I have been outlining may also be seen to undermine any clear distinction between 'natural' and 'revealed' theology. In any reading we start where we are, we learn more, we contribute, we learn how to learn more and how to contribute more. There is no clear break between what is 'natural' to us at any one point, and what we gain. Jumps and bumps, but no break (a break would not be revelation, it would be incomprehension).

This sort of understanding is an adult process, something it takes us a long while to gain the capacity to achieve. It takes time to acquire the ability to enter a foreign context, to realize that there is more to it than imagining me and my friends in fancy dress, to do more than make ancient times into a stage-set for contemporary drama, to be able to learn wider ways of being human. It can only be learned by doing it; but it is a shame to spoil the material by over-exposure too soon. The biblical writings are not child's play; nor should children be bored by homogenized and pre-digested gobbets from them.

New Testament (and other) exegesis and interpretation demand an enriched man willing to be further enriched. We can be grateful when we find the demand in some good measure met.

NOTES

1. On which see L. Wittgenstein, *Philosophical Investigations*, Blackwell 1953; and on what follows see his *On Certainty*, Blackwell 1969.

2. P. Winch, 'Understanding a Primitive Society', in D. Z. Phillips (ed.), *Religion and Understanding*, Oxford University Press 1967; N. Malcolm, cited in K. Nielsen, 'Wittgensteinian Fideism', *Philosophy* XLII. 161, July 1967, pp. 191f.; W. D. Hudson, in *Ludwig Wittgenstein*, Lutterworth 1968, and other writing. For a discussion see my 'Games, Families, the Public and Religion', *Philosophy* XLVII. 179, Jan. 1972.

3. Renford Bambrough in *Reason, Truth and God*, Methuen 1969; A. MacIntyre, 'God and the Theologians', *Encounter* 120, Sept. 1963; and 'Is Understanding Religion Compatible with Believing?', in J. Hick (ed.) *Faith and the Philosophers*, Macmillan 1964; T. Luckmann, *The Invisible Religion*, Macmillan, New York 1967, and writings by his associate, P. Berger, with recent reservations.

4. So G. Ebeling, in *Introduction to a Theological Theory of Language*, Collins 1973, though he has better things to say, too. Cf. E. L. Mascall, *The Secularization of Christianity*, Darton, Longman and Todd 1965; and see R. Barthes, *Elements of Semeiology*, Cape 1967.

5. Marshall McLuhan, various writings listed and commented on in G. E. Stern, *McLuhan Hot and Cool*, Penguin 1968.

6. In Ebeling, op. cit.; R. Funk, *Language, Hermeneutic and Word of God*, Harper 1967; C. E. Braaten, *History and Hermeneutics*, Lutterworth 1968.

7. N. Perrin, *Rediscovering the Teaching of Jesus*, SCM Press 1967, pp. 49ff. It is in answer to this that S. C. Brown has argued (in *Do Religious Claims make Sense?*, SCM Press 1969) that if the New Testament is foreign enough to need Bultmann's 'demythologizing' the latter must be impossible.

8. I think this is more accurate than R. G. Collingwood's account of 'thinking others' thoughts after them' (*The Idea of History*, Oxford University Press 1946). What I am suggesting ties in with my account of writing history as such in my *The Church and Jesus* (SBT 2.10), 1968, that we have to be content with a variety of attempts. But concern with others' thinking, as such, deserves more attention than I gave it there. Compare the pluralistic approach of N. Hampson, *The Life and Opinions of Maximilien Robespierre*, Duckworth 1974.

9. L. Wittgenstein, *Tractatus Logico-philosophicus*, 2nd trans., Routledge 1961; C. K. Ogden and I. A. Richards, *The Meaning of Meaning*, Routledge 1926; and *The Philosophy of Rhetoric*, Oxford University Press 1936; A. J. Ayer, *Language, Truth and Logic*, 2nd ed., Gollancz 1946.

10. I John 4.20f.; compare the οὖν of Rom. 12.1; Phil. 2.1; etc. This is the valid point in P. M. van Buren, *The Secular Meaning of the Gospel*, SCM Press 1963.

11. Compare C. F. Evans, *Resurrection and the New Testament*, (SBT 2.12), 1970.

12. R. Bultmann, *Jesus Christ and Mythology*, SCM Press 1960, pp. 64ff.

13. J. L. Austin, *Philosophical Papers*, Oxford University Press 1961; *How to do things with Words*, Oxford University Press 1962; D. Evans, *The Logic of Self-involvement*, SCM Press 1963.

14. On linguistics, J. Lyons, *Chomsky*, Fontana/Collins 1970; and as editor, *New Horizons in Linguistics*, Penguin 1970; N. Minnis (ed.), *Linguistics at Large*, Paladin 1973; Jean Aitchison, *General Linguistics*, English Universities Press 1972, esp. ch. 9, 'Meaning'. For the following argument (words and syntax) see especially B. Harrison in an article-review of *Semantic Theory* by J. J. Katz, *Mind* LXXXIII. 332, Oct. 1974, pp. 599ff.

15. I have gained a lot (I think) from wrestling from time to time with L. J. Cohen, *The Diversity of Meaning*, 2nd ed., Methuen 1966, though I find him closer to Austin and Wittgenstein than he thinks his arguments are.

16. Cf. e.g. Lucas Vischer (ed.), *New Directions in Faith and Order*, WCC Geneva 1968, section I 2 A, 'The Significance of the Hermeneutical Problem . . .', for a simpler form of these distinctions.

17. The following paragraphs are of course attempting to relate the foregoing to some of the issues in C. F. Evans, *Is 'Holy Scripture' Christian?*, SCM Press 1971.

11

A Partner for Cinderella?

DENNIS NINEHAM

IN his inaugural lecture at Durham[1] Professor Evans made the important point that Christian theology is not a discipline which can profitably be carried on by itself in isolation from other disciplines. To use his own analogy, 'theology . . . is always driven to look for a partner before she can dance to full effect'.[2] Doing theology, like dancing, is an activity for which the co-operation of at least one other person is needed. After dancing with philosophy more or less continuously for many hundreds of years, theology took on a new partner at the time when the critical study of the Bible arose, and has danced pretty consistently since then with history. The lecture suggested reasons for thinking that the time has now come when 'the historical method no longer suffices, and the theologian has to look around for assistance from another quarter',[3] but it left open the question who the new partner, or partners, should be. It did make the point, however, that the character and preoccupations of philosophy have changed radically since the days when theology used to dance with him; and that, at any rate as he exists in England, almost entirely preoccupied with linguistic and logical analysis, he is so earthbound, and his interests are so humdrum, that a return to an exclusive partnership with him would not be a good idea, even if he were willing.[4] Where then may other partners be found?

This essay is intended to advance a tentative plea for sociology, and more specifically for the sociology of knowledge, as a possible candidate. Perhaps if theology were to seek a partnership in that quarter, she might discover that there are new steps, and even whole new dances, to be learned of which she has previously known nothing; and she might also get an introduction to other partners with whom it would be well worthwhile to take the floor.

We must now drop the metaphor and even at the risk of some over-simplification[5] give a brief account of the present position with regard to theological method and how it came to be what it is. No one will dispute that the theological enterprise of the Christian church, as traditionally carried on, has taken as its basic datum the Bible, or rather the events and teaching reported and interpreted in the Bible. As it stands, this material displays a bewildering variety and lack of organization; but the theologians of the early Christian centuries, including some writers whose works are included in the canon, are generally credited with having discovered a way of interpreting it which revealed an underlying unity, in the light of which it could be reduced to systematic form.

The work of systematization was carried out not only by individuals —usually in the course of some controversy—but by councils and synods; and the creeds and definitions resulting from their work have usually been seen, if not as embodying *the* meaning of the Bible, at any rate as defining its meaning so far as the areas they cover are concerned. In practice the construction of a Christian system on the basis of the Bible was the result of bringing to bear on the biblical material questions, categories and insights derived from a widespread but fairly specific single philosophical position.[6] The period, however, was one of relative cultural stability and also relative cultural homogeneity. In the Western world to which Christianity spread, no philosophical tradition, or at any rate no philosophical tradition serviceable to a theist, was available except the one actually employed. Consequently the Christian system as it emerged came to be regarded as a constant quantum of truth and also as embodying the only possible reasonable interpretation of the Bible.

A coherent system is easier to handle than a mass of heterogeneous material, and for this reason if no other, a tendency naturally arose to treat the system, rather than the Bible itself, as the basis for further theological activity; or at any rate to use the Bible only as filtered through the system. To make such a statement is not for a moment to ignore the fact that the system itself has consistently been subject to revision in the light of the Bible. The Reformation alone suffices to prevent our ignoring that; and in fact a critique of the creeds on the basis of the biblical material has almost always been the ostensible—and very often the real—origin of other denominational and confessional divisions, and of differences of opinion within the denominations.

Eyebrows may therefore be raised, especially in Protestant circles, at our suggestion that it is very largely the creed, as understood in his denomination, which has effectively guided the thinking of almost every Christian theologian and exegete. A little reflection, however, will show what a large amount of truth this statement contains. For since the doctrines of the Trinity, the Incarnation and the rest, once they had been formulated, were thought to enshrine *the* meaning of the Bible, they inevitably provided both a framework of reference and also an ultimate criterion for all subsequent exegesis and theological investigation. Anyone, for example, working on a New Testament passage which referred to 'the Son' or 'the Spirit' now started from the conviction that the reference was to the Second or the Third Person of the Trinity as defined in the creeds and conciliar definitions. Thus, for example, John 14.28b ('the Father is greater than I') and John 7.39 ('as yet there was no spirit') now became *cruces interpretum* because they seemed *prima facie* to conflict with the Nicene and Chalcedonian doctrine. The orthodox doctrine of the Trinity indicated the area in which the correct interpretation of any such biblical text must lie, whatever the interpretation eventually turned out to be.

Examples could equally easily be cited in connection with other doctrines, so we may say that the work of the Fathers, based as it was on a partnership with the philosophy of the period, controlled subsequent exegesis in at least two ways. It controlled its general character because exegesis came to be understood essentially as the translation of biblical statements into the categories of the dominant philosophical tradition;[7] and secondly, as our examples have shown, it often went a long way towards defining the exegete's detailed conclusions.

In principle what has been said about the creeds of the 'undivided' church could be said about the detailed contents of the formularies of each denomination. In the Roman tradition, for example, the doctrine of the perpetual virginity of Mary has defined exegesis of gospel passages about 'the brethren of the Lord' which are *prima facie* incompatible with it. For the purposes of our argument, however, it will suffice to confine ourselves to the contents of the classical formularies accepted by the great majority of Christian groups—the doctrines of creation and of the Trinity and the Incarnation, the need for atonement, the divine foundation of the church and of the two main sacraments within it, and so on. In order to recognize how largely these have dominated subsequent theological thinking, even about the Bible, we have only to remind ourselves how far individual theologians have been from even the remotest suspicion that any work they might do on the Bible could conceivably call in question any fundamental doctrines of the creed.

In view of its character as a supposedly constant quantum of truth, we may perhaps symbolize the doctrinal system of the church as Q. If we then symbolize the Bible as B, we may represent what has been said so far, in diagrammatic form, somewhat as follows:

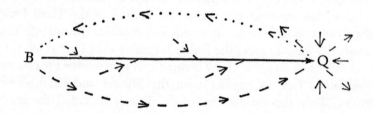

B originally gave rise to Q in cooperation with various philosophical influences ($\cdots\!\!\to\!\!\to$) and continues to exercise at least a negative critique of it ($\cdots\to\,-\,-\to\cdots$); but once Q has been established, it exercises its own retro-active influence on the interpretation, and thus the meaning, of B ($\,-\,\twoheadleftarrow\,-\,-\twoheadleftarrow\,$). It also stands in a reciprocal relationship to each culture in which it exists, exerting pressure on its surroundings through the work of its evangelists and other Christian spokesmen, but at the same time having its meaning significantly, if subtly, altered as a result of pressures from the environment, pressures which at the time were seldom recognized, still less exerted consciously.

If that is agreed, we may broadly differentiate the theological activities which have been proceeding on the basis of Q into two types. There is first what might be called 'theoretical theology', theological activity which takes Q, or some element of it, as an unquestioned datum and treats it rather as a physicist treats his experimental data, seeking to explain how it works and to understand what we might almost call the 'mechanics' of it—usually, as in the case of the physicist, with a view to taking more effective advantage of it. This is theology in its character of *fides quaerens intellectum,* and Anselm's *Cur Deus-Homo* is a typical example of it. Anselm accepts the traditional doctrine of the Incarnation of the Second Person of the Trinity (not, be it noted, the Johannine doctrine of the *logos sarx genomenos*) as an unquestioned truth and seeks to discover how the Incarnation worked, by what means it produced the desired result, why just that phenomenon, a God-man,[8] was necessary for the achievement of salvation. A little reflection will show how much traditional Christian theology has been of that type.

The other main type of Christian theologizing may be described as 'practical theology'. This seeks to discover what implications the truth of Q has for human behaviour, both individual and corporate. A characteristic example would be the Christian socialist movement of the turn of the century, which is connected with the names of Charles Gore and his circle. It is instructive to notice that here again the traditional[9] doctrine of the Incarnation was the unquestioned starting-point and basis. The constantly repeated thesis of this group was that God cannot be thought hostile or indifferent to material things and conditions because when men's salvation demanded it, he was willing to enter personally into the material world and immerse himself fully in it. God became man and in his human form busied himself about the physical, as well as the spiritual, needs of his fellow men. Any attitude which treats the material world or men's material needs with indifference or distaste is thus totally inconsistent with Q. The very nerve of the argument is the doctrine of the Incarnation of the godhead *as defined in* Q; yet the historical-critical method makes it difficult to find the doctrine in anything like that form in any New Testament passage, that is, in B. The incarnation of Yahweh would have been an unthinkable thought for any Jew and it is doubtful, to say the least, if any New Testament writer was sufficiently removed from Jewish categories of thought to have been able to entertain it. The appearance of the Messiah, or even of the *logos* of God, belonged to a very different universe of discourse from any involved in patristic theology.

If the steps to which theology has been accustomed are of that sort, a very short period dancing with the sociology of knowledge is likely to convince her that she must learn to cut some new capers. For almost the first advice her new partner will whisper in her ear is that if she wishes to dance with him, she must learn to contextualize any statement on any subject whatsoever with the question: 'Says who?'[10] He will explain that the meaning of any set of words is relative to the historical situation and cultural context of the person who speaks or writes them. Thus any interpretation or exposition must always be in terms of some specific set of presuppositions. To give a ludicrously crude example of the general principle, the word 'fire' will produce one understanding and response when shouted by an usherette in a crowded cinema, and quite another when shouted by an officer in charge of a firing-squad. Since almost all our presuppositions are so widely different from those of the people who laid down the main lines of Q,[11] any response their words evoke from us is likely to be quite appreciably different from the response they were originally intended to evoke. Phrases and images appropriate for expressing the meaning of the Bible in their cultural situations will be likely, to say the least, to convey a very different meaning in a situation divided from theirs by as wide a gulf as ours is. Consequently we cannot expect to be able to take over Q as the meaning of the Bible for us. If we are to express what the Bible means for us it will have to be in our own terms. In order to appreciate how different those are likely to be from the terms of Q, we have only to indulge for a moment in the fancy that immediately after its completion, the sole text of the Bible was lost until its discovery in a cave near the Dead Sea some few years ago. In that case, however deeply impressed modern readers might have been by the newly discovered text and however much they might have pondered over it, they would never have constructed on the basis of it anything like those essentially late-Hellenistic constructions, the doctrines of the Trinity and the Incarnation.

So we may repeat: what the Bible means for us must be expressed in our own way. If that seems a truism which has been recognized for a considerable time, it may be suggested that the problems involved have for the most part been sensed rather than carefully analysed, and the recognition of them has led to a rather hasty 'back to the Bible' movement on the part of many scholars. The aim—seldom clearly articulated—has been to bypass Q as far as possible and bring about a direct, and it is hoped creative, confrontation between the Bible and the modern world, as if for the first time.[12] Consciously or unconsciously, for example, some such intention seems to lie behind Bultmann's programme for demythologizing the Bible, where the idea is to confront the New Testament *kerygma* directly with the categories of Heideggerian existentialism.

Whether it is along Bultmann's lines or those of older liberal scholars that such an approach is made, one of the first results of it is to bring about the existence of two contemporary versions of Christianity. There is first the Christianity of the scholars, purportedly arrived at by the direct confrontation of the Bible with modern ideas,[13] and then there is the Christianity of more traditional clergy and laity who seek either to preserve Q, even if in a somewhat modified form, or at least to allow full weight to it in the formulation of a contemporary faith. If the present theological outlook is symbolized by the letter P, the two approaches might be represented as follows:

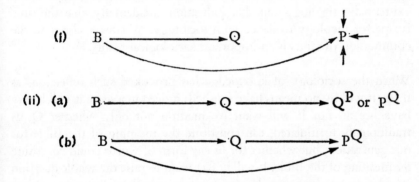

In both its forms (ii) seeks, in the language of the studbook, to produce P out of B by Q.

There is, however, a further difficulty about (i): it writes off the contents of Q altogether too precipitately. Although the contents of Q are not what *we* should have produced on the basis of B, and we may even on occasions have doubts whether they were primarily derived from B at all, they may still contain, couched in their own terms, truths which are deeply significant for us. For in many cases they were their authors' way of dealing with what are still real problems. If, as Leonard Hodgson used to insist, the Bible should always be approached with the question: What must the truth be now if people who thought as they did put it like that? there seems no reason to suppose that the posing of the same question with regard to Q would be any less fruitful, or at any rate that it would be entirely fruitless. Certainly failure to ask it will in practice doom any proposed solution of our problem. For some of the contents of Q have become so much part of the Christian consciousness, and are, quite justifiably, so deeply prized by most Christians, that any position which simply writes them off will prove unacceptable. The more enlightened among contemporary Christians may well be prepared to have Q confronted with some such question as Hodgson's in the sort of way that C. C. Richardson, Norman Pittenger, or, more radically, Erich Fromm, have confronted it;[14] they are not prepared to see it simply ignored. Indeed even to suggest the ignoring of it is to betray a basic failure to understand how things work either sociologically or psychologically; it is a symptom of the excessive individualism and the failure to apprehend the community dimension of the Christian religion which characterize much existentialist theology—another indication, incidentally, that the time is ripe for theology to dance with sociology. Whatever else it is, the communion of saints is an important sociological reality.[15]

When the sociology of knowledge has provoked such reflections as these, it will by no means have finished; indeed in a sense it will barely have begun. For it will want to question not only whether Q, as traditionally formulated, can constitute the meaning of the Bible for our generation, but whether for us *any* form of words could constitute *the* meaning of the Bible. It will in fact want to raise the whole question whether it any longer makes sense for us to talk of 'the meaning' or 'the message' of the Bible as something which can be formulated in set terms and used as an authoritative touchstone of what Christians are, and are not, committed to believing.

The argument is likely to go something like this. Sociology will insist that if every statement is to be submitted to the question 'Says who?', that must apply to the statements of the Bible, even the most central of them. Sooner or later, perhaps in relation to one of those luminous biblical passages Gadamer calls 'immanent texts',[16] theology will naturally want to reply 'Says God'. The sociologist, if he knows his business, will not dream of denying the propriety of such an answer in principle; but he will want to point out that the statement is one which needs very careful handling if the logic of it is not to be open to grave objections. He will point out that even insights derived from God must be conceived in the terms and categories of some particular culture if they are to find any recipients who can entertain them and so make them available to subsequent generations. The inspired status of B, if such it has, does not therefore exempt it from any of the relativist problems which arise in connection with Q.

So far as the biblical insights are concerned, they were conceived—or received—and expressed in the cultural terms of a single, evolving but recognizably continuous, religious tradition, the Judaeo-Christian tradition. It was characteristic of the Jews and the early Christians that they normally gave expression to the supernatural dimension of human affairs by incorporating the history of human life into a story—a story of God's actions upon, and interventions in, the world from creation day to doomsday. 'Story' is the word a twentieth-century westerner is more or less bound to use in this connection because the account of the past in the Bible, while it contains a fair amount of more or less accurate history, also contains many narratives—and those some of the most important—which from our point of view are wholly or partly mythical. The biblical writers have in places clearly allowed the demands of the story to modify the history; and they seldom give much sign of being aware that the mythical elements in their story, for example, the creation, the 'fall' of Adam and Eve, or the bodily ascension of Christ, were any less factual than the genuinely historical elements.

Modern readers cannot make such a mixture of myth and more or less accurate history their own in the way the original writers did. As Canon Bezzant put it, the story 'has been so shattered that the bare recital of it has the aspect of . . . travesty'. He added:

> Known facts of astronomy, geology, biological evolution, anthro-pology, the comparative study of religions, race and genetical and analytic psychology, the literary and historical criticism of the Bible, with the teaching of Jesus and the moral conscience of man-kind, have banished this scheme beyond the range of credibility.[17]

The difficulty which the biblical story presents to a modern reader, it will be noted, does not arise simply from its character as story. It may well be that any account of the ultimate significance—or even of the ultimate insignificance—of life must take the form of a story of some sort. The Marxists have their story and the humanists have theirs; there can be no objection to the modern Christian having his story too. The point is that it must be *his* story, doing full justice to all the types of knowledge about the present and the past to which Canon Bezzant refers.

It must also be emphasized that to say we cannot make the biblical story our own as it stands is not for a moment to deny that we can learn a great deal from it. Indeed no one would be likely to call himself a Christian unless he believed that the biblical story has almost inexhaustible truth to disclose. The question with which sociology confronts theology is precisely the question how the biblical story is to be used in helping us to see what the modern Christian story must be; and it is in this context that we can often get light from the use our Christian predecessors have made of the Bible in constructing their various stories, even though they were usually unaware that their story and the biblical story were not identical.[18]

There seem to be at least two ways in which the biblical story cannot be used by the modern Christian. He must not attempt to exempt certain passages of the biblical story from their status as parts of the story, absolutize them as if they were timelessly valid and culturally unconditioned, and then seek to weave them together as they stand in the hope that *that* will produce the modern Christian story. Biblical passages simply cannot be treated in that way. For example, the New Testament claim that 'Jesus is the Christ' got its very meaning from its context in the biblical story as a whole.[19] If such a formula is taken over direct as part of the modern Christian story, it will inevitably take on new meaning and then questions will arise what that meaning is and whether the formula is the best way of expressing it.

Secondly, once the character of the biblical writings as basically story is recognized, it will be seen to follow that there can be no question of extracting '*the* meaning' of it in any exclusive sense. For if there is one thing on which all modern literary critics and students of comparative mythology are agreed, it is the impropriety of attempting to extract from a myth or drama or story something which can be stated in alternative words and claimed as 'the meaning' of it. What modern literary critics and students of mythology seek to do through their studies is not to isolate '*the* meaning' of what they are studying but to leave it more meaningful than it was before they went to work. Biblical exegetes will have to learn to do the same. Working against successive cultural backgrounds, they can be relied on to discover ever new depths of meaning in the text. This will be of inestimable help to the dogmatic theologian, but it remains true that the task of discovering the appropriate story in which to body forth the relations of God and the world for the contemporary world will always remain a creative and subjective, or inter-subjective, one requiring radical trust in the guidance of God. However excellent and profound the work of biblical exegetes, the task will never become one of stating or drawing out *the* meaning of the text.

If anyone feels inclined to object that such a conclusion would rob the Christian faith of the future of any generally agreed content, let him consider the strength of many a literary critical consensus and how it is achieved. A recent writer on modern biblical study writes as follows:

> Isn't the real situation much more like that of literary criticism? The critic looks more closely at a text than others have done, brings new ideas to bear from a wider experience, and points out what the rest of us have overlooked. But in the end our agreement is necessary. As Dr Leavis once pointed out, the characteristic critical judgment takes the form 'This is so—isn't it?' Where something authentic has been said, the rest of us eventually answer 'Yes, of course'.[20]

One is reminded of Leonard Hodgson's often repeated claim that the characteristic theological judgment should be of the form 'This is how I see it; can you not see it like that too?' Certainly it looks as if dogmatic judgments in the future will have to take some such form and abandon any claim to demonstrative status.

NOTES

1. Published by Durham University in 1960 under the title *Queen or Cinderella*.
2. Ibid., p. 6.
3. Ibid., p. 22.
4. Of course the word 'exclusive' in that sentence is extremely important, as the work of a philosophical theologian such as Ian Ramsey showed.

5. The reader's indulgence is asked in advance for the number of very broad generalizations this paper will be found to contain. The excuse for them must be the need for brevity, and it is hoped that none of them would be found on detailed examination to need so much qualification as to destroy the validity of the argument. A case in point is what is said below about the relative homogeneity of the philosophical position presupposed by patristic writers.

6. See note 5 above.

7. Or at least of that form of it which appealed most to the exegete doing the work.

8. As the latest critical edition of Anselm's works (that by F. S. Schmitt, OSB, Nelson 1946+) makes clear, the title *Cur Deus-Homo* is best taken as meaning: why there needed to be a God-man. See Schmitt, II, 6ff., and cf. J. McIntyre, *St Anselm and his Critics*, Oliver and Boyd 1954, p. 117.

9. Gore's kenoticism does not prevent his doctrine of the Incarnation from being 'traditional' in the sense relevant to our argument.

10. See e.g. Peter L. Berger, *Invitation to Sociology*, Penguin Books 1966, pp. 79–80.

11. Just how widely is something still not sufficiently recognized by many theologians. The point will be developed further elsewhere; meanwhile for a brief but lively discussion see C. S. Lewis's inaugural lecture *De descriptione temporum*, now published in *They Asked for a Paper*, Bles 1962, pp. 9–25.

12. So far as bypassing Q is concerned, Albert Schweitzer put the point with characteristic vividness in his description of the nineteenth-century approach to the figure of Jesus. 'It loosed the bonds by which He had been riveted for centuries to the stony rocks of ecclesiastical doctrine, and rejoiced to see life and movement coming into the figure once more, and the historical Jesus advancing, as it seemed, to meet it.' Schweitzer, however, almost alone among his contemporaries, recognized the full dimensions of the problem. He went on: 'But he does not stay; He passes by our time and returns to His own' (*The Quest of the Historical Jesus*, ET A. & C. Black 1910, p. 397).

13. Cf. Martin Kähler's reaction against what he described as 'the papacy of the scholars' (*The So-called Historical Jesus and the Historic, Biblical Christ*, ET Fortress Press 1964, e.g. pp. 109ff.).

14. Cf. C. C. Richardson, *The Doctrine of the Trinity*, Abingdon Press 1958; W. Norman Pittenger, *The Word Incarnate*, Nisbet 1959; E. Fromm, *The Dogma of Christ*, Routledge & Kegan Paul 1963.

15. A fact attested independently by the literary critic Ian Robinson when he wrote recently, *à propos* the appreciative attitude of the translators of the Authorized Version towards earlier translators: 'For them the earlier versions were a guarantee, a sort of communion of saints, inspiring them, as ever, to the salvation of souls' (*The Survival of English*, Cambridge University Press 1973, p. 61).

16. See H. G. Gadamer, *Wahrheit und Methode*, Tübingen 1960.

17. *Objections to Christian Belief*, D. M. MacKinnon and others, Constable 1963, p. 84.

18. See p. 145 above.

19. In which, for example, the anointing or 'christing' of kings and priests was the accepted way of signalizing God's choice and appointment of them. Apart from that, as one scholar has remarked, the Greek phrase *ho christos* might well have been taken to mean 'the person who has just had a bath'—for it was mainly in connection with bathing that Greeks anointed themselves!

20. Father Laurence Bright, OP, in a letter to *The Times*, 18 June 1974.

12

The Uses Of 'Holy Scripture'

MAURICE WILES

IS 'HOLY SCRIPTURE' CHRISTIAN? is certainly a striking title
for a theological book.[1] Christopher Evans himself describes it
apologetically as a 'perhaps foolish title'.[2] It has a recognizably
impish quality about it, but characteristically it poses a question that
is searching, even uncomfortable, but far from foolish.

In the course of Christian history the distinctive character of 'holy
scripture' has often been asserted in ways which were epistemologically
absurd and religiously disastrous. Its composition has been ascribed to
forms of dictation which left the human writer no more than an
instrument in the hand of the divine author but ensured the inerrancy
of the resultant text. Then in obedience to its commands witches have
been burnt to the glory of God or else a divine authority claimed for
all one's own immediate concerns by the Midas touch of allegorical
interpretation. Modern scholarship has learnt long since to eschew all
such excesses. But the distinctive character of 'holy scripture' is still
frequently linked to accounts of revelation that carry less than universal
assent. Christopher Evans gives one such example in his discussion of
Cullmann's book *Salvation in History*.[3] Professor Mitchell has recently
suggested that if the concept of divine inspiration of the Bible is to be
retained, it will need to take the form of a belief 'that there are truths
which men could not have discovered by themselves, but which God
has found means of communicating to them'.[4] I do not intend to
discuss here whether any account of inspiration or revelation of this
kind can be sustained which would justify something like the degree of
distinctiveness traditionally ascribed to 'holy scripture'. That task is

one that appears to me to be a good deal more difficult than it is often assumed to be.

But in this paper I want to pursue a different question. It is this: suppose one were unable to provide any such account, would it follow that one ought to abandon the idea of a canonical scripture altogether? Or would there still be a place for a 'holy book' in the practice of Christian faith? Other religions which have very different ideas of revelation from the Christian tend to have their 'holy books' too. While the particular role of the Christian scriptures is undoubtedly related to the particular Christian understanding of revelation and of the unique incarnation of God in Jesus Christ, it would be surprising if Christianity's holy book did not function within Christianity in ways comparable with the role of holy books in other religious traditions. I propose therefore to offer some rather broad reflections on the way in which a holy book is liable to function in a religious culture, to consider how far the Bible functions in that kind of way and finally to attempt some evaluation of it in relation to those functions. I shall set out my reflections under three headings.

1. *Respect for antiquity*

Change always involves an element of loss. Even where change is clearly desirable, the past was seldom wholly evil and past good is often lost (it may be inevitably) along with the excision of the evil. Enthusiastic supporters of the New English Bible will normally be prepared to admit that where it replaces the Authorized Version there is loss as well as gain. In a pre-literate society where change is slow and the greatest danger is loss of old skills, religion is likely to fulfil an important conservative role. The myths speak of a golden age in the past, and much religious practice is designed to preserve or recapture it. Writing is an enormously important tool for this kind of preservative function. Books, when they first began to appear, would have had, in addition to their practical value, an aura of rarity and mystery which they cannot possibly have for us in an age of the paperback and the popular press. I remember a Nigerian student at the University of Ibadan, himself a first generation literate, telling me of the sense of shock with which in his first weeks at the University he had heard one of his tutors say that he did not agree with what a published book said. His sense of shock was very similar to that which a fundamentalist

Christian might feel on hearing for the first time someone say that he thought the Bible was wrong in some particular respect.

The charge of novelty is a powerful weapon of attack in making a religion look ridiculous. Celsus used it against Christianity; Roman Catholics (in less ecumenical days) used to use it against Protestants; and main-line Protestants use it against Christian Scientists and Jehovah's Witnesses. The Old Testament scriptures were important to the infant Christian church not only for internal guidance, but as a way of providing external respectability, of showing that Christianity was a religion with a past. On the whole people don't write 'scripture'; they write (very possibly believing themselves to be doing so by inspiration of the Spirit), but time has to pass before what they have written becomes 'scripture'. If they want to write scripture they do so pseudepigraphically in the name of some past saint or hero, or else they find it conveniently hidden in the temple.

Thus a written record hints at the changeless, primeval character of religion; it suggests that religion is concerned with the eternal rather than the ephemeral. It is a standing corrective against the shallowness of a religion that in its passionate concern with the present moment has lost its hold on that dimension.

That is an important function; and a religion without holy scriptures would be in grave danger of losing something vital. But can they fulfil that role without at the same time doing even greater harm? New knowledge arises; moral standards change (often for the better). The immorality of Homer's gods, for example, came to be regarded as intolerable. His poems as a result were to be excluded from Plato's ideal republic and he himself consigned (as in Pythagoras' dream) to Hades, where he was depicted suspended from a tree and surrounded by serpents, together with those who had neglected their wives, because of the things he had said about the gods.[5] Alternatively his lively stories could be allegorized into cosmogonical myths as by the Stoics. Christians too have often become involved in similar spiritual contortions, and indeed still do so to this day as pious congregations find themselves exulting in the hope of vengeance upon Babylon and singing, 'Blessed shall he be that taketh thy children and throweth them against the stones.'[6]

But there are other, less obvious, dangers too. Plato's suspicion of books, that characterized his later years, was more broadly based than simply on his objection to the immorality of Homer's gods. Books could never fully express the doctrine they were intended to convey; some readers were sure to misunderstand them and the book was unable to defend or to explain itself.[7] Moreover once books come to be revered as authorities, they encourage false short-cuts to knowledge. A. D. Nock declared that 'throughout the imperial period one of the conspicuous features of intellectual life is a readiness to accept statements because they were in books or even because they were said to be in books'.[8] So in later centuries the writings of Aristotle were regarded as rendering otiose the careful observations of the naturalist. Once grant that your book has the authority of God himself and such tendencies will be further exaggerated. Economic research and moral enquiry are not of central importance if the holy book already contains for you the essential insights into the proper ordering of society and an unchanging code of ethical behaviour. The use of the Bible to strengthen the forces of reaction is written large on the pages of history.

Now there is of course much else within the pages of the Bible that not only permits but insists on radical change. The New Testament's critique of the Old carries within it an implicit protest against the very way in which it has itself so often been regarded in the past. That respect for the past which the very existence of a holy scripture embodies and makes effective must for the Christian be dialectically combined with the ruthless criticism of life lived in the Spirit, that wind whose source and destination no man can tell.

2. *Escape from subjectivity*

For the most part the religious believer has (or should have) a healthy distrust of his own subjective judgments. He seeks escape from the smallness and the sinfulness implicit in a purely private, personal perspective. His faith is in that which is other than and greater than himself. He longs for objectivity, a sense of his faith as something given rather than something self-induced. So he sees holy scripture not merely as something coming to him with the givenness that belongs to the past as a whole; it is in some special way given by God. Thus the Old Testament law was not only found in the temple, some of it at least was written with the finger of God. A part of the Egyptian *Book of the Dead* was similarly found under a statue of the god Thoth and written in the writing of the god himself.[9] The Qur'an too was dictated by the angel Gabriel; and, as if that were not sufficient, later tradition (in direct contradiction of the text of the Qur'an itself) went on to recount how Muhammad ascended into heaven and received it directly from the very hands of God.[10]

But however strong the insistence on a direct divine source of holy scripture, it has never long been possible to avoid a balancing emphasis on the need for divine illumination of the reader also. Thus the Calvinist tradition has emphasized the need for the *'testimonium internum spiritus sancti'* and we find a Muslim Sufi declaring that 'no understanding of the Holy Book is possible until it is actually revealed to the believer as it was revealed to the prophet'.[11]

Such developments force us to ask how effectively a written record can fulfil its role as a source of genuine objectivity. Men certainly can evade its force by allegorical or other means and often do so, albeit unconsciously. Nevertheless it is some sort of check. It takes some getting round. Words have a firmer shape of meaning than symbolic acts or visual representation. And this, I take it, is at least a part of what lies behind the insistence of the Reformed tradition on the primacy of audition over against vision as the model by which knowledge of God ought to be construed—a theme much emphasized by Professor Torrance in his recent writings.[12] Words, and still more written words, have a tougher element of objectivity about them. We may be able to escape their implications by self-deception, but we would deceive ourselves more easily without them.

In the *Confessions* of Augustine there is an instructive discussion which serves to show how limited this provision of objectivity is. It is easier, he argues, to be confident of the fact of God's creation of all things visible and invisible than it is to be certain of what Moses intended by the opening verses of the book of Genesis. Our primary concern therefore has to be with what is true rather than with what is the meaning of the written text. He goes on:

> When [a man] says 'Moses did not mean what *you* say, but what *I* say,' and then does not deny what either of us says but allows that *both* are true—then, O my God, life of the poor, in whose breast there is no contradiction, pour thy soothing balm into my heart that I may patiently bear with people who talk like this! It is not because they are godly men and have seen in the heart of thy

servant what they say, but rather they are proud men and have not considered Moses' meaning, but only love their own—not because it is true but because it is their own.[13]

We are in no position to tell how fair Augustine is being to his critics. But there is no denying the shrewdness of his psychological insight. Men do undoubtedly read back their own meanings into the sacred text. And their capacity for doing so, albeit in good faith and without, at least at the conscious level, the perverted motives which Augustine ascribes to his opponents, is no harmless eccentricity. For having once convinced themselves that their meaning is the objective meaning of the sacred text, they then hold it with a renewed fanaticism as something which comes to them with the direct authority of God himself. It is a high price to pay for something that originates in a proper desire to escape from the dangers of subjectivity.

The question that then forces itself upon us is this. Can we be free of such dangers while still holding on to 'holy scripture' as a *symbol* of that objectivity, that otherness, that address to us which is at the heart of faith in a personal God? If we should no longer find it possible to see the Bible as characterized by that distinctive form of divine address which theories of inspiration have attempted to delineate, or if we have already become fully aware of the way in which any such divine address is inextricably intermingled with the fallibility of its human form both in its original expression and in its interpretation, can the concept of 'holy scripture' still fulfil such a role even symbolically? Or would any such idea be more likely to mislead than to serve the cause of truth?

3. *Focus of community*

Homer may have been consigned by Pythagoras to Hades, but the primary school-children of the Hellenistic world were made to inscribe in their exercise books, as their first essay in writing, the words 'Homer was not a man but a god'.[14] The poetic tradition, with Homer at its heart, provided for the Hellenistic age 'a fundamental homogeneity which made communication and genuine communion easier'. Men had in common 'the same metaphors, images, words—the same language'.[15] It ensured a basic unity of culture, in much the same way that the Bible and Shakespeare did in England a hundred years ago.[16]

In the same sort of way a fixed canon (like a fixed liturgy) provides a focus of unity for the Christian community, a common source of religious imagery; it needs to be large enough to provide for the rich variety of men's religious needs but compact enough to function as a source of common sensibility.

Its importance as a unifying agent can be illustrated historically. The fixing of the Mosaic canon is linked with Ezra's rebuilding of the Jewish state in conscious opposition to the surrounding peoples. It is no coincidence that the final fixing of the Jewish canon follows so swiftly on the heels of the fall of Jerusalem. The creation of the Christian canon was connected with the need to deal with the threats posed by Marcionites and by Gnostics.

But that method of securing unity over against the challenge of heretical ideas has its limitations. It is a card you can play only once. Having made the canon large enough to rule out Marcion and selective enough to deal with the Gnostics, there was need to find some other way of responding to the later challenges of an Arius or a Luther.

But there are more subtle dangers than those associated with the problem of heresy. The literary canon that is compact enough to be the basis of a common culture is unlikely to be rich enough to sustain that role indefinitely. The kind of situation which may then arise is vividly depicted by Peter Brown in his description of the Roman writer in the age of Augustine:

> Such a man lived among fellow-connoisseurs who had been steeped too long in too few books. He no longer needed to be explicit; only hidden meanings, rare and difficult words and elaborate circumlocutions, could save his readers from boredom, from *fastidium*, from that loss of interest in the obvious, that afflicts the overcultured man . . . Above all, the narrow canon of acknowledged classics had been charged with a halo of 'Wisdom': an intellectual agility quite alien to modern man, would have to be deployed constantly to extract the inexhaustible treasure that, it was felt, must lie hidden in so cramped a quarry.[17]

The natural outcome for the Christian writer in Augustine's day was the regular use of fanciful interpretations of an allegorical kind. But in eschewing the vagaries of allegorical method, we have not thereby freed ourselves from the fundamental problem. Are not some of the difficulties faced by the Roman writer whom Peter Brown describes shared by the authors of the continuous stream of biblical commentaries today? Do not many New Testament interpreters find themselves more or less forced into putting forward far-fetched interpretations in the desperate hope of saying something new, of being 'original' in the sense demanded by examinations for the Doctorate of Philosophy? The way in which a fixed canon provides a shared resource of faith and spirituality for all Christians is a blessing, but it is a mixed blessing.

These are not, of course, the only functions that holy scripture might serve in Christian faith. I have not attempted to explore uses of scripture which arise primarily from the distinctiveness of Christianity. But they seem to me to be three significant ways in which holy books in general, and the Bible in particular, have functioned. All three are religiously important functions which ought to find a place within the life of the church, even though they also have their inherent dangers. If 'holy scripture' is given too absolute a position, then the good that it can convey is likely to be outweighed by the evil that it can also bring with it. But it does not need to be given an absolutist position for the fulfilment of these three roles.

If then these are proper ways of understanding the role of holy scripture within Christian faith, what implications do they have for the interpretation of scripture? The Bible, we are sometimes told, should be studied and interpreted as any other book. That demand is one way of expressing the insistence that the Bible must not be exempted in deference to false piety from all appropriate forms of critical enquiry. But it is not a very satisfactory way of making the point. For how does one interpret 'any other book'? We do not interpret all books identically. To interpret a legal statute is not the same thing as to interpret a novel. They exist for different purposes and we therefore ask different questions of them in the two processes, although we use the one word 'interpretation' for them both.

What then would be involved in interpreting the Bible as 'holy scripture' in the light of the reflections that I have been pursuing here? It would mean discussing it and drawing out its meaning in ways which would enable it to function for us in the three ways that I have tried to describe. This would involve first of all letting it recall for us the primeval nature of those religious traditions out of which our faith comes and for which God cares as fully as he cares for us and for the future. There would be no call to feel ashamed of or try to cover up elements that seem to us strange or crude because they belong to the comparatively primitive origins of religious belief. These would not be in conflict with its role as holy scripture; they would be a proper part of it.

Secondly it would involve letting the Bible symbolize for us the 'over-against-ness' of God. This role stands closest to the traditional understanding of its authority as conveying otherwise inaccessible and wholly reliable knowledge of God. How can such a role continue in a symbolic way once we have come to recognize the need to use our critical judgment and discrimination in determining what is true and what is applicable to our own situation in the biblical record? We would need to be able to see it as something which addresses us in ways that we could not have thought up or invented for ourselves. That is a characteristic of all great literature and of any worthwhile account of occasions of great significance from past history—and clearly on any account the Bible is both those things. It would involve in addition the conviction that the literature and the events recorded are of a kind which (whatever else they may have done) have given rise to true belief about and response to God and have the potentiality of continuing to do so.

Thirdly it would involve seeing the Bible as a common resource of life and spirituality, the provider of a unity of feeling among Christian people. To facilitate its use in this way, what would be called for would be an imaginative development and assimilation of its leading themes and images. This is something that could co-exist (as indeed to some extent it already does) with very great diversity of specific beliefs. No canon, as we have seen, can ever fulfil such a function perfectly. Any selection of writings as an agreed corpus for such a purpose is bound to be somewhat arbitrary. But nor is it something than can be artificially determined by decree from on high. Attempts of that kind to impose a canon are doomed to failure. It is something that has to grow. In the canon of scripture the Christian church has such a growth. Seen in this context the restriction of the canon might more readily be grasped as blessing and not the 'curse of the canon' that Christopher Evans himself has been heard on occasion to describe it.

Critical study of the Bible has often been felt to be in conflict with its role as 'holy scripture'. So, on certain understandings of what constitutes something 'holy scripture', it has often been. It does not cohere readily with the conception that a holy book is first and foremost an authoritative utterance of special divine origin. But in relation to the uses that I have outlined here it would more readily appear as a tool in the service of 'holy scripture'.

NOTES

1. C. F. Evans, *Is 'Holy Scripture' Christian?*, SCM Press 1971.
2. Ibid., p. 36.
3. Ibid., pp. 29–30.
4. Basil Mitchell, *The Justification of Religious Belief*, Macmillan 1973, pp. 155–6.
5. See Diogenes Laertius, *Vitae Philosophorum*, VIII 21.
6. Ps. 137.9.
7. W. Jaeger, *Paideia*, Vol. III, Berlin 1947, p. 269; ET Blackwell 1945, pp. 194–5.
8. A. D. Nock, *Conversion*, Oxford 1933, p. 241.
9. S. G. F. Brandon, 'The Holy Book, the Holy Tradition and the Holy Ikon' in *Holy Book and Holy Tradition*, F. F. Bruce and E. G. Rupp (eds.), Manchester University Press 1968, p. 15.
10. G. Widengren, 'Holy Book and Holy Tradition in Islam' in op. cit., p. 219.
11. M. Iqbal, *The Reconstruction of Religious Thought in Islam*, Kashmiri Bazar, Lahore 1962, p. 181.
12. T. F. Torrance, *Theology in Reconstruction*, SCM Press 1965, pp. 21–2, 58, 87–8; *Theological Science*, Oxford University Press 1969, pp. 22–3. Torrance himself gives to the distinction a far more comprehensive epistemological significance than I have in mind here, or indeed am able to accept.
13. Augustine, *Confessions* XII. xxiv–xxv. 33–4.
14. H. I. Marrou, *Histoire de l'éducation dans l'antiquité*, 6th edition, Paris 1965, p. 246; ET, *A History of Education in Antiquity*, Sheed and Ward 1956, p. 162.
15. Ibid., p. 333 (ET p. 224).
16. See W. Jaeger, op. cit., Vol. II, p. 289 (ET p. 214). Jaeger compares its authority with that of the Bible and the church fathers in the Christian era.
17. P. Brown, *Augustine of Hippo*, Faber 1967, pp. 259–60.

13

The Myth of the Church
A Case Study in the Use of Scripture
for Christian Doctrine*

JOHN AUSTIN BAKER

'THE Myth of the Church' may seem a mere catchpenny title. God may be a 'myth'; the incarnation, the resurrection and the Holy Spirit may be 'myths'. The church is but too, too solid flesh, the only thing about Christianity which will not melt at the touch of the demythologizer. Nevertheless, the phrase is deliberately chosen and seriously meant.

'The church' is a term which can be used to refer to either of two very different things. The first reference is to that loose aggregation of millions of people all over the world associated by a single fact, namely that all their individual communities trace their origin ultimately to the person of Jesus. The church in this sense is not a myth; it is an empirical fact.

The second reference, however, is much harder to define. Here we are concerned with the 'church' of Christian doctrine: the body of the incarnate God, and his eternal, heavenly bride; an integral part of God's plan, conceived in the beginning, but a part that is to be perfected only at the ending of all things; the people of God, the elect remnant, but also the new human race, the sacrament of salvation to all mankind; the anonymous suffering servant, and yet one holy, universal,

*It was in the autumn of 1951 that the study of the New Testament suddenly came alive for me. The occasion was an essay on the meaning of 'being in Christ'; and the tutor who set the essay and made the dry bones live was, of course, Christopher Evans. It is in gratitude for a turning-point in my life that I (in this respect only one of a great army of students) offer here a lineal descendant of that juvenile but enthusiastic effort.

apostolic host, 'terrible as an army with banners'. There is no empirical reality to which this church exactly corresponds. It is, in this sense, a myth.

This is not another form of the old 'visible-invisible' distinction. The so-called 'invisible church' was always an empirical reality in principle, because 'the Lord knows who are his', even if we do not. The mythical church is non-empirical in principle for two reasons: first, because it is in part an eschatological reality, something which does not yet exist, even if it is on the way to existing; secondly, because none of its members in this life, however holy and faithful, measures up to its essential character. Yet the 'church' here is not being thought of simply as an ideal, a mental concept clothed in a variety of images in order to be a goal and stimulus of action. For bound up with this use is the conviction that these images are also realities, that they have taken on flesh and blood, and are, by some mysterious relationship, present in the world through the empirical church. Thus, Vatican II's 'Dogmatic Constitution on the Church' identifies the church with 'Jerusalem which is on high, the Mother of us all' in Gal. 4.26, and defines it as 'the kingdom of Christ, now present in mystery'. It is the holy city which comes down from God, 'when the world is made anew'. 'The life of the Church is hidden with Christ in God until she appears in glory with her Spouse.' The crux of the matter is summed up in the following passage:

> The society furnished with hierarchical agencies and the Mystical Body of Christ are not to be considered as two realities, nor are the visible assembly and the spiritual community, nor the earthly Church and the Church enriched with heavenly things. Rather they form one interlocked reality which is comprised of a divine and a human element. For this reason, by an excellent analogy, this reality is compared to the mystery of the incarnate Word. Just as the assumed nature inseparably united to the divine Word serves Him as a living instrument of salvation, so, in a similar way, does the communal structure of the Church serve Christ's Spirit, who vivifies it by way of building up the body.[1]

Such a treatment of the church is, of course, nothing new. It runs right back through Christian history to the sub-apostolic age, where we find it in Hermas, for example, or in the famous distinction in *II Clement* between 'the first church, which is spiritual, which was created before the sun and moon', 'the church of life, . . . the body of Christ', on the one hand, and the house that 'was made a den of robbers', on the other. It is, moreover, a characteristic of this very widespread and important stream in Christian thinking that it draws heavily upon New Testament images. Indeed, at first glance it seems to be more broadly and solidly rooted in the New Testament than almost any other department of Christian theology. It is, therefore, instructive to look at the New Testament material and to see how tiny in fact is the basis for it there; to ask what were the pressures and processes that produced it; and to realize that once again it is the feedback from the developed doctrine which makes so many Christians read the New Testament in a particular way. Only when we have done this can we ask if any practical conclusions on the use of the New Testament for doctrine suggest themselves.

To begin with the word ἐκκλησία: the background is in part, of course, the everyday environment of the Hellenistic world. Thus, in Acts 19 we find Luke using the word quite naturally both of the anti-Christian mob assembled in the theatre and of the lawful assembly which forms part of the government of the city. Another element in the semantic colour is the Old Testament qāhāl, the congregation of the people of God; and it is perhaps this sense which is most likely to underlie the use of ἐκκλησία in Matthew's gospel.

The word ἐκκλησία occurs in the New Testament III times. Of these instances, 44 refer to individual local communities of Christians; another 28 are in the plural and refer to such communities collectively. There are ten New Testament books in which the word does not occur at all: Mark, Luke, John, II Timothy, Titus, I Peter, II Peter, I John, II John and Jude. There are a further seven books in which it occurs only in the senses already mentioned, of a specific local church or churches: II Corinthians, I Thessalonians, II Thessalonians, Philemon, James, III John and Revelation. Of the other Pauline epistles, four—Romans, I Corinthians, Galatians and Philippians—add only one extra use, that is, to refer in a purely denotative way to the empirical church at large, the whole body of Christians everywhere. In Acts we find all these three uses plus four others. Two have already been mentioned. The others are: first, the rank and file of the Jersualem church, as distinct from the apostles and presbyters (15.4, 22—a strange reversal of later popular usage!); and secondly, the 'ἐκκλησία of God' (20.28), where the reference is to the local Ephesian church, but characterized as the *qāhāl* of God's elect people, 'purchased with his own blood'.[2]

This leaves four New Testament books: Hebrews, I Timothy, Colossians and Ephesians. Hebrews contains two instances: one, in the sense of *qāhāl*, is a quotation from Ps. 22 (Heb. 2.12); the other (12.23) comes in the phrase 'the festal assembly and congregation of the first-born, whose names are written in heaven'. The context is 'the city of the living God, heavenly Jerusalem, and myriads of angels', in fact, the country sought by that great company of 'just men made perfect', so magnificently surveyed in the preceding chapter. The composite phrase, πανηγύρει καὶ ἐκκλησίᾳ, is suggestive. πανήγυρις is a gathering of citizens for a great festival; hence in this context ἐκκλησία most naturally takes its neutral sense of 'assembly', the assembly of the inhabitants of the heavenly city. It may be doubted, therefore, whether either instance of the word in Hebrews has in mind the 'church' as such at all. I Timothy, however, most certainly does. In 3.5 and 5.16 the reference is to the empirical Christian community, thought of primarily as a household or family. In 3.15 this household is called ἐκκλησία θεοῦ ζῶντος, στῦλος καὶ ἑδραίωμα τῆς ἀληθείας: the Christian congregation is chosen by God to be in the world the 'pillar and buttress' of the truth about him and his salvation in Christ, presumably, if we follow the rest of the epistle, by denouncing and expelling heretics and by teaching a form of sound words. But the reference is still purely to an empirical group of people, God's household not in any mystical sense but because, like any secular household, they belong to the paterfamilias.

Colossians and Ephesians call for more careful examination. Col. 4.15f. creates a celebrated problem, but the sense of ἐκκλησία here is clear enough: the local congregation. 1.18, 24, however, open up new issues. 1.18 reads: 'And he is the head of the body, the church—he who is Beginning (ἀρχή), first-born from the dead, that in everything he might be one who is supreme.' The chapter as a whole is concerned to assert Christ's absolute priority and super-eminence over everything, visible and invisible, in heaven and earth, God only excepted. Thus, Christ is source and origin of the created order (ἀρχή = *rē'šīt*: Gen. 1.1), first of those glorified by the new creation, the resurrection, and ruler of the ἐκκλησία. Two points need to be noted here. First, the inclusion of ἐκκλησία in such a series—the whole creation, the army of the resurrected, the church—at once gives the church a more portentous role. We are taken far beyond the plain mundane fact of the local congregation, or even of the whole company of Christian people dispersed throughout the world. ἐκκλησία is now a work of mystery and power, a part of God's grand design, comparable to the creation and the raising of Jesus from the dead. Secondly, there is the explicit identification, both here and in 1.24, of Christ's body as the ἐκκλησία. Paul's high conception of the mystical union between Christ and the believer undoubtedly supplies a very suitable basis for this new vision of the cosmic significance of the church.[3] Nevertheless, it remains true that in the 'body' passages in Romans and I Corinthians the 'body'/ἐκκλησία equation is never explicitly made. There is here a small but crucial shift in language to which we shall return in a moment.

In Ephesians there are affinities with Colossians, but also important, if marginal, developments. In 1.22 we find the words, 'the ἐκκλησία, which is his body'. In 3.10 the hidden plan of God's complex wisdom is manifested to the celestial powers by means of the ἐκκλησία; that is to say, the church is the only place where mankind is unified by the abolition of the barrier between Jew and Gentile, and so is the only means of publicizing God's primordial and private intention. In 3.21 the writer coins, perhaps without much meaning, one of his grandiose phrases (which would hardly have come spontaneously to Paul): glory is ascribed to God 'in the ἐκκλησία and in Christ Jesus'.[4]

In 5.23–32 we have the famous parallel between a husband's best devotion to his wife and Christ's dealings with the church; but interwoven with this is another theme, that Christ's sacrificial death was undergone in order that he might in turn present the church to himself, washed pure in baptism, unblemished like a perfect sacrificial victim. In all this two main points are significant. First, in Colossians we have the wording 'the body, the ἐκκλησία' (1.18) and 'for the sake of his body, which is the ἐκκλησία' (1.24). There, ἐκκλησία is still primarily denotative: 'his body' = 'that identifiable group of people'. But in Ephesians the order is reversed: 'he gave him as head over all things to the ἐκκλησία, which is his body' (1.22). Here the attitude of mind has very slightly but significantly changed. Now, 'Christ's body' has become the definition of the ἐκκλησία; we have moved into the realm of a 'theology of the church'. This increasing concern with the metaphysical reality of the church shows itself more seriously in the second point: the church is now thought of less as God's instrument in saving the world, and more as the object and indeed the end-product of his salvation. This process had already begun in Colossians, where it was the vocation of the apostle to suffer for the sake of the ἐκκλησία (1.24). In Ephesians, such suffering is the vocation of Christ himself. It is no longer, as in John, 'God so loved the *world* that he gave . . .' (John 3.16), or, as in Paul, 'God was in Christ reconciling the *world* to himself . . .' (II Cor. 5.19), but 'Christ loved the *church*, and gave himself up for her' (Eph. 5.25).

But there is yet another change in language, in the very words just quoted, which is indicative of serious shifts in perspective. In Gal. 2.20 Paul speaks of 'the Son of God who loved *me*, and gave himself for *me*'. Eph. 5.25, as we have just seen, runs: 'Christ loved the *church*, and gave himself for *her*.' The exact correspondence of the other words only highlights the variation, which, moreover, is paralleled in another pair of quotations. In Col. 1.22 Paul wrote: '. . . in order to present *you* holy (ἀγίους) and unblemished (ἀμώμους) . . . before him'. Eph. 5.27, which is partly based on the Colossians passage, speaks of Christ presenting '*the church* to himself . . . that *she* might be holy and unblemished' (ἀγία καὶ ἄμωμος). This change of language is identical with one occurring in a pair of texts crucial to our present concern. In I Cor. 12.27 Paul had written: '*You* are Christ's body, and members in particular'; in Colossians and Ephesians, however, it is not 'you' but the ἐκκλησία which is the body.

We must now widen our scope to take in some material which is plainly not only relevant but important, but in which the actual word ἐκκλησία figures little if at all. First, let us look at the passage from which we have just quoted, Paul's most extended treatment of the body of Christ, I Cor. 12.4–27. The section falls naturally into two parts. In vv. 4–11 we have a catalogue of the gifts of the Spirit; in vv. 14–27 the diversity of these phenomena is explained in terms of the members of a body with their differing functions. Verses 12–13 are the logical link between the two parts. Christ himself is a body with many members, just like your body or mine (v.12); and at our baptism the one Spirit makes us part of that body, because it is Christ's own

Spirit, and just as man's own spirit is found uniquely in his own body, so Christ's Spirit is found uniquely in his body and anyone indwelt by that Spirit is *ipso facto* a member of that body.[5]

This is all the merest ABC of Pauline theology. But the vital point to notice in our present discussion is that the terminology which Paul uses to express his thinking is the personal terminology of union with the unique individual, Jesus Christ. Paul never speaks, as we so readily do, of being made a member of the *church* by baptism, but only of being united with *Christ*. From then on each one can say, 'It is no longer I that live but Christ in me.' The sometimes bewildering legerdemain with which Paul plays around with, 'I in Christ', 'Christ in me', 'the Spirit in me' and 'I in the Spirit', is due simply to the fact that all these expressions refer to the same experience of salvation. It is because Christ himself, through his own personal Spirit, lives in me and in every other Christian, that all of us are related to him as a man's body is to his spirit. But these are the primary categories: Christ, his Spirit, you and I.

The consequence of this, of course, is, and cannot but be, that the body of Christ is the empirical ἐκκλησία. Paul faces the challenge in all its rigour. Sin does not automatically eject one from the body. If it did, Paul could not ask the question: 'Shall I take the members of Christ and make them members of a prostitute?' (I Cor. 6.15). The notorious problem of I Cor. 5.5 underlines how difficult it is to get someone out of the body, so to speak, once they are in. It is the quarrels, arrogance and lustfulness of a community which is in fact the body of Christ which sadden and anger Paul. But he never takes refuge from his anguish in any convenient distinction between the body and the empirical ἐκκλησία.

This is all the more remarkable in view of another fact. To set out the evidence for this would in itself require far more space than the whole of this modest essay, and it must suffice to state the conclusion: Paul is the only New Testament writer who sees moral transformation as one of the works of the Holy Spirit. Apart from one or two possible hints or echoes elsewhere, only Paul looked beyond the charismata bestowed by the Spirit on some members of the ἐκκλησία only; in naming love as the supreme 'way' (I Cor. 12.28–13.13), and listing 'love, joy, peace, longsuffering, kindness, goodness, faithfulness, meekness, temperance' as 'the fruit of the Spirit' (Gal. 5.22f.), he was making a creative theological move unique in the New Testament. But, as we know, he was also creating an immense theological problem. He was prepared to invoke Christ and his Spirit as the only power which, by coming into a man, could deliver him from the tyranny of the sitting tenant, sin (Rom. 7.15–8.2). But how was this conviction to be reconciled with the failure of the empirical church to show forth the fruits of the Spirit? Paul, so far as I can see, offers no solution to this problem. One seeming solution was, however, temptingly available, and that was to distinguish between the 'true' body of Christ and the empirical community, to say, in other words, that the former alone was or would be free from sin's dominion.

We have seen already how a follower of Paul tried to deal with this perplexity: indeed, we understand the writer to the Ephesians much better, once we realize that this is what he is doing. A husband and wife are one flesh; so, in loving his wife a man is loving 'his own flesh', his own 'body' (5.28). But it is also a husband's duty to rule his wife, to be her 'head' (I Cor. 11.3: 'the head of a woman is her husband'—the apostle himself had said so!), and to use his authority to make her a good wife, everything a woman ought to be. So likewise Christ's body is the church, she is his flesh; and he loves her and cares for her, and, as her head, labours to make her everything a church ought to be. In this way, it is hoped, a sufficient degree of detachment is introduced between Christ and the church to allow of the church's sinfulness; and a sufficient degree of intimate mutual belonging is retained not to cut off the fount of saving life. But in fact the expedient does nothing to ease the difficulty. The tension is merely transferred to within the concept of the church itself, and leads in the end to a schizophrenic assessment of the church as simultaneously transcendent and perfect on the one hand, and a sinful body in process of being perfected on the other. We can see this incipient tendency developing if we compare yet again Eph. 5.26f. with Col. 1.21f. on which it is based. Colossians runs: ' . . . you who were estranged . . . he has now reconciled in his body of flesh by his death, in order to present you holy and unblemished and irreproachable before him.' This quite certainly concerns a projected perfecting of the empirical church, because it continues 'provided that you continue in the faith'. But in Ephesians there is no proviso. It is taken for granted that Christ will succeed in presenting the ἐκκλησία to himself in the divine realm of glory, to be his holy bride, the perfect oblation. What matters to you and me, therefore, is that 'when the roll is called up yonder' we should be there, that we should be of that number, 'when the saints go marching in'. The crucial necessity is to belong to the church, and, what is more, to the elect and perfect church. To this there is no plausible door save through the empirical church; but in that case there must be such a coinherence of the heavenly church and the empirical church that entry into the latter is also an assurance of access to the former. From this point onwards the creating of a 'theology of the church' is simply a matter of explication; the vital first moves have already been made.

Before turning to our concluding reflections on the relation of the New Testament to Christian doctrine, we must take a look at two passages in the fourth gospel which have also often been regarded as classic *loci* for a doctrine of the church, though in fact, as I hope to show, they are nothing of the kind.

Let us begin with the discourse on the vine in John 15.1–17. The first thing to note is that this is not a treatise about anything at all; it is a word of enlightenment and exhortation addressed to individuals both in themselves and in their relations with one another. These individuals are the 'friends' of Jesus, and they are told that their ability to make something of their lives depends entirely on their remaining wholly united with and supported by Jesus, as he is united with and supported by God. Since each is a friend of Jesus they must perforce be friends of each other, or their relationship with Jesus and his Father is contradicted, made nonsensical. The discourse then is indeed about a 'community', but the community is a product of a whole series of individual encounters with and responses to Jesus, and it is on these individual responses that abiding in Jesus and bearing fruit depend. If there were but one person left in the whole world, and he were to pick this up and read it, it could still, as it stands, speak significantly to him, because at its heart what it is about is Jesus as the one source of fruitful life for each human soul. 'I am the true vine'; not, 'I in my corporate extension, the church', but, 'I, Jesus, the individual who speaks to you'. The jump to the church can be made only by what are illegitimate exegetical expedients; by saying, for example, that since in the Old Testament the vine is Israel, here the vine must be the new Israel, that is, of course, the church, which is then understood as in some sense also Christ. But if Old Testament echoes are present, then the meaning surely is: 'I,

Jesus, am the new Israel, the true Israel, in my own person; and you, if you want to be saved, must join yourselves not in the first place to any society, but to me.'

There is in this passage a further feature which is of interest because it so clearly differentiates John's idea of the vine from Paul's conception of the body of Christ. In John, 'If a man does not abide in me, he is cast forth as a branch, and withers; and the branches are gathered, thrown into the fire, and burned' (15.6). Existence in the vine is something which depends wholly on the individual's abiding in Christ and in his commandments of love. This means that the vine may or may not at any given moment be co-terminous with the empirical church. The casting forth in the parabolic statement may allude to the last day; it is not, in the opinion of most exegetes, a reference to excommunication. John is here stating a truth of the Christian life which Paul too would have regarded as essential—personal union with Christ—but makes no attempt to define how this may work out in terms of membership of the ἐκκλησία or of the nature of that community. One possible reason for this could be that this is not the subject he thinks he is talking about.[6]

We must, I would suggest, dissent from the majority of commentators, when they find in this section a discourse on the church. C. K. Barrett's verdict is typical: ' . . . John's doctrine of the church is summed up in the two great symbolic discourses, that of the Shepherd . . . and that of the Vine'.[7] The one glorious exception is Bultmann. His exposition of this passage[8] is an absolute model in the way in which the balance and emphasis of the text are conveyed with scrupulous fidelity. The fact is that John is not interested in the church as such, because it is his view that, if—and only if—the basic essentials are right, then the church can be left to look after itself. It will just happen.

Much the same comment may be made about the other passage which Barrett notes as containing John's 'doctrine of the church', that of the shepherd (10.1–16). Indeed, the ecclesiological interpretation here is perhaps even more crass, because the concern of the passage is so obviously with mankind. Men recognize Jesus as the good shepherd because he is not concerned to exploit or oppress them, nor does he abandon them when they are in direst need. His only object is that they shall have life, even if it means the sacrifice of his own. This is the acid test; other leaders of men will not, when it comes to the point, make that sacrifice, because in the last analysis they are in the game for what they can get. Of Jesus alone is this not true, and men realize it, and trust him. And not only will Jews trust him, but men of all nations and races, who will find themselves forming one community because they hear the voice of the one shepherd.[9]

The time has come to relate our material to the formation of Christian doctrine, and to see what lessons, if any, it holds for us. The first and most obvious point to make is that the New Testament basis for anything that we might legitimately call a 'theology of the church' is minute.[10] Moreover, should any reader feel (not unreasonably) that some of the present discussion has sought to split some extremely fine hairs, it will be as well to point out that, had we not done so, there would have been no basis at all for that magnificent structure we call the 'doctrine of the church'. For it would not be hard to interpret even Ephesians so as to bring it into comfortable harmony with the rest. Nevertheless, to do so would, I am convinced, be mistaken. It is there (and there alone) that there is evidence of that small but significant shift in attitude which was necessary before the traditional doctrine of the church could be elaborated.

The second point—again an obvious one—is that, once this doctrine of the church has been formulated in its essentials, then all kinds of New Testament material that originally had nothing directly to do with it are drawn in and used to illustrate it; and this with such effect that thereafter, exegesis of the New Testament takes it for granted that these passages were originally written precisely in order to express a doctrine of the church. It looks, therefore, as though the particular form of ecclesiology we are considering must have some very powerful intrinsic attraction for Christians.

Nor is it hard to guess what this attraction might be. No man has seen God at any time; Jesus is no longer on earth; the Holy Spirit comes and goes; but the church is a contemporary fact that cannot be denied or disbelieved. Unfortunately the church is sometimes also a rather depressing and far from obviously salvific fact. But suppose that these somewhat unconvincing externals are truly the medium of divine and saving realities, that there is, as it were, at any rate a one-way *communicatio idiomatum*, so that 'when the church spits, her spittle is divine',[11] then the assurance of salvation becomes as solid as her buildings, as tangible as her eucharistic elements, as audible as her psalms, and our morale is rendered superhuman by the consciousness of belonging to a visible army against which even the gates of death cannot hope to stand.

But such confidence can in the end justly be reposed in God alone. The myth of the church, by creating a false ontological backing in the divine order for an earthly reality easier to rest in than God, actively comes between us and the one thing in which we ought to be trusting. By all means let us say that through the empirical church we come into a real relationship with God;[12] but let us also face the fact that this happens through an empirical church which is very often a disgrace and a disaster, and let us not pander to our reluctance to face this by inventing an imaginary ideal *persona* for our community. To do that is just as infantile for a church as for an individual (where we more readily recognize it). Much about the church is holy and beautiful, true and good; much is none of those things. Paul had to learn to live with that fact, and so must we.

It would be easy to draw the wrong conclusions from all this for our use of the New Testament in the Christian doctrinal enterprise. We might adopt the principle of taking, so to say, a majority vote of the New Testament witnesses, and calling the result 'the central message of the New Testament'. Or we might say, 'Anything in the New Testament is inspired, and the fact that, according to you, the doctrine of the church is supported only by a few sentences in one epistle is neither here nor there. It is in the sacred text somewhere, and that is what matters.' Or again, we could argue that if, starting from the New Testament, the church comes to some new apprehension of truth, then that is self-authenticating, and lack of biblical support is unimportant. No doubt it is improper to read such a doctrine back into the text if indeed it is not there; but that does not affect the worth of the doctrine in itself.

All these positions have been adopted in the past, and are adopted today; and the defects in all of them are well known. But if our case-study has any positive lesson for the doctrinal exercise, it is, I suggest, none of these. It does instead tell us two things. First, that when we come across a problematic element in our Christian thinking it is always as well to look back to the New Testament, because as like as not we shall find it there already in essence. And secondly, that when we do find it, we shall also find that the treatments of it are in many cases much freer and more varied than our own, provided always that we read them without the aid of our existing doctrinal spectacles. Nothing can exempt us from the duty of stating our own beliefs in our own words. But there are many false turnings on the roads of Christian dogma, and the New Testament more than any other part of our heritage can help us to retrace our steps.

NOTES

1. The Dogmatic Constitution of the Church, ch. 1, art. 3, 6–8, quoted from *The Documents of Vatican II*, ET ed. W. M. Abbott, Chapman 1966, pp. 16, 19–22.

2. This phrase implies what is arguably the highest christology to be found anywhere in the NT—if, that is, we could assume Luke to be a writer who set store by theological precision!

3. It is highly probable that the change from Christ as the whole body to Christ as the head of the body is prompted simply by the scheme of pre-eminence running through the section, and possibly also by an underlying dependence on exegesis of Gen. 1.

4. It is not proposed to discuss the notorious *pleroma*-clause of 1.22f. There is not space to do it justice, and any conclusions would be too tentative to advance our main theme.

5. This is entirely consonant with Paul's view of baptism in Rom. 6.3, where the union with Christ effected by baptism is so personal and intimate that the baptized person can be said to have passed in some real sense through Christ's own death and resurrection. Cf. Gal. 2.20.

6. The First Epistle of John does say something bearing on this subject (2.19: 'They went out from us, but they were not of us; for if they had been of us, they would have continued with us. But [this happened] that they might be made manifest as being, every one of them, not of us'). But this assessment seems simplistic and over-sanguine compared with other NT treatments.

7. C. K. Barrett, *The Gospel according to St John*, SPCK 1955, p. 82.

8. R. Bultmann, *The Gospel of John*, Blackwell 1971, pp. 529–47.

9. If the OT background is significant, then it simply reinforces this interpretation, since 'shepherd' in the OT is a term for secular rulers, or for God fulfilling the functions of such a ruler.

10. The obvious omission in our survey is I Peter 2. 5–10, which by means of a variety of OT images presents the empirical church as a replacement for the old Israel. Its influence in Christian theology has been considerable, especially through its references to Christians as a 'priesthood', but it is none the less not directly relevant to the particular strand in Christian theology we are considering. It therefore seemed better to draw attention to it but not discuss it in detail.

11. Cf. Athanasius, *ad Serap.* IV. 14: 'He spat as a man, and the spittle was divine.'

12. The passage from Vatican II quoted above does, it should in fairness be pointed out, conclude by saying precisely this.

14

The Preacher and the Biblical Critic

JOHN FENTON

THE practical problem with which we are concerned in this
essay arises every week: what is the preacher to do when, as a
result of historical criticism, his understanding of a biblical
text is considerably different from that of the congregation to whom
he is to preach? Should he declare his views, or should he conceal them?
Is he to look for some way of speaking, by which he can satisfy his
own conscience without disturbing the minds of others, or should
this not be his intention?

The areas in which the problem arises are numerous and well
known, but it may be worth mentioning three, at this point. First,
the authenticity of sayings attributed to Jesus in the gospels; particularly in John's gospel, but not only there. Do you say, 'Jesus said
that he was the good shepherd', if you do not believe that he did?
Do you say, 'Jesus promised to be present where two or three had
met together in his name', if you do not think that this saying is
authentic, in the sense that it was said by Jesus before the crucifixion,
which is probably how most people would understand 'Jesus promised'?[1] Second, the historicity of certain events, not only in the
Old Testament but also in the New. The preacher who uses the gospel
lections provided by The Book of Common Prayer (1662) has to deal
with a feeding miracle three times a year (Lent IV, Trinity VII and
XXV): is he to mention the fact that some commentators have seen
many problems in these stories and that it may not be possible to say
anything as to what actually happened? Third, there is the area of
beliefs held by biblical writers, which seem to many people no longer
tenable in the form in which the biblical writers held them: for ex-

178

ample, the opinion that epilepsy is caused by demonic possession, or the belief that Christ will soon return to the earth for the last judgment.

A partial solution can be dealt with immediately, both because it is uncontroversial, and because it is only a partial solution. Everybody who admits the existence of the problem will also agree that not all situations are the same, and that in certain circumstances there need be little doubt what the appropriate procedure should be; in particular, that the ability of a specific congregation may be such that a full-scale treatment of the matter will be in order. An example that immediately springs to mind in this connection is the series of sermons which Professor Evans preached in Pusey House Chapel in the Hilary Term of 1963.[2] In that situation, surely, the preacher was right to think that his hearers would be helped rather than hindered through being asked to consider questions raised by biblical criticism: for example, *à propos* the miracle at Cana:

> May not the symbolic truth have flowed over into the story of the event, and moulded it to an exact expression of itself? May not in some cases the spiritual truth have created the event?[3]

Or, *à propos* the stilling of the storm:

> So, then, the storm in the sea is a demon, and the great calm is produced by the expulsion of the demon. Behind this lies a very old semitic idea of the sea, or the legendary sea-monster, as the source and embodiment of chaos in the world, and in this story it joins up with a later Jewish idea of demons as the cause of frenzied disturbance in the world. And we do not believe it.[4]

It is interesting to compare Professor Evans' method with that of the late Dr Farrer, who continued and concluded the course in the same place and in the same term: neither in these four sermons, nor, I think, elsewhere in his published sermons, do we find the same direct treatment of historical and critical problems, as in those of Professor Evans; and in some of Dr Farrer's writing this refusal to deal with problems of this kind weakens the force of what he is saying: see, for example, the sermon on the temptations for Lent I[5], and the longer treatment of the subject in *The Triple Victory*; e.g., 'I hold it to be utterly pointless to discuss what evidence St Matthew had for the detail he supplies.'[6]

Everyone will agree that it is appropriate in certain circumstances for the preacher to enter into a consideration of critical problems, and that the criterion is the ability of the congregation to profit from this kind of discussion: a service for students might be thought to be such an occasion, and others would be gatherings of clergy, lay-readers, sixth formers, and so on. Nevertheless, this is a minute fraction of the total. What is the preacher to do on a normal occasion, or when the congregation consists of people of mixed ability?

A solution that has often been proposed starts out from the observation that the business of preaching is to be distinguished clearly and strictly from the business of preparing a sermon, and proceeds to the point that there is no need for the preacher to 'show his working' in the course of preaching the sermon itself. He should apply to the text all the tools of criticism, to the best of his ability, in his study; but in the pulpit he should preach the word which he has heard, without disclosing the method by which he has received it. This way of dealing with the problem, it could be claimed, can be applied in all situations, whatever the ability of the congregation.

Thus, to take the three areas already mentioned: in relation to the authenticity of sayings of Jesus, there is no need to attribute sayings to Jesus at all. The gospel is not that Jesus *said* he was the good shepherd, but that he is. Secondly, in relation to the historicity of events, there is no need to speak of events as though they happened. What matters is what they mean. Thirdly, in relation to outmoded biblical beliefs, what you *say* is what the belief represents, and not the belief in its first-century form.

There is nothing new in this proposal. In the final section of the first and second editions of *The Life of Jesus Critically Examined* (1835–6), D. F. Strauss raised the question how the theologian is to proceed in the church; he saw four possible ways: (i) 'To elevate the church to his own point of view'; (ii) 'To transport himself to the point of view of the church'; (iii) to forsake the ministerial office; (iv) to adopt 'a positive mode of reconciling the two extremes—the consciousness of the theologian, and that of the church'. This last was the way he recommended, and this is how he describes it:

In his discourses to the church, he will indeed adhere to the forms of the popular conception, but on every opportunity he will exhibit their spiritual significance, which to him constitutes their sole truth . . . Thus . . . at the festival of Easter, he will indeed set out from the sensible fact of the resurrection of Christ, but he will dwell chiefly on the being buried and rising again with Christ, which the Apostle himself has strenuously inculcated.[7]

There is much to be said in favour of this method. For example, it recognizes that preaching is meant to be positive, the proclamation of good news, from faith to faith; and it distinguishes clearly between criticism and the opinions of men on the one side, and the gospel on the other. Again, it takes full account of the unsuitability of the sermon as an occasion for introducing historical, literary-critical and philo-sophical arguments; these, it recognizes, are much better kept for situations in which there can be discussion and questions (e.g. study-groups or lectures); they do not fit easily into liturgical occasions, at least as liturgy has been understood and practised in the past. Thirdly, it avoids the consequences of the fact that biblical scholars do not agree among themselves; if the preacher is not required to show how he has travelled from the biblical text to the message which he proclaims, but is simply to proclaim the message itself, then the contradictory opinions of the scholars on all the problems—authenticity, historicity and credibility—need never come into the open. Points such as these can be made in favour of the proposal that the methods of criticism be kept separate from the activity of preaching, much as the sound of hammer and axe was not heard in the temple while it was being built; yet there is much to be said on the other side.

First, this procedure is open to the charge of clericalism, paternalism, élitism. The preacher is deciding that it is appropriate for him to study scripture critically, but that it is not appropriate for the congregation to whom he is preaching. On what grounds does he make this judg-ment, and is he justified in making it? May he not be deluding himself into thinking that he is a superior being, and that others are not fit to be admitted into the secret circle of gnostics to which his training and ability have given him entrance? How can he be sure that he is not surrendering to the temptation to make things easier for himself? Since we would expect the bias to be in favour of proceeding by the easier way, we should doubt the validity of the arguments that seem to favour it.

Secondly, this way of dealing with the matter, for all its good and positive aspects, does nothing to change the situation; it leaves it as it finds it: the gap between the preacher's understanding of scripture and that of the congregation is perpetuated. It cannot be right that this should be so. On the one side, it places the preacher in increasing isolation from his hearers, and neither is this good for him, nor does it make for effective preaching; and on the other side, it leaves the congregation in a vulnerable position, because they will have no defence against those who attack the naiveté of their faith.[8]

Further, there is what can only be described as a certain faithlessness in this approach to the problem. It separates the inspiration of the biblical critic from the inspiration of the congregation, as if the source of each were not identical. If God is one, and truth is one, then there is nothing that is to be kept secret from the congregation on the grounds that it belongs only to the province of criticism.

To put it another way: the preacher, we hope, has found through the application of historical and literary criticism to the biblical texts a way to a clearer understanding of the gospel. He will want to share this with others. He believes that the last two hundred years of biblical study have been a blessing. What is good for the preacher will be good for those to whom he is to preach, always allowing for their real differences in temperament, ability and circumstances. Therefore the proposal that the problem of the church and criticism should be dealt with by means of a rigorous separation of the two, the pulpit and the study, preaching and preparing, message and method, for all its obvious attractiveness, is inadequate, unconstructive and unfaithful.

There is, however, a further aspect of the problem which we have not yet considered; but when we do, the case for the separation of functions falls to the ground. To put the point crudely and bluntly, the fact of the matter is that the preacher who has accepted the methods of biblical criticism holds a faith that is in certain respects different from that of the man who does not; therefore the preacher who conceals his method from the congregation also withholds his faith. This can be illustrated in various ways.

For example, what are we to believe about the activity of God in the world? According to the biblical writers, God speaks directly to prophets, and intervenes in the course of history through sending war, famine and pestilence; he heals the sick and raises the dead. The world is open to direct action by God, or the devil, and secondary causes are ignored. One of the results of the application of critical methods to the study of scripture, on the other hand, is to qualify this way of thinking. No one would accuse F. H. A. Scrivener (1813–91) of being a radical ('His attempt to defend the *textus receptus* has now been almost universally abandoned'[9]), but the opening paragraph of his *Plain Introduction to the Criticism of the New Testament* illustrates the new way of looking at miracles which is part and parcel of the critical method:

> When God was pleased to make known to man His purpose of redeeming us through the death of His Son, He employed for this end the general laws, and worked according to the ordinary course of His Providential government, so far as they were available for the furtherance of His merciful design. A revelation from heaven, in its very notion, implies supernatural interposition; yet neither in the first promulgation nor in the subsequent propagation of Christ's religion, can we mark any *waste* of miracles. So far as they were needed for the assurance of honest seekers after truth, they were freely resorted to: whensoever the principles which move mankind in the affairs of common life were adequate to the exigencies of the case, more unusual and (as we might have thought) more powerful means of producing conviction were withheld, as at once superfluous and ineffectual. Those who heard not Moses and the prophets would scarcely be persuaded, though one rose from the dead.[10]

The passage expresses an attitude that is not found in the Bible. The biblical writers believe that there is no limit to what God can do: Scrivener notes that he is economical in his use of miracles. God can do all things and to him nothing is impossible, but the question is whether in fact he acts in this way; and Scrivener points out that he does not. The difference between these two points of view may be illustrated by the case of petitionary prayer: on a simple and literal reading of the Bible, the believer is promised that whatever he asks in Jesus' name he will receive; others would be uncertain whether it is ever God's will that we should pray for a miracle to happen, believing that we must live within certain conditions, one of which is the non-reversibility of events. The preacher who expounds, for example, the miracle of the raising of Jairus' daughter, without bringing into the open the problems that such a story raises, leaves the congregation in the state of mind to think, if this happened then, why not now? Why do we not pray for the restoration to life of the victims of bombs, car-accidents, plane-crashes, etc.? Am I responsible, because of my lack of faith, for the sickness and death of my friends?

Secondly, the difference between the faith of the Bible reader and that of the critic may be illustrated by their different understandings of the humanity of Jesus. The latter says that the evangelists' portrayal of Jesus has been coloured by religious attitudes and motives to such an extent that his humanity has almost been concealed: he is portrayed as one who knows the future, predicting not only his death but also his resurrection; who has supernatural powers, and is aware of himself as standing in a unique relationship with God which existed before his birth—before Abraham was. To the biblical critic, these are mythical ways in which the post-Easter communities expressed their faith in Jesus after the resurrection; they are not reports of what Jesus said and did in the days of his flesh. The Bible reader is always in danger of becoming a docetist; and the preacher who evades the historical problems leaves his hearers exposed to that heresy.

A third and final example of the difference between the two understandings is the way in which either side uses scripture. If the Bible is presented without any explanation, if it is expounded uncritically and unhistorically, the congregation can only assume that it is some kind of infallible authority, which solves problems and issues directions, if only one knows one's way around it.[11] Whatever the view of the Bible critic is, it is certainly not that. He is aware of the relativity of the books of the Bible, their variety and the different historical contexts in which they were composed and for which they were designed. The application of scripture to life is not as simple as the use of a rule-book in playing a game. If this is not made clear, then the congregation is understandably confused when questions such as the ordination of women and the marriage of divorced persons are discussed as though there could be any doubt about the answers.

D. F. Strauss listed four possible ways in which the theologian might proceed; his fourth is the one which he himself recommended (though he was not allowed to pursue it) and which has in fact been followed by the majority—the way of concealing the differences. The question is, whether we have now reached a time when that way is no longer viable: partly because of its inherent defects; partly because we live in a world of more rapid communication in every direction, so that, for example, the opinions of scholars can be made available universally and instantaneously. The theologian cannot any longer treat the church as something inferior, to be protected from the truth. Strauss's first suggestion is the way forward: the theologian must try 'to elevate the church to his own point of view'.

If this were agreed, then perhaps one practical point might follow, and it may be worth mentioning it here. There used to be those who said that there should be no celebration of the eucharist without a preaching of the word: and we understood their point, even though we did not always follow it in practice. Might it not be as appropriate and as impractical to suggest that there should be no reading of scripture, in liturgy, without exposition? It would follow, no doubt, that there would be less reading of scripture: but might this not be an advantage?

Biblical criticism is the preacher's best friend; it directs his attention to what he should say, and will not allow him to say what he should not. It shuts the door on the kind of preaching that is merely historical reconstruction and moralizing thereon, and demands of the preacher that he use the texts in the only way that is left—as testimony.

New Testament criticism has led us to see that the subject of the texts, whether they are gospels, acts, epistles or apocalypses, is always the risen Lord, who is present with his congregation. The writers of the New Testament books bear witness to Jesus as they believed on him in the post-Easter period, whatever the form of the document they were writing. What the preacher has in the biblical text is therefore the faith of a first- or second-century believer; and what he must do with it, if he is to preach on it, is to re-create this faith in his own idiom and in that of those to whom he is to preach. He proclaims the same faith because he proclaims the same Lord.

It is not the case that biblical criticism has destroyed the facts and left everything uncertain. It has indeed brought what were once thought to be facts into doubt: for example, the so-called 'life of Jesus';[12] the historicity of Acts; the authorship of various books; but it has brought into clearer light another set of facts: that believers believed in the Lord in this way, and proclaimed and worshipped him thus. And *these* facts are what matters, because Christianity is faith in one who died and is alive; present, not absent. But no one can believe in him without testimony; faith is never spontaneous. The preacher is one who testifies; and one of the sources of his testimony is the faith of the first and second generations of believers. New Testament criticism compels the preacher to see the texts in this way; it thus opens up to him a wealth of material that he must make his own, in order to make it available for others.

NOTES

1. Cf. F. W. Beare, 'Sayings of the Risen Jesus in the Synoptic Tradition: An Inquiry into their Origin and Significance', *Christian History and Interpretation: Studies presented to John Knox*, ed. W. R. Farmer, C. F. D. Moule, R. R. Niebuhr, Cambridge University Press 1967, p. 175.

2. Christopher Evans and Austin Farrer, *Bible Sermons*, Mowbray 1963.

3. 'This Beginning of Signs', op. cit., p. 5.

4. 'What Manner of Man?', op. cit., p. 20.

5. 'If Thou be the Son of God', op. cit., pp. 45ff.

6. Austin Farrer, *The Triple Victory*, Faith Press 1965, p. 13.

7. David Friedrich Strauss, *The Life of Jesus Critically Examined*, SCM Press 1973, p. 783.

8. This was written before the publication of an article in *The Times* of 11 May 1974 by the Right Reverend R. P. C. Hanson, 'The dangerous gulf between pulpit and pew' and the correspondence that followed, all of which seems to confirm the point. I should however add that I had heard Dr Hanson read an excellent paper on this subject at a conference in Oxford in September 1973, and was much influenced by what he said.

9. F. L. Cross (ed.), *The Oxford Dictionary of the Christian Church*, 1957, art. 'Scrivener'.

10. F. H. A. Scrivener, *Plain Introduction to the Criticism of the New Testament*, 3rd ed., Cambridge 1883, p. 1.

11. Cf. James Barr, *The Bible in the Modern World*, SCM Press 1973, p. 142.

12. 'So-called' because, as New Testament writers use the expression, the life of Jesus began at the resurrection; see II Cor. 4. 10f.; the only exception is Matt. 27.63, but note who is speaking.

15

New Testament Scholarship and Liturgical Revision

TOM BAKER

THE purpose of liturgy, sacred or secular, is to celebrate the most cherished and central traditions of a society, to express the common convictions which give that society cohesion, and to manifest those living symbols which are necessary for its vitality and continued existence. It is therefore a characteristic of liturgy to be resistant to passing fashions of thought and experience, even at times of change and revision. The modern critical approach to the New Testament texts is notoriously subject to such fashions, its conclusions always tentative, and subject to further revision. It is hardly surprising then that its influence on liturgical revision should not be direct, obvious or immediate. We may be thankful that this is so. The mind boggles at the thought of a liturgy or lectionary dominated by any one particular school of New Testament scholarship and interpretation. It is a great comfort that we have never had to endure the Burkitt rite or the Bultmann rite, or the rite of the New Quest. All the varied phases of New Testament scholarship have made their contribution to our understanding. But if any one of them had been allowed to become petrified in a liturgy or lectionary, how impoverished, strait-jacketed and ephemeral that liturgy or lectionary would have been.

Yet the truth remains that the growth and development of the critical approach to the New Testament over the past two centuries has had a most profound and lasting effect on contemporary theology. Granted the provisional nature of particular hypotheses or conclusions, the methods of modern study remain fairly constant, and the use of these methods have led to quite fundamental changes in theological perspective. These changes, now familiar enough, may be summarized under four heads: (*a*) The Bible can no longer be thought of either as an encyclopaedia of general knowledge, or as a collection of oracles, guaranteed by divine sanction against all error, and directly applicable to present circumstances. Every saying, or episode, must be understood within the context of its historical situation and cultural milieu, and having regard to the literary form in which it is expressed. A great deal of the biblical literature is now seen to be the end-product of a process of use and adaptation within the religious life of the community, and thus to be the literary deposit of a living tradition, which both preceded it and continued to flow beyond it. The New Testament is indeed a book wide open at both ends. (*b*) For this and other reasons revelation is no longer thought of as being communicated through propositions, but rather through what the late Bishop Ian Ramsey has taught us to call 'disclosure situations', that is to say, through the impact of specific events and experiences upon the minds and hearts of those involved in them. The interrelation of event and interpretation is, we know, a battle-ground amongst New Testament scholars. But that the 'locus' of revelation lies at some point within that interrelation, and not primarily in verbal propositions of any kind, would seem to be common ground. (*c*) The variety of religious thought and practice revealed in the pages of the New Testament is considerably greater than was formerly realized. Redaction criticism has done its work all too well. The attempt to find some pristine and unifying principle which can be verbalized and conceptualized is suspected to be a wild goose chase. Harmonization reduces everything to a shapeless pulp. No longer is it easy to speak of *the* New Testament doctrine of this or that. (*d*) For all these reasons there is no direct line from exegesis to exposition and application. The horizons of New Testament thought are very different from our own. The enterprise of 'translation' or demythologization is inescapable in some form or other. The essential religious experience of the New Testament authors is too closely bound up with its first-century conceptualization and imagery to be easily detached and applied direct. Nowhere is this problem more acute than in those passages which have exercised the greatest influence on liturgy, and in which the element of first-century mythology and imagery is at its highest—for example, the sending of the Son, his descent from heaven, the birth from a virgin, the resurrection, the ascension, the heavenly session, the coming again in glory at the Last Day.

Now in view of the function of liturgy to provide a vehicle of worship common to Christians of widely different temperaments and religious experience, and bearing in mind its inevitably conservative bias, it would be unreasonable to expect that these developments in the understanding of the New Testament, comparatively recent as they are, should exercise an immediate and far-reaching effect upon it. At the same time, bearing also in mind the real sea change which these developments have made in contemporary theological thought, one might at least have hoped that they would show themselves in some degree, if only indirectly. There are in fact *some* traces of such an influence in recent liturgical revisions. For example, in the 1922 lectionary for the daily office (taken over, with some revisions, in the Prayer Book as proposed in 1928) the readings from the first three gospels are often conflated in a harmonizing fashion. More recent revisions of the lectionary allow for the reading of each gospel in turn, and in shorter and more digestible portions. The new Calendar and Lectionary adopted in 1969 by the Church of England Liturgical Commission allows for a much wider choice of readings at the eucharist by following a two-year cycle. It also overcomes the imbalance of the 1662 Book of Common Prayer selection of Epistles and Gospels, with its predilection for the more muddy and obscure passages from the epistles, and its excessive number of miracle stories in the gospel readings. More generally, the unbalanced and almost exclusive emphasis of Cranmer's communion service on the passion and death of Christ has been corrected in recent revisions in a way which does greater justice to complementary New Testament themes of resurrection, joy and hope. There are signs too that recent New Testament scholarship on the eschatological mould of New Testament thought has exerted an influence. Thus in the Lord's Prayer 'Lead us not into temptation' has become 'Do not bring us to the time of trial'. Recent research into the connotations in Jewish religious thought of the word *anamnesis* (memorial) has had some impact on the wording of the eucharistic prayer.

So there are traces of influence, but the list is quite small, the influence marginal. Its modest scope stands in contrast to the considerable influence exerted by recent research into the early liturgies. This is obvious and far-reaching. Indeed it may have been too great. There are those who think that the eucharistic prayer contained in the Communion offices of Alternative Services Series 2 and Series 3 has been unduly influenced by the unproven hypotheses of such scholars as Gregory Dix and E. C. Ratcliffe on the original text of the *Apostolic Tradition* of Hippolytus (c. AD 215), and more generally by a purist and 'archaeological' tendency to treat the second and third centuries AD as the golden age of liturgy. Be that as it may, the tender concern of the revisers for modern *liturgical* studies stands in contrast with their comparative unconcern for recent *New Testament* scholarship.

Nor is there any absence of concern for conservative opinion. The extent of this will be well known to any of those who took part in the debates of the General Synod of the Church of England on liturgical revision, and who know from the inside the influence of party interests on the final shape of the revision known as Series 3. It will suffice to give a few examples. The believer in the verbal inerrancy of sacred scripture is sure to be gratified that, at the end of the lessons from the Old Testament and the epistles, the reader is invited (though not obliged) to say 'This is the word of the Lord'. At the end of the gospel reading he is obliged to say 'This is the gospel of Christ', thus using the word 'gospel' in a sense hard to defend even on pre-critical assumptions. Puritan feeling is fully met by the inclusion (though optional) of the Ten Commandments, and by the heightened tone and temperature of the general Confession and Absolution. Strict adherents of the doctrine of the all-sufficiency of Christ's atoning death will be reassured by the reappearance of the words 'his perfect sacrifice made once for all upon the cross'. The phraseology of the *epiclesis*, the invitation to communion and words of administration is clearly intended to allow for receptionist views of the eucharistic presence. The omission of all manual acts during the recitation of the Last Supper narrative protects the susceptibilities of those who object to any idea of a 'moment' of consecration, or of consecration by formula. Adventists are catered for by the substitution of the words 'we look for his coming in glory' for the less explicit 'we look for the coming of his kingdom' in Series 2. Those whose noses are keen to smell out any whiff of the 'sacrifice of the mass' will be happy that the explicit offering of bread and cup, contained in the first version of Series 2, has been omitted in all subsequent revisions. Lastly, the defenders of strict credal orthodoxy must be more than satisfied by the fact that the Creed is virtually repeated a second time in the first half of the eucharistic prayer.

So plenty of consideration has been shown to conservative, and more particularly conservative evangelical, opinion. That is not to be deplored. But can we trace any comparable concern to take account of New Testament scholarship, with its profound effect on contemporary theological thought? We must remind ourselves at this point that not too much is to be expected, for the reasons already given. Nevertheless, apart from the comparatively minor influences mentioned above, contemporary theology in general, and critical scholarship in particular, have been largely ignored. Perhaps it would be more accurate to say that, as a result of a certain insensitivity of treatment, the insights which it offers have been obscured, and the problems it raises made more acute. Admittedly this is a subjective judgment, not easy to defend or to refute. A closer look at three examples may help to make the point a little clearer.

1. As we saw earlier on in this chapter, the general tendency of recent New Testament study has been to blur the distinction between scripture and tradition, to call in question the notion of the Bible as a 'holy book', standing on its own as a wholly unique authority, its meaning clearly intelligible and directly applicable. Even before the advent of critical scholarship, the Church of England has in general appealed to tradition and reason as necessary adjuncts (to put the matter at its lowest) to the authority of scripture. Yet the Series 3 revision has resulted in a rite even more heavily and exclusively biblical than before. For now there are *three* biblical lessons instead of only two; and the rubrics allow, indeed encourage, a psalm or a canticle (usually biblical) in no less than three places. This means that Christian hymns and songs are likely to be replaced, and the time available for the sermon to be curtailed. Thus the element of '*sola scriptura*' is emphasized at the expense of later tradition enshrined in hymns, and of contemporary interpretation provided by the sermon. There is a certain irony that at a time when the Bible is advisedly being given a less exclusive place in Religious Education syllabuses, the liturgy should become even more heavily biblical than before. It is understandable that the Roman Catholic church, in the first flush of enthusiasm at its recent rediscovery of the Bible, should tread this path, but the Church of England might have been more wary.

One wonders whether the members of the Liturgical Commission ever gave thought to the possible inclusion of extra-biblical literature amongst the lessons, at least for optional use. We have seen recently the publication of a book called *The Fourth Lesson in the Daily Office*.[1] Mostly modern, but including some material from earlier sources, it is an anthology of passages from Christian authors, designed to be read as part of the Daily Office ('Morning and Evening Prayer, Series 2 revised'). The same principle could have been applied to the readings at the eucharist. It has been objected that the reading of set passages of non-biblical material alongside the biblical lessons might give the impression that both are of equal authority. Yet it is difficult to see why the inclusion of certain Christian writings in the liturgy, on a temporary and changing basis, should be held to attribute canonical authority to such writings, any more than canonical authority is attributed to the liturgical sermon. On the other hand it might have the beneficial effect of breaking down the idea that the Bible has some kind of intrinsic, almost magical, authority and sacredness. It might remove the impression that the inspiration of the Holy Spirit came to an end with the closing of the canon of scripture, and so help to fill in the desert which exists in the minds of most worshippers between 'the world of the Bible' and our own day. We might even follow up Christopher Evans' invitation to take a long, hard look at the very concept of canonicity. Nor should it be forgotten that in the pre-Reformation church passages from the lives of the saints and the acts of the martyrs were read out during divine service. In the circumstances of his day Cranmer was probably quite right to have removed them from the lectionary. The clearing away of some of the rank overgrowth of legend and superstition which had cluttered up the liturgy, so that the Bible itself might come into clearer view, must have come as a great liberation, and a welcome simplification. Perhaps the need today, in different circumstances, is for some enrichment of the liturgy from extra-biblical sources, in order to relieve the aridity of an exclusively biblical diet. In Cranmer's day the problem about the Bible was unfamiliarity, today it is in part over-familiarity. There is the further problem that, as the world of the New Testament recedes further and further into the past, so the issues with which we are faced today become incapable of solution by direct appeal to New Testament texts. There is also some evidence to suggest that, as human history develops, the past, and especially the distant past, is losing its hold upon the minds and imagination of men. All this, it may be said, is no argument for failing to give pride of place to the New Testament in the liturgy. For better or worse the Christian faith stands or falls by the doctrine of the Word made flesh, and is therefore firmly anchored in the past, in the historical figure of Jesus of Nazareth. Yet there is also the doctrine of the Holy Spirit, who continues to speak through the prophets. Both theological and pastoral considerations suggest a certain caution against so overloading the liturgy with biblical material that little room is left for anything else.

2. The impact of modern studies has made it all the more difficult to make a direct identification of the Word of God with the written words of the Bible. Yet this is directly encouraged by the rubric which exhorts the reader of the epistle to finish the reading with the words 'This is the word of the Lord'. It is true that, in the final revision of Series 3, these words are optional. But experience so far suggests that their use will become very widespread. The older and more modest formula 'Here endeth the epistle' had the great merit of not committing anybody to any particular interpretation of the passage, nor to any particular view of biblical inspiration. Some of the passages set for the epistle contain words of St Paul written in moments of unreflective exasperation or even perhaps of sheer bad temper. It may well be that such passages *contain* a word of the Lord, if treated sensitively in their context. But to equate them directly with the word of the Lord is positively misleading, and wrongly provocative. I well remember an argument I had once with a very devout old lady on some subject or other, the exact nature of which I have forgotten. Feeling myself getting the worst of it, I appealed to something in one of Paul's epistles. 'Ah, yes', said the old lady, 'but that's where Paul and I disagree.' Her instinct, I like to feel, was right.

Further to this, it is odd and ironic that in the Series 3 revision great care is taken not to make a direct, one-to-one, identification of the consecrated bread and wine with the body and blood of Christ. Thus the *epiclesis* contains the words (derived in fact from the Roman canon) 'grant that by the power of your Spirit these gifts may be *unto us* his body and blood' (my italics). The Series 2 words of Administration, 'The Body of Christ', become in Series 3 'The Body of Christ keep you in eternal life', presumably to avoid the impression that the bread is without qualification to be identified with the body of Christ. The same motive may lie behind the omission of all manual acts during the recitation of the so-called 'words of institution'. Yet there is no such scruple in avoiding a direct, one-to-one identification of the words of scripture with the Word of God. Admittedly this refers only to one rubric, and it may seem a niggling kind of criticism. I am however inclined to think that it has considerable and somewhat alarming significance. Superstition about the Word can be just as damaging as superstition about the Sacrament, perhaps more so.

3. The third point I find much harder to explain. It concerns the need to 'translate' in some way those parts of the New Testament where the element of 'mythology' is at its highest, and which are most closely bound up with the first-century world view (more particularly with its apocalyptic framework), and which have crystallized out into credal formulae. Now the New Testament, taken as a whole, does not invite us to over-systematize here. There is a bewildering variety of such quasi-credal material and a rich interplay of patterns and images. In St Paul's writings, as C. K. Barrett has pointed out,[2] we find a subtle blending of the mythological and the existential, such as defies exact analysis or systematization. The type of language which is used (the sending of the Son, the sitting at the right hand of the Father, the coming in glory on the clouds of heaven) belongs to the discourse of poetry rather than prose. It is language which points beyond itself to a mystery which cannot be contained by or fully expressed in any set of propositions. The language is elusive, teasing, evocative, not to be codified or tied up into a system. Now it is surely reasonable to expect that a modern liturgy will handle such language with delicacy and imagination, and with some sensitivity to the problems which it raises today. But what could be more hard, wooden and prosaic than the first part of the eucharistic prayer in both Series 2 and 3, with its dull formalizations, its tiresomely repetitive 'through him' formula? Granted that this part of the liturgy must celebrate the gracious work of God in creation and redemption, that does not mean that it has to read like a grocery list or an inventory. The 'mighty works' of God are too richly mysterious to be listed. The case is not the same with some other revised liturgies. The various forms in the new Roman rite, and in such unofficial rites as that used by the Sisters at West Malling, avoid this tendency to itemize, and are more conducive to the sense of mystery. The trouble with the Anglican forms is not simply that they are by comparison dull and prosaic, but that, because of this very fact, they

invite a hard and literal interpretation of the words that are used.

On the same subject, what are we to make of the acclamation in the very midst of the eucharistic prayer 'Christ has died, Christ is risen, Christ will come again'. It does seem a pity that, at the very heart of the eucharistic mystery, and just at the point where concentration and devotion should be at its deepest, I am bound to perform a series of complicated mental somersaults. For how can I say such words as 'Christ will come again' without such an exhausting exercise? In the first place the language of 'coming *again*' is hardly characteristic of the New Testament. In the second place the hope of the Lord's Parousia was something of an embarrassment even to some of the New Testament writers (let alone to us moderns); and was subject to various transmutations within the New Testament literature itself, most notably in the fourth gospel. I am by no means objecting to a forward-looking and indeed eschatological reference in the eucharist, far from it. But it might have been hoped that it would be expressed in less blatantly apocalyptic language than this. It is true that this acclamation appears in the revised Roman rite, but other versions are offered as alternatives, in words which do not so clearly invite belief in a literal and datable second coming.

These are just three areas in which the new rites fail to do justice to fresh theological insights resulting from the modern approach to the New Testament, or show an insensitivity to the issues which that approach has raised. There are a number of other incidental items of the same kind. Is it only pedantry which regrets the highly questionable attribution of the 'Comfortable Words' to Christ, St Paul and St John as in the 1662 communion service? Then there is the Proper Preface for Ascension Day which runs: 'because in his risen body he appeared to his disciples, and in their sight was taken up into heaven, to reign with you in glory'. It is now almost a commonplace even of Sunday School teaching that the ascension is not to be thought of as a journey upwards into space. It is further an accepted datum of New Testament criticism that Luke's idea of a temporary restoration of the risen Lord to quasi-earthly conditions, followed by the ascension as a second and separate 'destination event', is by no means characteristic of New Testament thought on the subject. Must the intellectual difficulties raised by the reading of the Lucan ascension narratives in the lessons be rubbed in yet further by inclusion in the very heart of the eucharistic action? Other forms of biblical words are available in abundance. On quite another subject it is surely a matter for regret that in the Series 3 lectionary for the Holy Week eucharists we have lost the traditional reading of each of the four passion narratives in turn, and in full. The practice of such solemn recitation of the passion narratives as an essential part of the liturgy of Holy Week not only provides a most moving spiritual experience, it is also fully justified by all that form criticism and redaction criticism has to tell us about the nature and purpose of these incomparable narratives. Reading only two of them (in rather abbreviated form) together with little snippets from the others, is an impoverishment.

We must be fair to the liturgical revisers. Of all the rites now available in the Church of England, Series 3 is still the best bargain, and on balance an improvement on its predecessors, at least for modern use. *The real problem in finding a living and relevant liturgy for today is presented by the Bible itself.* No amount of modernization of the liturgy, however skilful, can remove the inescapably archaic character of the biblical readings and allusions. Indeed modern translations serve only to make the archaism even more obvious. While the church in general searches for a fresh approach to biblical interpretation, a liturgy must continue to be by and large conservative in its use of biblical material.

However, while allowing this to be true of public and formal liturgies, would it not be good if the small, often ecumenical, groups which are a growing feature of modern church life, were encouraged to be more adventurous in the eucharistic expression they give to their common life? In some places this is already happening, but in a rather half-hearted and stealthy fashion. If there were more widespread and freer experiments at small group level, with open lines of communication, then in course of time some very valuable lessons might be learned, and some answers to the problems raised in this chapter brought nearer to solution. The impact on the public liturgy of the church might follow in due course. There are plenty of precedents. In the earliest times, as we know, the president at the eucharist improvised the anaphora. Later on there was a great flowering of local rites of rich variety, as in the Mozarabic and Gallican rites. Modern Pentecostalism has a tradition of spontaneity in eucharistic worship within a broad framework. No doubt the churches were wise to cut back on over-luxuriant growth, and to seek a greater measure of uniformity. But, as with Cranmer's reform of the lectionary, circumstances have changed, and the growing acceptance of pluralism in contemporary thought suggests that a greater diversity in liturgical expression is to be welcomed. This may best come about at small-group level, rather than by producing a welter of official and alternative forms of public worship. I would like the bishops to be bold, and positively to encourage such free eucharistic expression. All that would be required is the issuing of certain basic and mandatory rubrics, along these lines:

1. The president shall take bread and wine, with or without words.
2. The president shall give thanks for God's goodness, making the memorial of Christ, and including in his prayer one of the New Testament narratives of the Last Supper. He shall pray in his own words, or in words chosen by him, or in words agreed on by the group.
3. The president shall break the bread, with or without words.
4. Those present shall eat the bread and drink of the cup.

Nothing more than this is needed to constitute a valid eucharist, except perhaps some directive about the Orders of the president, and the baptismal and communicant status of the participants. Anything more than this would inhibit the required freedom. In other words let the public worship of the church continue to be according to the authorized form or forms. But let there be a return to the days of Justin Martyr in the conduct and development of eucharistic worship at small-group level. And let both be freely accepted as conducive to the church's health.

NOTES

1. Christopher Campling, *The Fourth Lesson in the Daily Office*, Darton, Longman and Todd, Vol. I 1973, Vol. II 1974.
2. C. K. Barrett, *From First Adam to Last*, A. & C. Black 1962, pp. 83-91.

16

Walking in Newness of Life

SYDNEY EVANS

MANY, varied and sometimes strange have been the ways in which the church-community of the centuries has used the biblical literature for the directing and correcting of its interior and exterior life.[1] Many, varied and sometimes strange have been the ways in which individual Christians have expressed their understanding of discipleship. The biblical literature has been used as a quarry by writers on the spiritual life, by constructors of liturgies, by the artists of the frescoes and mosaics of Byzantine churches in which walls, arches and domes so treated provide the worshipper with an illustrated Bible. In our own times new experiments in discipleship continue to find expression and continue to seek in the Bible for support and direction; we need only mention the community at Taizé, the Little Brothers and Sisters of Jesus, the Iona Community, St Christopher's Hospice, industrial mission. The search for a true Christian inwardness is as eager within the church community today as is the urge to explore fresh ways of caring for the victims of the contradictions, injustices and sicknesses of humanity's experience. The question that calls for an answer is the question as to how searchers for true Christian inwardness can be guided to make best use of the biblical resources.

An intellectual task is involved, however reluctant some searchers after spirituality may be to admit this. There can be little stability in a spirituality which avoids facing doubt about faith, uncertainty about old authorities and all that questioning of former assumptions which follows from the new knowledge which continues to circulate in the modern consciousness. What is actually happening around us and the questions arising from within us must be faced and sifted and assimilated by those who are to act as guides to others in the contemporary phase of the moral and spiritual quest. Whereas on the one hand modern intellectualism threatens to destroy civilization unless it can become permeated with the corrective insights into the human condition that come from faith and prayer, on the other hand faith and prayer are often casualties of a modern consciousness that has not been adequately analysed, criticized and put into proper perspective.

In pursuing the intellectual task the Christian scholar will inevitably disturb some minds while he enables others to rediscover the possibility of belief. Unexamined assumptions must needs be investigated if there is to emerge a more adequate apologetic for Christianity as the support as well as the encouragement of faith. To stand firm in a confidence of faith in the cross-currents of challenge and change which characterize our open society requires honesty in faith and honesty in prayer. Patterns of prayer that faithful men and women have been able to use even in the recent past are now being found by them to be no longer real.

For the sake of deeper faith and of better prayer we need to explore afresh those earliest Christian responses embedded in the writings of the New Testament—those crystallizations of the primary vision. Already help in this area is coming from New Testament scholars who are regaining confidence in their handling of the biblical material as a result of the long critical reappraisal that has marked this century.

C. F. D. Moule's *The Birth of the New Testament*[2] is a notable example of a New Testament scholar reinterpreting the inner dynamics of the early Christian consciousness, helping the reader to understand better what he is reading and with what assumptions he should approach the reading and pointing the way towards what the author calls 'the ethical translation of the gospel'. In selecting the word 'ethical' he would appear to be including what we might call inner attitudes and spirituality as well as outward behaviour. In a different style J. A. Baker in his book *The Foolishness of God*[3] explores afresh the significance of Jesus in the context of today's climate and critique and in the final chapter 'Man in the Presence of God' investigates the 'ethical translation of the gospel' in terms of spirituality as well as of morality. In a book subtitled 'An Essay on the Biblical Basis of Christian Spirituality', E. J. Tinsley has written of the concept of *The Imitation of God in Christ*[4] as one of the unifying themes of biblical ethics. In *Christ and Spirit in the New Testament* G. M. Styler has examined 'the basis of obligation in Paul's christology and ethics'[5] showing 'how tightly Paul holds together the work of Christ, our inclusion in it, our continuing life and our future hope'. Human obligation as such he finds to be connected with human creation in the image of God; the Christian's 'transformed world of obligation' he finds to be connected with the new creation:

> In some way, then, which it still remains hard to express, Christ in his very person is the point at which human ideals and obligations are renovated and transformed. What went before is now seen as a foreshadowing of Christ; and Christ himself marks the goal of life as well as its origin. He confronts us with human obligation in its ultimate form; and does so not just by the legacy of teaching or insights that he has bequeathed, nor just because of the life that he lived and its consequences; but because of the life that he lives, which is ours to live also.

I am reminded of two observations by Henry Chadwick when writing of Origen in *Early Christian Thought and the Classical Tradition*:[6]

> The gospel brings to actuality what is present in men potentially and its 'newness' consists in the concrete example of Christ himself.

> The gospel is the republication of the law of nature implanted by creation. It does not bring a new morality but a recognition of the highest ethical aspiration.

Chadwick's phrase 'concrete image' suggests a Jesus of the past, a past paradigm with continuing influence; it needs to be transposed into Styler's 'not just because of the life that he lived and its consequences; but because of the life that he lives, which is ours to live also'. But Chadwick's further insight is particularly helpful in this whole area of spiritual guidance. In speaking of the gospel as 'the republication of the law of nature' he helps us to see how the gospel vision and vocation can be related to those strange inner workings of human emotions which often inhibit spiritual growth. Freud, Jung and their followers have helped us to understand the 'law of nature' in respect of the inner dynamics of fear, guilt, projection, repression. There are many who cannot receive the gift of the new life of the gospel until they have been helped to understand, disentangle and re-assimilate lived emotional experiences of the past. Depth psychology offers help towards religious faith and life in the spirit just as some forms of depression yield only to a change in the mix of the body's chemistry. But what is offered by the gospel is more than the recovery of the ability to live more comfortably with oneself.

Sir Edwyn Hoskyns used to start his lectures on Christian ethics by announcing the subject and then saying to his audience: 'We will begin therefore with the resurrection.'

Over against the current tendency to reduce the stature of a human being by such language as that which speaks of a 'naked ape' in the 'human zoo', Christianity stands for the estimate of humanity of which Irenaeus can be quoted as exemplar: 'The glory of God is a living man: the life of a man is the vision of God.'[7] One form of the New Testament statement of this vision which both awakens awareness of the way things are really and invites exploration of life in the light of this awareness is 'the glory of God in the face of Jesus Christ'.[8] At once we are confronted with the paradox: no mere Jesus of history, but a historical Jesus experienced by others and interpreted by them in the light of their experience of him. The only Jesus we know is the experienced Jesus. We know him only through the reactions to him of those who experienced him in the pre-Easter and post-Easter paradox. We know him only by entering ourselves into that knowing of him that animated a community of people who expressed their knowing of him in worship, in preaching, in writing, in loving, in martyrdom.

Always therefore we must begin with the resurrection. Nothing of what they experienced would have happened had there not been that conviction about the significance of his death which they called the resurrection. Whatever else it means to walk in newness of life it certainly means entering into that experience which the New Testament writers are speaking about when they speak of the risen Christ. And when they speak about the risen Christ they are saying something fundamental about God and about ourselves, about the truth of the way things are. The resurrection of Jesus is not an isolated event to be marvelled at or dismissed as incredible. It belongs within a new understanding of the real dimensions of the life we are already living.

Within the purpose of this offering of essays and within the emphasis of this particular small gift we turn to C. F. Evans' *Resurrection and the*

New Testament.[9] In turning to that publication of lectures delivered on different occasions we turn to what may not inappropriately be called 'preliminary sketches for a future canvas'. But we turn the more confidently in the knowledge that this New Testament scholar and critic is not only a priest for whom the ministry of word and sacraments is central to his life, but also a priest from whose wise spiritual and human insight and counsel many men and women have learned the better how to live godly in Christ Jesus in their individual circumstances. In turning, albeit briefly, to this work we will select the final chapter entitled 'The Resurrection Faith'. For whatever the problems the resurrection narratives may pose for the critical mind (and these are faced frankly in preceding chapters) there is no possible doubt that the faith by which the early Christian community lived was the resurrection faith. This is the fact which has given Christianity its distinctive character and continuing influence as insight, interpretation and inspiration. 'As dying, and, behold, we live.' Those who have criticized Christopher Evans for being too tentative or too negative in respect of the reliability of the gospel accounts of the empty tomb and the resurrection appearances have usually failed to acknowledge how positive is his affirmation of resurrection faith.

By what process the radical reorientation of the first disciples' expectations was brought about we can never discover by any independent investigation outside the Christian community and its literature. Some will be disposed to accept what the documents say in spite of their inconsistencies and problematic aspects: others will find themselves withholding belief about the manner in which Jesus crucified, dead and buried became known as the animating presence of a new quality of life in relationship. What matters is whether it is true that Jesus is risen and that his resurrection releases power to enable us to walk in newness of life.

It is the truth of this faith that Christopher Evans examines in the final section of his book. He begins:

> The central place of the resurrection faith in the New Testament is hardly what was to be expected either from contemporary Judaism or from the preaching and teaching of Jesus as it has been recorded.[10]

He goes on to examine the various ways in which the New Testament writers interpret the significance of the resurrection; the relation of resurrection emphasis to exaltation emphasis; the relation of exaltation emphasis to the gift of the spirit; the contrast between the time sequence of events in the synoptic gospels and in Acts and the all-inclusive Johannine interpretation of the cross as the glory. The two themes of resurrection and exaltation are found awkwardly related: none the less:

> Resurrection as the more concrete and cruder term directs attention not only forwards but backwards also. As reversal and resuscitation it is the recovery intact from death of this particular man and of what made him the particular man he was. Like Janus it looks both ways and in opening into what is new brings with it that which is old and otherwise past . . . It was this sense of the recovery of the past as raw material of the eschatological future which led to the repetition and transmission in tradition of the words and deeds of Jesus, and eventually to the writing of the gospels, in their present form of accounts of his earthly ministry, as accessories to belief in the risen Lord.[11]

Whatever the resurrection may have been as event 'it is now seen to be the *fons et origo* of Christian faith in the lordship of Jesus'.[12] 'It follows that resurrection is also the source of the existence of the church and its knowledge of itself as the community of the risen Lord and Messiah, the community of the last days'[13]—no mere sect or reformist group but the true Israel with a mission to the world.

To quote from a carefully extended argument is inevitably to distort. But if by quoting I send the reader back to the original work I shall have done what I want to do. For when Christopher Evans moves on to deal with Paul's thinking about resurrection he brings us to a more intimate understanding of the inwardness of discipleship as dying and rising with Christ. He finds in Paul's thinking an understanding of resurrection not as a means to a further end but as

> a new and permanent form of existence characterized by the relationship expressed in the words 'with Christ'. The preposition 'with' . . . marks for Paul the parallelism between the career of Christ and that of the Christian, who co-suffers, co-dies, is con-crucified and co-buried with Christ, is raised with him, is con-formed to him and made to sit with him, is co-heir, co-ruler and is con-glorified with him.[14]

Resurrection itself is now interpreted as a mark of Christian living.

In II Corinthians, Paul finds in dying and rising with Christ the clue to the understanding of what has been happening to him and the means of drawing from it positive conclusions of complete confidence in God.[15]

The resurrection of Jesus when understood as bringing to light 'the inner moral quality of obedience and righteousness' becomes the source of new and 'specific trust in the God who is able and powerful to fulfil his purpose and his promises'.[16]

It is thus of the essence of the Christian faith that within the temporal order a real beginning is possible which is new and which is from God. Paul expressed this in terms of death and resurrection with Christ.[17]

The eucharist in the continuing life and worship of the Christian community affirms this conviction and enables the worshipper to enter more deeply into the meaning that it affirms. Writing of the eucharist in some unpublished retreat addresses Christopher Evans takes our thinking a stage further:

Now—and here comes something more difficult—it seems that the consecration of things to God involves some form of death. I think this would be so even in an ideal world. We would not be able to pass from what is temporal, finite and limited to what is eternal, infinite and complete—and back again and then finally and once for all without any coming back—without something like death. We cannot imagine simply growing from here to there or evolving thither. There would have to be some form of transformation, some change into a different way of existing, something like death. Anthony Bloom—one of the still-centred men—says repeatedly that we cannot have a satisfactory philosophy of life without a philosophy of death. For even in ideal conditions death is a boundary, a boundary of life and thought, of feeling and desire, of intention and will. It is the place where we have to stand from time to time in imagination in order to understand life. Then we see that our life cannot give a total satisfaction because it is not intended to do so if we are divine creation. 'Thou has made us for thyself, and our heart is restless till it rests in thee.' That is either nonsense or true; and if true it has immense implications.

We know this chiefly because of Christ. The sacrament is the sacrament of Christ and not only of his body but also of his blood, of his death in the world as it is. This also is for the Christian one of the given things whatever we make of it—much, little or nothing. The gospel is at its core the gospel of the death and resurrection of Christ. You cannot have the gospel without it. The Son of man goes as it is written of him; the Son of man must suffer.

The Son of man—who is he? He is the man who knows his whence and his whither; the man for whom the world and life in it does not add up apart from its givenness, from its divine source in the Creator Father; the man whose words and actions are bent to making that truth real; so the man who makes the future God present and the distant God here. In a world of contradiction, of blurred perspective, of misguided desire and perverse will, this man can only die. Conflict is inevitable—and is indeed written all over his life—and if neither side will compromise the conflict is to the death. So then the consecration, the making holy, the devoting to its proper end which accords with its nature can only be via death. This is what God has stamped on life by the gospel whatever we make of it. To grow as a Christian is to grow in the apprehension of it and the sense of it. This is the form the intelligible mystery now takes.

All this needs to be heard, pondered and freshly assimilated by Christians in these days when various kinds of meditation techniques are being peddled as prophylactics against tense and fretful living. Christian prayer is not a prophylactic technique. Christian prayer is a way of being in this world in faith relationship with the crucified and risen Christ so that the raw material of one's given temperament and circumstances is pressed interiorly like grapes into the vintage wine of Christ-lovingness towards God and towards other people. A spirituality which evades or avoids the harsh realities of historical experience is other than Christian. Life in Christ is life in the path and in the spirit of the Jesus who was obedient to the death of the cross. To be a disciple of Christ is to understand that the way to real life is through death to false alternatives: the resurrection is the sign which authenticates the route.

What we are found to be by others, what value others draw from our lives, depends largely on whether or not we have learned in the crucible of a heart of love to do something creative with the raw materials of our personality and our circumstances. Unless faith and prayer enable us to make this sort of difference it becomes harder to see why we should bother to pray or to believe. But when what we see to be true about the way in which Jesus handled the raw material of life as it came to him begins to come true again in other persons and even, dare we say it, even in ourselves, then our confidence grows in the genuineness of a spirituality which by its joyfulness authenticates the faith from which it springs. What else is the purpose of New Testament exegesis if not to make more possible this kind of existence?

NOTES

1. D. E. Nineham (ed.), *The Church's Use of the Bible, Past and Present*, SPCK 1963.
2. C. F. D. Moule, *The Birth of the New Testament*, A. & C. Black 1962.
3. J. A. Baker, *The Foolishness of God*, Darton, Longman and Todd 1970.
4. E. J. Tinsley, *The Imitation of God in Christ*, SCM Press 1960.
5. G. M. Styler, 'The Basis of Obligation in Paul's Christology and Ethics', *Christ and Spirit in the New Testament: Studies in honour of C. F. D. Moule*, ed. Barnabas Lindars and Stephen S. Smalley, Cambridge University Press 1973, pp. 175–88.
6. Henry Chadwick, *Early Christian Thought and the Classical Tradition*, Oxford University Press 1966, p. 105.
7. Irenaeus, *Adversus Haereses*, IV. 20.7.
8. II Cor. 4.6.
9. C. F. Evans, *Resurrection and the New Testament* (SBT 2.12), 1970.
10. Ibid., p. 132.
11. Ibid., p. 142.
12. Ibid., p. 148.
13. Ibid., p. 149.
14. Ibid., p. 163.
15. Ibid., p. 165.
16. Ibid., p. 167.
17. Ibid., p. 168.

17

A Change of Diet?

JANET DYSON

WHAT place has the New Testament in religious education in state schools? Up to ten years ago the answer to this question was clear enough. We need only look at the agreed syllabuses of religious education to realize that large slices of the Bible sprinkled with small bits of church history and spiced with a few of the personal and social problems of young people was the prescribed diet for religious education lessons.

The compilers of the syllabuses had no doubt at all that 'religious instruction in accordance with an agreed syllabus' as laid down in the 1944 Education Act meant Christian education, and this was to be based largely on the Bible. The following may be regarded as representative of the aims of that time: 'to present the revelation of God given in the Bible';[1] 'The goal will be a life of worship and service in the Christian community';[2] 'To teach Christianity to our children is to inspire them with the vision of the glory of God in the face of Jesus Christ, and to send them into the world willing to follow him.'[3]

Clearly the presuppositions of the compilers were: the Bible is the common meeting point for all the Christian denominations and its contents are suitable for inspiring and developing faith in the young from the infant to the secondary school; Christianity is the faith which most people in society accept; Religious Instruction is religious *instruction*, the transmission of agreed knowledge about the Christian religion with the hope that those instructed will make a favourable response and take their place in the Christian community.

Are these presuppositions of 1944 those of 1974? Is the diet prescribed for the post-war years the right one for the last quarter of the twentieth century? Three official reports on education thought the diet was basically correct. The Newson Report of 1963 acknowledged the 'mixed society in which we live' where there are controversial views about religion. Nevertheless it stressed that 'religious instruction in accordance with any local education authority's agreed syllabus is instruction in the Christian religion.'[4] It considered that those who equated Christianity 'with simple moral instruction' . . . were wrong. A teacher must 'know his Bible and its teaching, he must have thought about the relation of religion, and religious knowledge, to other fields of human activity and ways of knowing'.[5] Clearly it accepted that the 1944 settlement was right in that Christian education was quite specifically the task of the state school.

The Gittens Report on *Primary Education in Wales* was also quite explicit that the aim of teaching is to establish the Christian faith:

> The aim of using Bible stories is to teach right ideas about God and develop attitudes towards him. . . . The Bible is used to help children grow into a relationship with Christ so that they will wish to pattern their lives on his.[6]

The Plowden Report which investigated the education of children up to twelve years in England was not so explicit as this, yet the opinion of the main body of the committee was that religious education was induction into Christian belief, but this was to be related to situations within the children's experience.

> Young children need a simple and positive introduction to religion. They should be taught to know and love God and to practise in the school community the virtues appropriate to their age and development.

It was sure that some stories about the life and teaching of Jesus could be taught to children at an early age and that children 'should not be confused by being taught to doubt before faith is established'.[7] The minority report however wrote a note of reservation in which it questioned whether children under twelve could understand Christian beliefs.[8] It suggested that religious education should be 'to supply children with a moral basis'. 'The school has a considerable part to play in inducing the children to accept an adequate set of moral, social and aesthetic values,' but it questioned whether this should be tied to theology. Bible stories along with classical stories and legends should be taught as part of the cultural inheritance from the past.[9]

During the last decade these three official reports have reinforced the view that religious education should aim at the establishment of Christian faith and that Bible stories, particularly from the New Testament, are an important means to this end. Yet these assumptions are increasingly coming under fire. Is the Bible a suitable textbook for inspiring and developing faith in the state schools? Do the majority of people in society want Christianity taught to the young in school? Is instruction the same as education?

First of all, let us look at the question of the Bible. Does religious education based on such large doses of the Bible 'work'? Have young people with ten years of religious education a satisfactory understanding of the Bible stories? Empirical research has shown that factual knowledge of the Bible, quite apart from its religious understanding, was minimal among fifteen-year-old pupils.[10] However, because they were deeply interested in personal, social and moral questions, Loukes[11] suggested that the study of these problems in the light of Christian insight should replace the study of the Bible. His approach has been termed the 'implicit religion'[12] approach, for it seeks to help pupils in their search for meaning to life, 'a conversation between the older and younger on the simple question, "What is life like?"'[13] Such an approach is of great importance, but it must be rigorous and informed to prevent the lesson becoming 'aimless chatter in which the blind lead the blind'.[14]

The work of Ronald Goldman showed that children are not understanding religious insights from the Bible because they are unintelligible to them in terms of their experience. Children are not intellectually ready for religious teaching until they have developed the capacity for abstract thought. Teaching biblical concepts too soon develops crude literalisms and distortions which last into adolescence and contribute to its rejection as childish. 'It is an impossible task to teach the Bible as such to children much before adolescence.'[15] It is an adult book.[16]

Goldman therefore suggested a drastic reduction of Bible material for children before the age of twelve years and made a distinction between teaching the Bible and teaching *from* the Bible. He called for 'a programme of developmental religious education' in which the exploration of 'life-themes' based on the experience of children and illustrated at times from the Bible should replace the traditional pattern. In this way religion and ordinary life will not be separated in the minds of the children.

Teaching through themes has become very common in the last few years and this approach has been adopted by the new agreed syllabuses. The Durham Report supports the thematic approach particularly with younger children, for it not only meets their developmental needs but 'it provides a framework in which emotion can be nurtured, apprehension widened, sensitivity deepened, perception stimulated and relationships built'.[17] Goldman's justification for themes was: 'We are putting real life experience alongside religious truth, so that knowing ordinary life at depth becomes a religious experience'.[18] But why should a theme on sheep and shepherds develop into Jesus the good shepherd? And why should the importance of bread turn into the Last Supper? Does this not suggest that we are making ordinary life a preliminary to the material of a specifically religious nature, that religion and life are very different after all? John Hull shows that there can easily arise a conflict between belief and method.[19] The belief that a religious experience is a normal experience understood in a certain way convinces the teacher that he may introduce a child to a religious experience through exploring the meanings of everyday life. Yet in his method of development he then brings in specifically religious material particularly from the gospels and thereby implies that it is this which is really religious. Hull suggests that themes are 'probably more faithful to themselves and less prone to turn into something else if they do not contain Biblical material'. However, he argues that thematic teaching is compatible with biblical theology, for the God of Israel acts in history through the experience of the nation and the lives of individuals. He reveals himself through human affairs. Such an understanding of religious education by thematic teaching will 'heighten sensitivity to the basic religious quest of man and show the roots of human experience from which religion springs'. But he argues that for Christian education themes are not enough, for God's revelation is seen supremely in the death and resurrection of Christ.

But does society still want *Christian* education in its schools? The evidence of a few years ago suggests that it does.[20] In addition it is often argued that not only is Christianity the principal religion of

England, but it has contributed to our historical and cultural development to such an extent that a proper understanding of western civilization would be impossible without a knowledge of it. But there is a growing recognition that England is no longer religiously homogeneous. Not only is there a sizable group of humanists who question the intention of religious education in schools, there are also non-Christian religious communities, such as Hindus, Sikhs, Moslems, as well as Jews. Of course it is possible for adherents of non-Christian philosophies and religions to be withdrawn from the class, and this was the answer in the past for Jews and indeed for Roman Catholics. Now the problem is greater because of the numbers involved and the integrated approach to learning. But much more important, this would reinforce the view that religious education appears in the curriculum for dogmatic or confessional reasons, not educational ones. If religious education is important as an aspect of education, then it is essential that the contents and aims be such that no groups are thereby forced to be excluded.

This point leads us to consider the third presupposition of the Act: to instruct in the hope that children will choose Christianity. But the view of a teacher as an instructor has changed radically. There has been a shift away from emphasis on the subject *per se* given on the authority of the teacher to a greater concern with the interests and needs of children at varying stages of their development. What is important is not imparting facts but enabling children to learn from a variety of experiences. 'The child is the agent in his own learning.'[21] This understanding of education has been termed 'child-centred', but perhaps 'child-related'[22] is better, for the selection of material is made on the basis of the child's capacities. Sten Rodhe[23] prefers the model of an ellipse with two foci of content and pupil to that of a circle with the child at the centre. The teacher's job then is to promote a dialogue between child and content.

Is it possible or desirable to exclude religious education from this concept of learning? Clearly not. The change in terminology from religious instruction to religious education may be evidence of this. To regard religious education as instruction in Christianity with the hope of acceptance is to seek to indoctrinate and to argue for its inclusion in the curriculum on confessional rather than educational grounds. It may possibly be said that religion is such a different subject from others, quite unlike the empirically verifiable subjects, that it cannot be approached experientially in the same way, and that some authoritative instruction is necessary. But are there not also other subjects (e.g. poetry and art) which are not empirically verifiable, yet where we would deplore telling children what to think? We ask them rather on the basis of their limited experience and understanding of the poem or work of art to make their own response. Can we inhibit the critical and value judgments which we encourage in all other good teaching by appealing to answers given on authority? Cox puts the position like this:

> It would seem more realistic to regard training in religious ideas as educationally similar to those of other subjects, basing them on the children's interpretation of experience, thus making them more genuine if less extensive.[24]

It is this educational role of religious education which all recent writing stresses. The Durham Report states: 'It is a subject with its own inherent educational value and must have its place on the curriculum for educational reasons.'[25] It argues that throughout history man has sought answers to questions which his life poses, 'questions which are a part of the human condition'[26] in which young people share. 'They should have some opportunity to learn that religion is a feature of this condition, and for some men a deeply significant area of human knowledge and experience.'[27] The report thus sums up its educational rationale by saying:

> The aim of religious education should be to explore the place and significance of religion in human life and so to make a distinctive contribution to each pupil's search for a faith by which to live.[28]

The new agreed syllabuses reflect this educational approach to religious education and have made suggestions based on the needs, interests and abilities of the pupils. Clearly the work of Goldman and Loukes has made its mark. These syllabuses are concerned with the relevance of religious education to real life and they are more liberal in recommending the study of non-Christian religions and philosophies, usually in the fifth and sixth forms. Nevertheless they are basically Christian syllabuses and still largely biblical, particularly in the secondary school. The sub-title of the Northamptonshire syllabus, part 1, is 'An exploration into Christian faith for primary schools' and this same phrase occurs in part 2 for secondary schools as 'the purpose of the syllabus'.[29] The Lancashire syllabus, *Religion and Life*, states: 'In the forefront of our thinking has also been the need to present the Christian message in a way that is relevant . . . '[30] Goldman too had been convinced that religious education was about Christianity but that it should be taught only when pupils had developed the capacity for abstract thought. 'Christianity should be taught because it is true.'[31]

What we have in fact is an open-ended approach to Christianity in which some allowance is made for other views and ideas but presented through the filter of Christian thinking. This approach which is that of all the new agreed syllabuses[32] has been termed 'neo-confessional'. It puts emphasis on the search for meaning through a life-centred approach in which there is much discussion and questioning of values, attitudes, beliefs and practices. It recommends that teachers should look at the whole evidence, following where the argument leads, but because the presuppositions are Christian it is difficult to see just how open-ended the discussions really are. J. W. D. Smith acknowledges that such a study 'may be open-ended in the sense that it leaves pupils free to accept or reject the Christian position but it may become an open-ended approach to a closed system of belief and practice.'[33] Earlier Lionel Elvin had raised a similar point when he questioned if a Christian could really be so open as to doubt the existence of God. 'The crux about the open approach will be over these basic theological points.'[34]

The debate on open-ended Christian education brings back into the foreground the whole question of indoctrination. Clearly the old approach may be described as such when its avowed intention was to induct pupils into the Christian faith, but is this true of the new approach? Or to put it another way, does commitment preclude real openness in teaching? The attempt of Stenhouse[35] and to a certain extent John Wilson[36] shows that 'procedural neutrality' on the part of the teacher may lead to rather sterile results in which too much emphasis is put on the intellectual arguments. They thought that opinions expressed by the teacher would influence the pupils, and as they believed so much in the autonomy of the pupils to make up their own minds about the subject under discussion, they saw the teacher's role as that of a chairman. Colin Alves in his splendid little book *The*

Christian in Education rejects this approach as being too restrictive, for, in insisting that the teacher should operate as the arbiter between various views and not express his own, it suggests that what is of paramount importance is the development of rationality and factual accuracy. But 'many basic educational processes start from the impact of person upon person, the whole person upon the whole person, not just mind upon mind'.[37]

Basil Mitchell discusses 'indoctrination' in an appendix to *The Fourth R* and distinguishes two aspects to which critics object, the content and the aims. Indoctrination takes place when a person persuades another to believe a debatable or controversial statement without adequate reasons, 'teaching of reasonably disputatious doctrines as if they were known facts'.[38] Or indoctrination involves getting a person to believe things in such a way that he will not revise his beliefs even if given good arguments against them. After discussing the extreme positions he concludes by drawing a parallel between being educated and learning to build a home. The extreme liberal leaves the novice completely alone to build his house, offering him only incidental technical information; the extreme authoritarian helps by planning and building the home for the novice in such a way that later alteration is difficult. The sensible educator advises but is careful not to impose his own views, allowing freedom of choice during the process and the possibility of later alterations and developments.

To the question, 'Does open-ended Christianity necessarily lead to indoctrination?' the answer is 'No', for openness does not mean being without presuppositions or viewpoints.

> Openness consists in consciously recognizing the existence of presuppositions, of recognizing their status as presuppositions and not as unchallengeable facts or dogmas, and therefore being ready to consider arguments against them.[39]

One of the great merits of *The Fourth R* was the way in which it tried to combine 'openness and commitment, exploration and conviction'.[40] It stressed that school religious education was not to press for acceptance of any particular faith or belief system, but only for 'conversion from a shallow and unreflective attitude to life . . . commitment to the religious quest, to that search for meaning, purpose, and value which is open to all men.'[41] But on the question of content it argued that in this country it 'should consist mainly of the exploration of the literature and beliefs of the Christian faith',[12] although pupils should be acquainted with the basic facts about other religions. The justification for this was twofold. First, Christianity is the religion with which most pupils are already familiar and so the appropriate one for exploring 'the place and significance of religion in human life'. But secondly a religion cannot be properly understood without studying its religious tradition, and it would be both impracticable and un-realistic to expect pupils to study the scriptures of other religions. Nevertheless *The Fourth R* cannot be termed neo-confessional, for it argues for Christianity for most pupils on educational, not dogmatic, grounds. However, it acknowledges the wish of some parents for their children to be educated in the Jewish or another faith and so in rather a curious way the confessional situation is brought again into the picture. In some cities this could point to possible visits from the imam, rabbi, priest and even guru to conduct classes for children who may have been withdrawn 'to be taught their particular faith'.[43] What had been so cogently argued against in the report has reappeared in a foot-note.

But is open-ended Christianity, which still consists mainly of Christian teaching based on the Bible with bits of non-Christian religions and philosophies, open-ended *enough* for the situation of today? J. W. D. Smith asks for the non-Christian, 'Must "learning for living" be done within the pattern of Christian belief and life?'[44] The answer from some Christians is 'No'.

Ninian Smart has argued that religious education in schools should not be different in principle from religious studies at university level and should concern itself with the study of the phenomena of religion and alternatives to religion. He distinguishes between teaching *that* and teaching *how* and draws a parallel with history in which a skill is learnt, 'the capacity to do history—to think historically, to judge about historical issues, to understand some of the forces at work in major historical events, etc'.[45] In the same way he thinks of the aim of religious education as that 'of creating certain capacities to under-stand and think about religion'.[46] Thus religious education becomes teaching *about* religion, an objective academic discipline which the Schools Council Working Paper refers to as 'explicit religion'.[47] Christianity is part of the programme studied alongside and in dialogue with other religions. Instead of being left until the fifth or sixth forms, the project team suggest that other religions can be looked at by much younger children if it is remembered that religion is 'multi-dimensional'. Smart has distinguished six dimensions: doctrinal, mythological, ethical, ritual, experiential, social.[48] The first three 'represent the teaching of a religion; they sum up its *Weltanschauung*; they express the perspective in which the adherent views the world and himself'. They are the parahistorical claims and as such are open to debate. The second three are 'the primary data of religion in the world' and probably provide the best introduction to the study of religion.

Sten Rodhe,[49] in his address to the Inter-European Commission on Church and School in 1970, put forward a universal model for the teaching of religions based on the development in Swedish schools. He argued for a descriptive teaching about living world religions, concentrating on answers to the existential questions which are given by the many religions. Such teaching should be based on primary sources and should be given as a separate subject to all pupils with due regard to what is most suitable at the varying ages. Such an approach, which is rightly receiving more attention,[50] tries to make the young understand religion and the part it has played and still plays in human experience. It aims to make them literate and intelligent about religion in a world context. No one religion takes pride of place and controls the material, although clearly the religions of the immediate environment will provide the basis for study at the earliest stages. Thus Christian studies become part of a larger programme of religious education. In an editorial to *Learning for Living* John Hull wrote:

> The religious education offered by the State to children and young people today must be offered to the Christian family, the Muslim family, the humanist family, and to members of all other traditions without favour and without discrimination. It must be a religious education based not on an assumption that Christianity is true but on the belief in the importance of the study of the place of religions in the life of mankind.[51]

The recipe is being rewritten both in terms of the list of ingredients and the method of procedure, and hence the diet in religious education, but at present there are few takers.

What then can we say about the New Testament in this changing diet? First, it needs to be said that the New Testament belongs to the church. It was written in the church, by the church, for the church. It was written from faith to faith; the various writings were produced by early Christians at particular points in the first century to deal with situations in the life and thinking of many churches of their day. Not one of the authors thought he was writing for generations other than his own, nor did he think he was writing 'holy scripture'. These church documents, whether gospels, letters or apocalypse, were written for specific purposes which can in most cases be determined from a close analysis of the books themselves against the background of the first century. But all were concerned with the meaning and significance of Christ as experienced within the church and were written to elucidate this for the contemporary Christians. The language and thought-forms are first-century, reflecting various mixtures from Jewish to Hellenistic thinking. These writings were not the only ones produced within and reflecting the Christ event, but they were the ones which the church of a later day believed to be apostolic or near-apostolic and to contain a 'right' understanding of Christ against which developments could be checked. The idea of the New Testament canon emerged some time towards the end of the second century, although its contents were in dispute for another two hundred years. Nevertheless, in accepting a second canon of books alongside the Jewish scriptures the church declared that this new collection was authoritative for its life and thought—it was 'holy scripture'. The reading of the New Testament within the liturgy, the interpretation of it in sermons and the appeal to it as sacred ensured that it 'lived' within the church. Although the New Testament was the point of nearest contact the church had with Jesus of Nazareth, the writings were not used to develop this but rather were the means of teaching religious and moral lessons, challenging a response of faith and commitment to Christ.

And so it is today for those who have imbibed church teaching for years. The precise meanings of expressions may not be fully understood, but within the church there is a certain associative effect of the New Testament on those who believe it as a divine source of revelation. C. H. Dodd wrote in 1938:

Most of us in this country today could say that whatever stands for religion to us has from our earliest days found expression in the speech of the Bible. No wonder when we hear it read at the solemn assembly its words carry 'overtones' of association.... Given certain conditions, religious feelings of real value may be evoked by such a use of the Scriptures even without clear understanding.... They owe their effect, not in the first place to their intelligible meaning, but to the 'aura' of sacred association surrounding them.[52]

But now it is 1974 and there are comparatively few, the regular church-goers, for whom this can be true. This cannot be true for a non-believing adult community, nor for a state school. The question may be asked, 'If the New Testament belongs to the church what is it doing in a state school?' When the aim of religious education in schools was the establishment of the Christian faith, the New Testament had a clearly defined role, even if in being separated from the worshipping community it was difficult to fulfil that role. But now that the aims and content of religious education are changing so much, just what place does it have? As theology was demoted from its position as the queen of the sciences in the university, so the New Testament has to cease to be the *prima donna* in the school. No longer can the New Testament claim a dominant position as of right. If it has a position, and I believe it has, it will be of a different kind. In the new religious education of the last quarter of the twentieth century the New Testament will be studied less frequently, and probably only in the secondary school (although introductory points about the Bible may be looked into at an earlier stage, and maybe some of the great stories told to illustrate Judaism or Christianity). It will be one of the phenomena placed alongside other holy books such as the Qur'ān, the Bhagavadgītā, the Upaniṣads and the Buddhist scriptures, as well as non-Christian interpretations of life such as *The Humanist Frame*.[53]

Clearly when we multiply the amount of material in the curriculum without increasing the time allocation, the approach to the material must be different. Christianity will be studied as one of the major religions in the world and the New Testament will be seen as its unique sacred scripture. It will be necessary to give up the Bible-study approach in which stress is put on the knowledge of the Bible contents against the background of the history and geography of the Mediterranean world, often with the closing questions: What does this mean for us?

What does the message of Jesus say to us about such-and-such a problem of modern living? What can we learn from Jesus' view on wealth? Instead of this fairly subjective approach, I am suggesting an objective one in which we look at the nature of the material in the New Testament, the different kinds of literature from which it is composed, the meaning of first-century thought-forms and the symbolic language in which it was written. Instead of going through the parables, miracles, life and ministry of Jesus, the Acts of the Apostles, week after week for four or five years (and being faced with the questions Is it true? Did it happen?), the New Testament should be approached by means of selections of different types of material (miracle, parable, myth, hymn, symbolic story) to enable the young to understand their use in the New Testament context and to ask: What did this mean for the writer and the people for whom it was written? What does the story take for granted? What do Christians mean by this? How can this best be expressed in today's language? Questions of historicity will inevitably arise and should be discussed, but the pupils should be enabled to understand that the questions we wish to ask are not always ones which can be answered from the nature of the material. They should also realize that Christians have different opinions on the matter. Some account of the ways in which Christian scholars approach the Bible is of the utmost importance to enable pupils to understand that the belief in the incarnation, for example, does not rest upon the stories of a virgin birth which come to us only in Matthew and Luke, where the details differ. Nor does the belief in resurrection rest on a reanimated body and an empty tomb. The New Testament interpretation will obviously vary according to the abilities of the pupils (and I am particularly aware of the great difficulties which exist with slow learners who lack much verbal ability), but it should reflect the kind of thinking which Christian theologians are saying about the New Testament.

Such study will be done at intervals in the secondary school. By the time many pupils leave school at sixteen years, they should know that the New Testament is *not* a Christian Qur'ān. They should know something about the way the New Testament was put together. They should know that each story has a job to do in the writing of which it is part. They should be able to bring out the meaning for the people of the day, give some account of how later Christians have understood it, how Christians today understand it, and what it means for the man who believes it to be true. They should be able to appreciate the importance of Jesus to the church.

On this approach to the New Testament the pupil will not be able to reproduce the details of Jesus' teaching in parables, nor to give a connected account of Paul's second missionary journey. But this is to be welcomed, for New Testament scholarship shows plainly that the parables, although part of the original tradition, have undergone changes during the oral period with the result that their meaning in the gospels is related to Christian experience of later days rather than to the message of Jesus for his own generation. The Acts too, often a favourite for inclusion in the third form or 'O' level class, is not the primary source material for an understanding of Paul, but is the second part of a two-volume theology in which the details of history are subservient to much greater issues in the witness of the church.

In addition to this objective study of the New Testament there will be need to look at the problems of life and death, suffering and evil, and the personal, social and moral concerns of the young—the 'implicit' approach to religion. Humanism and other religions will provide views for consideration, and the New Testament will be part of the Christian interpretation. However, in this problem-solving approach there is great difficulty in using the New Testament, for the problems of today are not those of the New Testament church. To dip into the New Testament atomistically for the clues to solve today's problems may often distort its real meaning. No one wants the young to quote verbatim from the New Testament with 'The Bible says' as if this provided a ready solution. Yet the New Testament does contain assertions and Christian responses which may be considered as part of the evidence for discussion. But again the pupils should be made aware that there are many Christian responses to most problems.

The recipe is being rewritten. I venture to suggest that in the next ten years we shall see a complete change of diet in the direction of a more explicit study of religions alongside Christianity. Consequently the New Testament will cease to be the *prima donna* and become part of the corps de ballet. Certainly one of the great benefits of this approach to the teaching of religions is the attempt to understand *religion*. However, in the end all depends on the way in which the meal is served. It could lead to a hotch-potch resulting in indigestion or simply a boring recitation of a world-wide catechism. Misunderstanding of religion, boredom and unthinking rejection may come from a diet of snippets from other religions as much as from an overweighty dose of biblical stories.

NOTES

1. West Riding Syllabus of Religious Instruction, 1947, p. 29.

2. County Borough of Sunderland Syllabus of Religious Instruction, 1944, p. 13.

3. *Religious Teaching for Schools*, the Cambridgeshire Agreed Syllabus, CUP 1949, p. 9.

4. *Half our Future*: report of the Central Advisory Council for Education (England), HMSO 1963 (Newsom Report), section 166.

5. Ibid., section 169.

6. *Primary Education in Wales*: report of the Central Advisory Council for Education (Wales), HMSO 1967 (Gittens Report), p. 371.

7. *Children and their Primary Schools*: report of the Central Advisory Council for Education (England), HMSO 1967 (Plowden Report), section 572.

8. Ibid., pp. 489–93.

9. See Lionel Elvin, 'Standpoint of a Secular Humanist', *Religious Education 1944–1984*, ed. A. G. Wedderspoon, George Allen & Unwin 1966, p. 175.

10. University of Sheffield Institute of Education, *Religious Education in Secondary Schools*, Nelson 1961, p. 44.

11. H. Loukes, *Teenage Religion*, SCM Press 1961.

12. Schools Council Working Paper 36: *Religious Education in Secondary Schools*, Evans/Methuen Educational 1971, p. 34.

13. H. Loukes, *New Ground in Christian Education*, SCM Press 1965, p. 148.

14. J. W. D. Smith, *Religious Education in a Secular Setting*, SCM Press 1969, p. 99.

15. R. Goldman, *Readiness for Religion*, Routledge & Kegan Paul 1965, p. 8.

16. See C. F. Evans, 'Should the New Testament be taught to Children?', *Is 'Holy Scripture' Christian?*, SCM Press 1971, p. 40; and *The Fourth R*, National Society/SPCK 1970 (Durham Report), para. 230.

17. Ibid.

18. Goldman, op. cit., p. 114.

19. John Hull, *The Theology of Themes*, Teacher's Department paper of the Christian Education Movement 1972, originally published in the *Scottish Journal of Theology* 25, 1972, pp. 20–31.

20. NOP, *New Society*, May 1965; P. R. May and O. R. Johnston, *Religion in our Schools*, Hodder & Stoughton 1968.

21. Plowden Report, section 259.

22. F. H. Hilliard, *Learning for Living*, November 1965, p. 15. See *The Fourth R*, para. 246.

23. Sten Rodhe, 'The Teaching of Religions', *Teaching about Religions*, ed. G. Parrinder, Harrap 1971, p. 89.

24. E. Cox, *Changing Aims in Religious Education*, Routledge & Kegan Paul 1966, p. 64.

25. *The Fourth R*, para. 201.

26. Ibid., para. 204.

27. Ibid., para. 205.

28. Ibid., para. 215. See also para. 202.

29. Northampton Education Committee, *Life and Worship*, 1968, p. 15.

30. Lancashire Education Committee, *Religion and Life*, 1968, p. 1.

31. Goldman, op. cit., p. 59.

32. At the time of writing the City of Birmingham syllabus has not been published, but it should prove to be an exception to this statement. This syllabus will be more concerned with the study of religions in a multi-cultural community. Already its proposals have met with much criticism, particularly because it includes sections on Communism and Humanism. The Department of Education and Science has, in fact, ruled that the proposed syllabus is illegal, and the working party which drafted it has been reconvened.

33. J. W. D. Smith, op. cit. (note 14 above), p. 101.

34. Elvin, art. cit. (note 9 above), p. 177.

35. Schools Council Integrated Humanities, *The Humanities Project: An Introduction*, Heinemann 1970.

36. John Wilson et al., *Introduction to Moral Education*, Penguin Books 1968.

37. C. Alves, *The Christian in Education*, SCM Press 1972, p. 38.

38. Antony Flew, *Studies in Philosophy and Education*, vol. V, no. 2, 1967, p. 277 (quoted in *The Fourth R*, appendix B, p. 354).

39. *The Fourth R*, para. 483.

40. Ibid., p. xii.

41. Ibid., para. 217.

42. Ibid., para. 214.

43. Ibid., footnote to para. 212.

44. J. W. D. Smith, op. cit., p. 69.

45. N. Smart, *Secular Education and the Logic of Religion*, Faber 1968, p. 95.

46. Ibid., p. 97.

47. Schools Council Working Paper 36 (note 12 above), p. 36.

48. N. Smart, op. cit., ch. 1.

49. Rohde, art. cit. (note 23 above), pp. 77ff.

50. See E. Cox, 'The Aims of Religious Education', *Religious Education in Integrated Studies*, ed. I. H. Birnie, SCM Press 1972, p. 40.

51. *Learning for Living*, March 1971.

52. C. H. Dodd, *The Authority of the Bible*, Nisbet 1938, p. 4.

53. Julian Huxley (ed.), *The Humanist Frame*, Allen & Unwin 1961.

18

'*Who's In, Who's Out*'

CLARE DRURY

THE four canonical gospels are widely held by Christians to have special authority as the only books which give true information about the life and ministry of Christ. But there are other accounts, the apocryphal gospels, books containing stories similar to those in the New Testament gospels and dating in some cases from the same period. Between the two a clear line is drawn: Matthew, Mark, Luke and John (despite the differences between their accounts, which is a separate question altogether) are held to offer the authentic and authoritative account, while apocryphal literature is regarded only as imaginative elaboration of the true story. But the line is blurred and less straight than we are led to believe.

Consideration of the Christmas story will quickly show that the purity and authority of the canonical account have long been overlaid by popular and elaborate accretions, most vividly exemplified in the words of many Christmas carols and artistically in every conceivable medium. Take, for example, the crib which almost every church in this country displays throughout the Christmas season. Mary and Joseph are to be seen in a stable with the infant Christ, watched by an ox and an ass. A star hangs overhead while shepherds and/or three kings bearing gifts stand by and worship. The details of the scene have become so familiar that we do not think to question them, but a quick glance at the text of the narrative reveals that the accounts of Matthew and Luke's birth narratives—and they are the only canonical evangelists to describe the nativity—are almost invariably muddled together in popular tradition. What is even more remarkable is the lack of detail and colour in their descriptions of the scene itself compared with the rich detail of our imaginations, prepared by centuries of artistic, literary and musical representation of the subject.

> Now when Jesus was born in Bethlehem of Judea in the days of Herod the king, behold, wise men from the East came to Jerusalem, saying, 'Where is he who has been born king of the Jews? For we have seen his star in the East, and have come to worship him' . . . and lo, the star which they had seen in the East went before them, till it came to rest over the place where the child was. When they saw the star, they rejoiced exceedingly with great joy; and going into the house they saw the child with Mary his mother, and they fell down and worshipped him. Then, opening their treasures, they offered him gifts, gold and frankincense and myrrh (Matt. 2. 1–2, 9–11).

We are not told how many wise men came to offer gifts, and the tradition that there were three, and that they were kings, is totally unwarranted from the biblical account: they were magi or wise men. We are given no hint of what they looked like, but the picture we are accustomed to presents them as three crowned figures, one old and bearded, one in the prime of life and often a negro, and the third a mere youth. Where then did these details arise? The number three is probably a simple deduction from the number of gifts, and the tradition of showing one as a negro started in the late middle ages when theologians taught that the magi had been prefigured by the sons of Noah, thus symbolizing all the races of men in the world; the names Caspar, Melchior and Balthasar which they are often given are first found in the sixth century. The notion that they were kings arose much earlier, however, for Tertullian (AD 160–220) calls them *'reges fere'*,[1] perhaps on the basis of Ps. 72.10, 'May the kings of Tarshish and of the Isles render him tribute, may the kings of Sheba and Seba bring gifts!'

The origin of the tradition of the ox and ass at the nativity is easier to trace. The apocryphal gospel of Pseudo-Matthew[2] (a late work incorporating much earlier tradition) explains their presence as follows:

> On the third day after the birth of our Lord Jesus Christ holy Mary went out from the cave, and went into a stable and put her child in a manger, and an ox and an ass worshipped him. Then was fulfilled that which was said through the prophet Isaiah 'The ox knows his owner and the ass his master's crib' [Isa. 1.3]. Thus the beasts, ox and

ass, with him between them, unceasingly worshipped him. Then was fulfilled that which was said through the prophet Habakkuk: 'Between two beasts are you known' [Hab. 3.2 LXX]. And Joseph remained in the same place with Mary for three days.

The ox and ass have become such an acceptable part of the traditional nativity picture that their presence has become almost indispensable, even though they are not to be found in the canonical accounts. A different fate awaited other sections of Pseudo-Matthew, especially those describing the flight into Egypt, a potentially romantic journey only baldly described by the evangelist: 'And he rose and took the child and his mother by night, and departed to Egypt' (Matt. 2.14). This was elaborated by miracles performed by the child Jesus, stories popular in Middle Ages which are now generally forgotten and of which artistic representations have become rare.

Every traveller in Italy, or student of Byzantine and western medieval art, will be familiar with pictures showing the life of the Virgin and the story of her parents Joachim and Anna. The stories are told in a document dating from the second century, the Protevangelium of James.[3] Joachim and Anna were an aged couple full of sadness and remorse at their failure to produce offspring. Joachim reproached himself because he found that all the righteous men of Israel had produced children:

And Joachim was very sad, and did not show himself to his wife, but betook himself into the wilderness; there he pitched his tent and fasted forty days and forty nights; and he said to himself; 'I shall not go down either for food or for drink until the Lord my God visits me; prayer shall be my food and drink.'

Anna meanwhile was lamenting her barrenness at home and being taunted for it by her servant Judith; she went into her garden.

And she saw a laurel tree and sat down beneath it and implored the Lord, saying: 'O God of our fathers, bless me and hear my prayer, as thou didst bless the womb of Sarah and gavest her a son, Isaac.' . . . And behold an angel of the Lord came to her and said 'Anna, Anna, the Lord has heard your prayer. You shall conceive and bear, and your offspring shall be spoken of in the whole world.' And Anna said: 'As the Lord my God lives, if I bear a child, whether male or female, I will bring it as a gift to the Lord my God and it shall serve him all the days of its life . . . And Anna stood at the gate and saw Joachim coming and ran immediately and hung on his neck, saying: 'Now I know that the Lord God has greatly blessed me; for behold the widow is no longer a widow, and I, who was childless, have conceived.'

Mary was duly born, and after a remarkable infancy was presented to the temple, as her mother had promised, where she lived until she reached marriageable age when a husband had to be found for her. The high priest entered the sanctuary to pray for guidance:

And behold, an angel of the Lord suddenly stood before him and said to him: 'Zacharias, Zacharias, go out and assemble the widowers of the people, and to whomsoever the Lord shall give a sign, his wife she shall be.'

Joseph, who like the other widowers had brought a rod with him to the temple, received the sign of a dove coming out of the end of it and alighting on his head, so he became Mary's husband. Thereafter the Protevangelium of James tells the story of Christ's nativity, generally following and combining the stories of Matthew and Luke's accounts until the point of John the Baptist's execution, but with the author's own theological interpretation. He adds, after a more miraculous account of Christ's birth, a doubting midwife named Salome who tested Mary's virginity with her finger, but because of her doubt her hand withered. 'I have tempted the living God; and behold, my hand falls away from me, consumed by fire!' She prayed to the Lord that it might be healed,

And behold, an angel of the Lord stood before Salome and said to her: 'The Lord has heard your prayer. Come near, touch the child and you will be healed.' And she did so.

There is nothing intrinsically objectionable about such stories so simply and poetically told, especially as they often seem to be derived from canonical stories, as this one from doubting Thomas (John 20.26–29). There are, however, other collections of stories about the child Jesus which are extravagant to the point of being fairy-tales, telling of miraculous and sometimes cruel pranks he played on his friends. They frequently try to make the same point as canonical stories—illustrating for example Christ's overruling of the sabbath laws, such as the one recorded in the gospel of Thomas, when as a boy of five Jesus fashioned twelve sparrows on the sabbath day, and when reprimanded by Joseph he clapped his hands and off the sparrows flew. Such stories are not edifying in any way, but bear witness to their authors' unwillingness to believe that Christ was ever an ordinary human being, which led them to attribute magical powers to him in his infancy as the best way they could imagine of expressing his divinity. Since all the stories are based on the belief that Jesus Christ is the Son of God, and since some of the material goes back to very early times, often contemporary with the canonical gospels, and since it is usually orthodox if a little bizarre, it should not suffer the neglect with which it is treated at present, especially as this magical element is not absent from the canonical accounts (e.g. Matt. 17.24–27, the story of the coin in the fish's mouth). Some of the apocryphal gospels are readable in their own right and may lead to a clearer and richer understanding of the New Testament.

For it is only recently and in northern climes that complete rejection has occurred. The traditions about Christ's parents and extra details surrounding his birth have been used and recommended from very early times by theologians such as Justin Martyr and Origen, and, despite attacks from purists throughout the centuries, became more and more popular and elaborate as the cult of the Virgin grew stronger in both East and West. Artistic evidence in churches all over Europe and the Near East points to this: in eastern churches pride of place in the internal decorative schemes is given to the life of the Virgin and her assumption; in the decoration of the Capella Scrovegni in Padua, for example, Giotto included scenes from the story of Joachim and Anna; and Flemish and German artists continued to paint scenes from the Protevangelium of James and other infancy gospels right up to the Reformation. In the middle ages, therefore, the distinction between canonical and apocryphal was blurred: apocryphal scenes were as commonplace and acceptable then as are the ox and ass and the three kings today.

Perhaps then the modern rejection of much apocryphal tradition is unwarranted. Stanley Spencer, after all, who has a claim to be the best modern English religious painter, used the story of Joachim and

Anna, and other extra-canonical material might be found to be as acceptable as the three kings and as valuable. It seems to be popularly assumed that a sharp line can be drawn between canonical and apocryphal gospel stories: that in the former the narrative interest is secondary to the theological, while the reverse is true of apocryphal literature. Further, it is asserted that the canonical gospels reveal a sobriety and christological concern lacking in the apocryphal gospels, or, to put it in a nutshell, that the canonical gospels are 'true' while their apocryphal counterparts are not. This attitude is questionable, especially since it is often assumed without a careful and unbiased study of the motives, presuppositions and sources of the writers of both 'sorts' of gospel, and without a real comparison of the two, for it was the belief of all the writers that Jesus Christ was the Son of God who had saved the world.

If the development of this belief in the different books within the New Testament canon is studied, further light may be shed on the problem. A systematic development is clearly discernible from the earliest Pauline literature to the latest gospels. The first account of Christ's saving work is a very brief summary:

> For I delivered unto you as of first importance, what I also received, that Christ died for our sins in accordance with the scriptures, that he was buried, that he was raised on the third day in accordance with the scriptures and that he appeared to Cephas, then to the twelve . . . (I Cor. 15.3).

This is comparable in its cardinal points with the hymn in Philippians 2, which describes the incarnation in dramatic mythological terms. In both passages it is the death of Christ which is emphasized as the supreme saving event, not the incarnation itself (though it obviously has more soteriological importance in Philippians than in Corinthians). But throughout the Pauline literature it is the crucifixion which shatters the status quo, and it is no romanticized crucifixion but the cursed death of a man hanging on a tree. Without the death of Christ as a ransom for many, the salvation of the faithful at the imminent 'eschaton' would not have been possible. Nowhere does Paul discuss the virgin birth or how precisely Christ took flesh (apart, that is, from the vague term 'emptied himself' in Philippians, and Gal. 4.4: 'God sent forth his Son, born of a woman, born under the law').

Mark, the earliest evangelist, reveals the same soteriological pattern as Paul, but he takes it further back into the life of Christ. The crucifixion provides the climax of the gospel, and the theological significance is similar to Paul's—only the death of the Messiah in an unacceptable and degrading way could break through and open up future salvation. The enigmatic ending of the book serves only to highlight the importance of the death itself. But in Mark the end time, 'the eschaton', is taken back further into the ministry of Christ; his teaching points towards it and his miracles help bring it about. For, in Jewish mythology, before the end a great battle must take place in which good will finally overcome evil, and Christ's healing miracles are seen as victories over demonic powers; battle is already joined during his lifetime.

Matthew's gospel illustrates the 'backwards' tendency developing further, for he takes the story back beyond Mark's starting point of the Baptist's appearance, to the circumstances surrounding Christ's birth. As time went on people were becoming more and more curious about Christ's life and more firm in the belief that the Messiah must have led an extraordinary life from the beginning. Matthew recorded the events, not as a modern historian would, accompanied by dates and evidence, but, with his concern to show that Jesus is the long-awaited Messiah of the Jews, writing his own version of the story. Believing that Old Testament scripture embodied the will and purpose of God, his concern was to show whenever he could that Jesus fulfilled messianic prophecies, or to turn the point around, the Old Testament became a source to him, for what was prophesied of the Messiah in the scriptures *must* be true of Jesus. This is most obvious in the story of Christ's entry into Jerusalem, where, true to his source (Zech. 9.9), Matthew records Christ entering on an ass *and* on its colt. His birth from a virgin was prophesied by Isaiah (7.14); he was the Son of David and so must be born in David's city of Bethlehem; he was the great lawgiver prophesied by Moses (Deut. 18.15), so his infancy was surrounded by similar tragic events and his parents fled to Moses' land of Egypt. This use of the Old Testament as a source is of course not peculiar to Matthew: Pseudo-Matthew's use some centuries later of prophecy to supply the ox and ass (perhaps suggested by the manger in Luke's birth narrative) is precisely the same.

Moreover Luke's account of Christ's nativity, although very different from Matthew's, uses the Old Testament as a source in a similar way.

Each evangelist, for example, makes it possible for Jesus to be born at Bethlehem, even though he was well known as a Galilean from Nazareth. Matthew sets the scene in Bethlehem from the start, and gets the family to Nazareth on the return from Egypt:

> When he heard that Archelaus reigned over Judea in place of his father Herod, he was afraid to go there. . . . And he went and dwelt in a city called Nazareth, that what was spoken by the prophets might be fulfilled, 'He shall be called a Nazarene' (2.22f.).

Luke, on the other hand, starts the story of Christ's nativity at Nazareth with the annunciation, and transfers the family to Bethlehem for the birth itself by means of a census which he had heard took place at about the same time. Luke, however, does not show prophecies being slavishly fulfilled as Matthew does, but transmits a general Old Testament feeling in his narrative; first of all in taking the story back even further to John the Baptist's birth he presents a typical Old Testament mysterious birth from aged and barren parents, like those of Isaac (Gen. 17–20), Samson (Judg. 13.2) and Samuel (I Sam. 1–2), and the songs he puts in his characters' mouths are highly reminiscent of Old Testament ones (e.g. Hannah's song of thanksgiving, I Sam. 2. 1–10). This desire to delve ever further back into the past is continued in the apocryphal gospels, where we find an extension of a tendency already perceptible in Matthew and Luke. Arising from the assumption that the birth and conception of the Messiah must have been exceptional, the idea developed that even his mother and grandparents must be special, and that he must have been a child of extraordinary gifts himself. The motives of the later writers were as praiseworthy as those of the canonical evangelists; for instance, when the author of the Protevangelium of James is concerned to defend Mary's virginity by the story of the doubt of Salome, derived as it is from the account of the doubt of Thomas in John, he also clarifies the problem of Davidic descent, which in Matthew and Luke comes through Joseph, by attributing it to Mary.

Since, therefore, the motives and methods of the writers of both canonical and apocryphal gospels seem to be broadly similar, and since many apocryphal stories emanate from the same period and the same world, it is necessary, in order to discover why the latter were excluded from the canon, to turn to the first two centuries of the Christian era.

For the earliest church, Christ was the supreme revelation of God, but of the same God whose will and purpose was set out in Old Testament scripture. The law and the prophets continued to be valid, but through Christ they were interpreted in a new way, for they all pointed to him. Thus the church had a double authority, two entities, Christ and scripture standing side by side without contradiction, indeed each serving to support and interpret the other. For nearly two hundred years there was no thought of supplanting the authority of scripture, or of adding to it by new writings. Moreover, none of the writers of what we know as the New Testament thought of attaining canonical status when they took up their pens; far from it. What then was the purpose of an evangelist when he sat down to write? They did not set out to provide a straightforward and comprehensive picture of all Jesus had done and said, but, like any writer, they were selective and creative and wrote with a particular purpose and a particular sort of readership in mind:

> Now Jesus did many other signs in the presence of the disciples, which are not written in this book; and these are written that you may believe that Jesus is the Christ, the Son of God (John 20.30f.).

> Inasmuch as many have undertaken to compile a narrative of the things which have been accomplished among us, just as they were delivered to us by those who from the beginning were eyewitnesses and ministers of the word, it seemed good to me also, having followed all things closely for some time past, to write an orderly account for you, most excellent Theophilus, that you may know the truth concerning the things of which you have been informed (Luke 1.1–4).

Several points are worth noting in these two passages: the importance given to apostolic authority, as is also the case with the apocryphal gospels, Luke's assertion that 'many' have written about Christ and that the author in organizing and ordering the material undertook to present the truth. From the moment Mark's pen touched paper the tradition became of necessity less fluid and began to be fixed. It was not, however, as clearly fixed as some would like to believe, as is seen from the three synoptic gospels, so alike and yet so fundamentally different. Thus there was at this stage absolutely no suggestion of the officialized sanctity of the gospels, of their completeness and infallibility, as began to appear by the end of the second century. Moreover it was a long time before all four became universally accepted. Just as it is possible to trace the use of one gospel as a source for another, and the Old Testament as a source for them all, so in the apocryphal writings, scripture and Christian writings are used as sources. The Protevangelium of James is obviously dependent on Luke to a great extent, both in detailed quotation and in general style. Anna sings songs of lament and praise highly reminiscent of the Magnificat and Luke's other songs. The curious thing is that while people do not hesitate to admit the dependence of Pseudo-James on the Old Testament, allowing creativity and free use of sources for non-canonical works such as this, they seem to find it difficult to accept the same creativity and use of the Old Testament as a source when they are ascribed to Luke.

When the history of the canon is studied, however, and the slow and gradual choice of authoritative documents, the havering, the differences according to area are seen, then perhaps the sharp line separating canonical and apocryphal seems more blurred. The fourth gospel, for example, was not universally accepted for a long time because it seemed so strange alongside the synoptics. The motives for fixing a canon of authoritative documents are not entirely clear, but the tension between a desire on the one hand for unity, and on the other for variety, seems to have been largely responsible, alongside a growing desire to clarify what was orthodox in the face of the fast multiplying sects and heresies. The initiative may well have come from the heretic Marcion with his decision to substitute gospel and apostle for law and prophets. He rejected the Old Testament as the work of the evil God, now overcome and superseded by Christ; having purged them of all Jewish interest Marcion presented Luke and a corpus of Pauline epistles as his canon. The orthodox reaction to this was to emphasize the importance of having more than one gospel. On the other side 'masses of books' were being produced all over the empire by gnostics and other sectarians. The church followed Marcion in his bipartite canon, but did not limit it to one gospel. Even so this multiplicity of gospels was found difficult, as can be seen from Tatian's attempt in his Diatessaron to unify and harmonize the four accounts; and a similar purpose is explicitly set out in Luke's prologue. However, Irenaeus Bishop of Lyons about AD 180 speculated on the reasons for the fourfold gospel, claiming that as there were four winds and four cardinal points, so there must be four gospels. This argument, far less plausible now than in the second century, was put forward to counter the quantity of gnostic material being produced. And even when the four gospels had attained an authority similar to that of Old Testament scripture, the apocryphal stories continued to be read, loved and studied as much by theologians as by the people.

The sharp modern distinction between the two is therefore unwarranted, for the apocryphal material is often of higher quality than is suggested; sometimes, indeed, it has crept in upon the orthodox tradition unawares, and canonical authors used the same sources and methods as are often deprecated in their apocryphal counterparts. Furthermore, in the past, even when the distinction was noted, the value and richness of the Apocrypha was appreciated. Of course not all apocryphal material is of the same quality and has had the same impact on popular tradition as have the gospel of Thomas, Pseudo-Matthew and the Protevangelium of James, and perhaps not all is worthy of resurrection, but at various levels it is all valuable—to strike the popular imagination, to enable a richer understanding of medieval art and poetry, and to help scholars gain a clearer picture of the motivations of early Christian writers—even canonical writers.

NOTES

1. Tertullian, *Adversus Judaeos* 9.
2. Extracts from the gospel of Pseudo-Matthew in *New Testament Apocrypha* I, ed. E. Hennecke and W. Schneemelcher, ET ed. R. McL. Wilson, 2nd impression, SCM Press 1973, pp. 410-13.
3. English version of the Protevangelium of James, *New Testament Apocrypha* I, pp. 374-88.

19

Dear Christopher, . . .

ELLEN FLESSEMAN-VAN LEER

Dear Christopher,

To have chosen the form of a letter for a contribution to this volume may need some justification, so let me explain a little. When I received the invitation to write an essay in honour of your sixty-fifth birthday, my first reaction was a feeling of great pleasure. For, quite apart from the purely personal aspects, this invitation was proof to me that the discussions we have had in the past on biblical hermeneutics and their presuppositions, which have been very significant to me, must have been important to you too.

My second feeling, however, was one of dismay. For when I considered the subjects which were suggested to me for an essay, I felt at a loss. I am, as you know, merely an amateur in biblical scholarship, so a paper on any purely New Testament theme was ruled out. There remained subjects of a formal nature, dealing with methods and presuppositions rather than with the content of Christian faith; but in that field too I knew myself unable to write an essay which I could dare to offer as a tribute to you with any confidence. Another thing may also have played a part: though I realize that these 'formal' questions are indispensable for the thinking through of Christian faith, I am not sure whether I am, deep down, still vitally interested in them. After having immersed myself in them for quite a length of time, I have come to feel that they are somehow barren as compared with the more 'material' questions.

So, rather than refuse to contribute to your *Festschrift* at all I have chosen the form of a letter to indicate that what follows makes no pretension to be any more than a few personal remarks.

You may remember that when we both participated in the study project of the Commission on Faith and Order on biblical hermeneutics, I was in the interesting, but trying, position of participating in two regional working groups, discussing the same subject: one group, the great majority of whom were German scholars, the other the British group, of which you too were a member and in which I had the rare privilege of being the sole continental representative. In those years I was in danger of becoming theologically schizophrenic. For I was being torn between the serious, profound and intense German group with its conviction that biblical exegesis and hermeneutics were matters of life and death, and the British group, much more relaxed and down-to-earth, but rather sceptical and relativistic.

When the study on biblical hermeneutics was planned, nobody, I think, had quite realized to what extent the fundamental basis of our respective beliefs would come to be questioned. We knew of course as a matter of empirical fact that the Bible functioned differently in different churches. But many of us had hoped—rather naïvely in retrospect—that a concentration on hermeneutics would show that the theologians of the various churches were nearer to each other than the observable dogmatic differences would seem to suggest. If we had paused to think about it, we should all presumably have agreed that biblical hermeneutics is to those who come from a *sola scriptura* background a more urgent matter than it is to those who do not share that Reformation doctrine. But what I, for one, had not fully realized beforehand was that the hermeneutical question in the terms in which it had come to be stated was to some not only unanswerable, but even quite beside the point. Hermeneutics, as understood in the Faith and Order inquiry, is not merely concerned with trying to describe the method by which the original meaning of a given text can be ascertained. The formulation of such a method offers no insurmountable difficulties to biblical scholars, who have been reared in the school of modern literary and historical criticism, as was clearly brought out in the discussions in our British study group and in the other regional groups. But the real thrust of the hermeneutics inquiry was the endeavour to state as clearly and concisely as possible how what has been expressed in scripture can be brought to life for, and communicated to, men of today. And it was to that issue that the continental group in which I worked directed its efforts though it was not able to bring them to a recognizable solution. (Nor, by the way, did Faith and Order in its final study report succeed in stating any definite rules.) It was, however, the very possibility and necessity of this task which was put in question by our British working party.

Looking back on our discussions today after a good eight years, I wonder whether we pinpointed the differences among us correctly. Perhaps we made too much of the problem of the canon and of the authority and normativeness of canonical scripture. Quite a few of the arguments brought forward at the time I recognized in some of the essays in your book *Is 'Holy Scripture' Christian?*[1] In the same way, Dennis Nineham's article, 'The Bible in Modern Theology',[2] and James Barr's book, *The Bible in the Modern World*,[3] would perhaps not have been written, and certainly not written in the way they are, had it not been for those discussions. However, I am no longer sure that it was only your rejection of a fixed canonical scripture as (testimony to) the authoritative word of God which caused you and Dennis Nineham in particular to put a question-mark against our whole hermeneutical exercise. Is it not true that on the basis of your thinking one just cannot really be overmuch concerned about hermeneutics, because one has fundamentally no need for it? Biblical hermeneutics presupposes a time-gap between the truth of the Bible and present-day man, which has to be bridged. This time-gap does not really exist for you, for biblical truth has been preserved in and by the church right up to the present time. We have here, in essence, the old problem of scripture and tradition, about which you too, Christopher, had some very pertinent things to say in the first essay in your book just mentioned.

Up to some twenty-five years ago most theologians thought that the main controversial point in that issue was whether the concept of traditions as orally transmitted truths, not to be found in scripture, was affirmed or rejected. It seemed to many who worked in the field that much was gained for an understanding between the 'Catholic' and the 'Protestant' churches when it was agreed that the real point in question was not these so-called unwritten traditions, but the one tradition, divine truth handed down through the ages. And when a growing number of Roman Catholic theologians defined this tradition as *traditio interpretativa*, and when Protestant theologians conceded that that concept was by no means incompatible with the Reformation doctrine of scripture, many believed that one more controversial question was being solved. Actually it might well be that this newer concept of tradition covered up, and actually constituted, a more basic disagreement. For if tradition is understood as a living and changing reality transmitted in the church from generation to generation, instead of being a static whole in the past, scripture becomes more rather than less superfluous. Christian truth is what lives in the church today; in the last resort it is the mind of the church. In the 'two sources doctrine' the Bible stood, side by side with tradition, and in a way independent of it, over against the church; according to the present view the Bible is taken up into, and actualized in, tradition and consequently becomes indistinguishable from it. Therefore there is no longer any need for biblical hermeneutics. There is no time-gap to be bridged, for in tradition the Bible has become contemporary and actualized and interpreted.

I realize that in the above I have overstated your views. Still, I believe that there is enough truth in it to show why the problem of hermeneutics as stated in the Faith and Order study seemed to you a not very interesting and somewhat artificial one, which begged the real questions. But we never actually talked in those terms in our British group; we were too intent on attacking or defending the doctrine of the Bible as source and norm of Christian faith.

One of the things I have become convinced of by our discussions is that it is not possible to formulate an exact and conclusive doctrine of scripture. Do not misunderstand me. I have not come to attach less value to the Bible; I still believe that it is the reference point for the thinking, teaching, preaching and acting of the church. I know full well, and I accept, the traditional arguments that the biblical writings are a form of tradition, written down by the church at a comparatively early stage, that the fixing of the canon was a decision of the church, defended by a sincere but mistaken belief in apostolic origins, that scripture is dependent for its interpretation on the church, and that thus it is embedded in the church on every side. I know all this, and yet it remains an indisputable fact that both in the history of the Christian community and in the life of many individual believers the Bible has as a matter of fact been experienced time and again as a word addressed from 'the other side'. However much it may be embedded in the church, it has never been fully swallowed up by it. Thus it can become —as has actually happened in many instances—an independent entity, changing and correcting the very tradition of which it is part. However, when I try to systematize these experiences into a well-rounded doctrine of scripture I am at a loss, for such a doctrine can be attacked on many points. But perhaps the mistake lies in even trying to formulate such a concise doctrine. It can be shown from experience that scripture can work; what is more, I think that even the most radical sceptic in our British study group would affirm that he has experienced its power in his life. The quotation, repeated three or four times in your book already mentioned, can be adduced as proof: 'Here are these books; we believe them to be profitable books from experience.' The remark in your essay on Resurrection, that the New Testament writings are at the least 'guide-posts' and the 'raw material' for the exploration of faith-truth, points in the same direction. And to quote Dennis Nineham:

> You will all have had again and again the experience . . . of finding that it is only as you go back to the Bible that you regain your balance, . . . your unfaith is rebuked, your fears and frettings removed, your path made clear.[4]

In view of the article from which this quotation is taken the little word 'only' seems to me quite remarkable. I even wonder whether Dennis would not have erased it, if it had been pointed out to him. For in this incidental little word something of the exclusiveness of *sola scriptura*, so obnoxious to him and to you, seems to shimmer through.

But the experiences we have had in connection with scripture point to the power which certain passages or books of the Bible have exercised over us, never to 'the Bible' as a whole. That is to say: we can speak experientially about the Bible *in usu*, not *extra usum*, and not about the Bible as a whole, but only about those parts or thoughts of it which have impinged upon us or upon the community of which we are part. Might that not be the reason why it appears so hard—or even impossible—to formulate a doctrine of scripture? For such a doctrine will have to speak of the Bible as a whole (which exists in its facticity, but never works as a whole) both *extra* and *ante usum*.

Thus, my conviction that scripture somehow can bring man into contact with, and mediate to him, the power of God remains unshaken; and the same goes for my conviction that it is somehow the ultimate source of, and norm for, what Christian truth is. But the word 'somehow' indicates that I cannot give a full and exact description of how that norm works. I can only say what I do not mean by it: not a norm in any legal sense, nor in any proof-text sense, nor in the sense that whatever is said in the Bible must necessarily be believed today. (As if anything is ever *to be* believed!) But I am not particularly worried about the fact that I cannot convincingly state or defend a doctrine of the Bible. The less so because every alternative view which I have heard stated seemed to me equally vulnerable to criticism.

Isn't it rather significant that the majority of your essays end with explicit or implicit question-marks, and that the only two essays in which you take a more affirmative stance are those on the resurrection and on the church? When you were writing on a subject in your own field of New Testament scholarship you could apparently draw a line from the New Testament data to contemporary Christian faith without being able or bothering, I take it, to state by what rules exactly you did it. I would suggest that in this respect you are typical of British, and especially Anglican, scholarship. It is of a very high quality indeed, but it hardly ever produces anything like a *Glaubenslehre*. And exactly at this point the difference in climate in the two hermeneutics groups in which I participated came to the fore. The main strength in the British group lay in their asking critical questions. In making positive statements they were rather weak. In the German group it was the other way round. They worked from too many unquestioned assumptions, but they stated positively what they believed.

I asked you once in one of our many discussions why you were devoting so much of your time to studying the New Testament when you considered it neither authoritative or normative, nor a primary source of faith-truth. I vividly remember the answer you gave me: that in all that it did and thought the church should have the Bible at its elbow and that therefore it was necessary that biblical scholarship should go on.

Is this not a fairly élitist answer? If it is agreed that the Bible is and should be a factor when the church makes up its mind—and on this minimum we are all agreed—is it enough to assign its study to a few academics? Are we not thereby widening the gap between scholarship and ordinary believers, reducing them to children under age, to be nurtured in the bosom of good, wise mother church? Moreover, as long as scripture was considered to be the authoritative word of God, its place in the church was secure, even if it was often used, if at all, in a way scholars would find untenable and obscurantist. Taken up into the teaching and preaching of the church, it could always become a living force once again. But if the doctrine of biblical authority is discarded (as—perhaps rightly—you advocate) and if at the same time the study of the Bible is delegated to a few people working somewhere in an academic corner, the net result will be that the Bible will drop out of Christian consciousness. And I think all of us would consider that something to be highly regretted. It leaves the church shut up in a monologue with itself, with nothing it can appeal to except its own consciousness.

Therefore I want to make a plea that the Bible should be taught to adults—if not, as you cogently argue, to children in school—in such a way that the question of its authority is for the time being left on one side and that modern biblical scholarship is taken into account at every step.

I do not know whether it is possible in your British and Anglican situation to carry out what I have in mind. In my own church I can fall back upon a long tradition of lay Bible groups as a generally accepted feature of parish life. It is true that this tradition is not entirely an advantage, for the Bible is often used in these groups in such a harmonistic and dogmatic way that it merely functions as an endorsement of convictions and doctrines already held. This tendency is reinforced by the very familiarity of many key texts, which immunizes the readers against their impact. Therefore a process of alienation or 'defamiliarization' is necessary; for only when a text has become unfamiliar again is it possible to look at it with new eyes. I believe that critical biblical scholarship is an extremely suitable tool to bring about this shock effect of defamiliarization. For one thing, it can show up the strangeness of a text by placing it in its own time, place and mode of thinking, all of them far removed from ours. Also, by pointing out the varieties of textual reading, translation and interpretation even in the case of texts traditionally adduced as proofs for basic doctrines, it can break down views previously regarded as certain. Moreover, lay people, especially those who have come to reject an excessively 'pietistic' and 'edifying' use of the Bible, often welcome this more intellectual approach and are as a rule highly interested to look into the theological workshop. And why shouldn't they? I myself and you too, Christopher, find it equally stimulating and not seldom exciting.

But the main point I want to make is that in thus working with lay groups some of the main problems we so fervently discussed in our hermeneutics sessions are being solved, or at least bypassed without any loss. Take the question of the canon, on which we spent a lot of time. When one is in charge of a group, one has to pick passages which in content and relevance seem to be interesting and to offer material for discussion. Whatever might be said theologically about the canon, in practice one makes a conscious choice. It may be observed parenthetically that the same goes for expository preaching, whether one follows a given lectionary or chooses one's own text. It must be admitted that it is always only a segment of the Bible which actually functions. I do not see any sense in solidifying that fact into a doctrine of a canon within the canon, the less so because the part that functions will vary according to differences of time and situation. If an emphatic defence of the canon appears to be untenable, an emphatic attack upon it appears to be something of a tilting against windmills.

Or take the other problem which stood out in our British meetings and which we indicated in a kind of shorthand by the distinction between 'what it *meant*' and 'what it *means*'. Whether one likes it or not, the question what the meaning of a given text is for us will unavoidably be raised in any lay group, and the answers of the participants are likely to vary greatly. The assertion that one cannot speak of *the* one and only meaning of a text, it being mostly polyinterpretable, is substantiated in nearly any group discussion. Moreover, there always will be those who maintain that the text does not mean anything to them, while there are others who point to an analogy or a connection between the text and today, by which they are struck. And once in a while that produces an 'aha *Erlebnis*'[5] for some one to whom the text originally had made no sense.

It is an interesting experience to perceive how, when lay people study the Bible together in an intellectually responsible manner, the critical observations of scholars like you and many others are manifestly borne out, and yet the Bible holds its own. I have learned a great deal from you and generally from my work in the British working party, in particular to take less for granted and to ask more critical questions. For that I am very grateful. But I have learned from my *praxis* that the Bible can break through preconceived and traditional ideas and that it can be a source of power, giving people a basic trust and the freedom to speak out against the *status quo*. That is the reason why you did not succeed in convincing me that I do not meet in the Bible a word 'from the other side'.

Affectionately yours,

Ellen

NOTES

1. Christopher Evans, *Is 'Holy Scripture' Christian?*, SCM Press 1971.
2. Dennis Nineham, 'The Bible in Modern Theology', *Bulletin of the John Rylands Library* 52, 1969, pp. 178–99.
3. James Barr, *The Bible in the Modern World*, SCM Press 1973.
4. Nineham, art. cit., p. 198.
5. An 'aha *Erlebnis*': an experience which gives rise to an exclamation of surprise.